Bodywork Maintenance and Repair
including Interiors

By Paul Browne
and the Autobooks team of Technical Writers

Autobooks

Autobooks Ltd. Golden Lane Brighton BN1 2QJ England

Acknowledgements

The Publishers wish to thank the following
organisations and firms for their assistance
in the preparation of this book:

The Automobile Association (Engineering
 Staff)
Bintex Limited
Burgess Power Tools Limited
Calbrook Cars Limited
Cooper & Company (Coachbuilders)
DRIVE Magazine
Dunlop Engineering Group
Guy Performance (Alcester)
Holt Products Limited
Imperial Chemical Industries Limited
 (Paints Division)
International Pinchin Johnson Limited
Price Enfield Glass Company
Raydon Racing (Burgess Hill)
Tucker Fasteners Limited
Yarsley Testing Laboratories
Ziebart (GB) Limited

Cover Photography: Walter Gardiner

First Published 1975

© Autobooks Ltd 1975

ISBN 0 85147 578 7

652

Printed and bound in Brighton England for
Autobooks Ltd by G Beard & Son Ltd

Contents

Foreword

A great many motorists today are meeting the problem of the rising cost of running a car by carrying out their own maintenance. For them it can be rather depressing to find that in spite of the careful attention paid to routine servicing and mechanical repairs the value of the car is drastically eroded by deterioration of the bodywork, which all too often threatens to disintegrate into a mound of rust while most of the mechanical parts are still serviceable. One object of this book is to help the owner with average handicraft ability to prolong the life of the bodywork of his or her car to approach that of the engine. This will not avoid depreciation of the car's value, which is based mainly on age, but such a car will command a high trade-in price rather than a low one – a difference of several hundred pounds in some instances, and considerably more than will have been spent on the work suggested. But the possibilities for do-it-yourself attention to the bodywork do not end with preservation. Repair techniques, sheet metalworking, painting methods and materials, the use of glass reinforced plastics, and work on upholstery, trim, windows, doors and structural woodwork are all discussed, information useful in restoring an old car as well as repairing a new one. And the techniques can also be applied to the bodywork modifications that go with mechanical tuning for increased performance, or simply to the process of creating a different, more stylish vehicle. For the young in heart, customising offers a chance to add fun and gaiety to everyday life, and almost unlimited scope for artistic ability. The pages that follow explore the possibilities and limitations of the available techniques, so that the reader can start on the right lines and avoid expensive mistakes.

Paul Browne

CHAPTER 1

Rust: causes, effects and prevention

There can be little doubt that the major enemy of the motor car is rust. Rust is most often what finally defeats a car at the end of its life, and in some cases that life can be alarmingly short. Almost certainly, more cars have to be scrapped because of rust damage than for any other reason. Mechanical components can always be repaired, rebuilt or replaced, even if the process is expensive, but rust damage to the car's structure, if neglected, can eventually become irreparable. This chapter looks at the causes of rust, its effects and their implications and some of the ways in which they can be avoided, including preventive maintenance.

1:1 Why do cars rust?

Iron, which is the major constituent of the steel used in car bodies, has a natural tendency to go into solution in the presence of pure water, in the form of positively charged ions. For this to happen an equivalent number of positive ions of some other element must be displaced. The material displaced is hydrogen, which gathers on the surface of the metal. This primary reaction would not continue long on its own because the film of hydrogen would separate the water from the metal, but two secondary reactions enable it to continue. Some of the hydrogen bubbles off as a gas, and some unites with dissolved oxygen in the water. Either of these reactions enable further ions to be released into the water, where they are oxidised and precipitated as ferric hydroxide (rust). In practice the corrosion rate is determined by the amount of dissolved oxygen in the water.

Directly a car leaves the factory it is attacked not only by rainwater, which is rich in dissolved oxygen, but by dilute sulphuric acid, which is formed when rain absorbs

sulphur dioxide from chimney smoke. The chemicals used for crop spraying produce a similar effect in country areas. Salt-laden sea breezes in coastal districts are also corrosive, and ten per cent of British cars are used in these areas. The growing use of rock salt to melt ice and snow on roads in the winter months is another cause of corrosion, particularly under the floor and wheelarches. Salt-impregnated mud stays damp so that the chemical reactions can continue unchecked.

When part of a car's metal is exposed to acid-laden water the metal covered by water becomes an anode, and the remainder becomes a cathode. The reaction is similar to that deliberately induced in a car battery, and the anode slowly dissolves as a result. The more acid in the water, and the warmer the atmosphere, the quicker the corrosion takes place.

It is not the outside of the body that suffers most. Although the bonnet takes the brunt of wind and weather, it is the quickest to dry, and gets washed most frequently by the rain, reducing the build-up of corrosive materials. The danger is greatest where damp dirt collects and water lingers while it slowly evaporates leaving acid behind. Box sections are very vulnerable, because they are neither watertight nor ventilated, and in many cases they miss the phosphating and priming treatments. Condensation can do as much damage as salt spray in these cavities. The drain holes are often inadequate and badly placed, so that they are clogged or let in water thrown up from the road. Large ventilation holes cut in the upper parts would be more useful.

Box sections and other closed cavities are incorporated in the sills of most cars and in places like crossmembers, doors and the back ends of front and rear wings. **Section 1:5** describes typical structures in more detail.

Foot well corrosion:

Rust on the upper surface of the foot wells is caused by water coming in around loose or worn door weather-strips, through holes left by missing carpet studs, or water brought in on passenger's feet. Another common cause is condensation under rubber mats and other kinds of carpeting. A surprising amount of water is brought in on passenger's shoes, and the only way to get rid of this is to mop it up, or take the mats out. Manufacturers do not help by eliminating press-studs and fixing the floor carpet under trim strips which have to be unscrewed – more than anyone can be expected to do at the end of a long day.

Corrosion traps:

Some of the corrosion traps on a car body are created by the designer in trying to give the bodywork 'eye appeal'. Bright trim strips and light clusters are fixed to the body with unplugged rivets and fasteners made of a metal chemically dissimilar to the trim. The jolly trim line is intended to break up the slab side, but add a drop of acid-laden rainwater and you have a jolly little primary cell, which breaks up the side with bi-metallic corrosion. Nearly all rusted-out car bodies show a line of rust just above the horizontal trim-strip, where water has run down from the crown of the wing and evaporated, and there are larger rust patches corresponding to each trim clip.

1:2 Rust-proofing in production

The kind of priming and painting received by a metal surface has an important bearing on its resistance to rusting. Finishing paints will not adhere well to bare metal, and the difficulty is compounded by grease and oil used for protection and lubrication during storage, cutting and pressing of metal components.

Manufacturer's basic treatment:

When a mass-produced car body leaves the spot-welding line as an assembled shell it is cleaned and degreased by dipping in a succession of alkali emulsion baths, then rinsed in water. It is then dipped in manganese phosphate or some other proprietary phosphating solution, which leaves a fine crystalline surface to act as a key for the primer. It also retards rusting, but only for a short time, as many thousands of motorists know to their cost. After phosphating, the body is rinsed again in water, then given a chromic acid rinse to neutralise or 'fix' the phosphate coating.

Any untreated phosphate salts lurking in crevices will cause corrosion within four years. A bigger menace in car production is the paint-line blemish or accidental damage on the trim line. Such cars go back to a hospitalisation track, where they are buffed down to the bare metal and re-painted. The buffing removes the phosphate coating, making the car a candidate for early rusting. Automobile Association engineers say that up to one third of all cars have been doctored in this way.

Doors, bonnets and boot lids are also phosphated, but some manufacturers do not apply any primer/sealer to hidden surfaces such as the insides of door panels and box sections, which are notorious condensation traps.

The bottom of an unprotected steel door has a life of four or five years before it is eaten through with rust.

The outer paint covers the rust for a time and then begins to blister. Owners have been known to attribute this to leaving the car in the sun. In fact it is the rain, not the sun, that does the damage. It is not unusual for a distributor to find water in the doors of new cars which have been stored in fields, and rusting which has gone beyond the superficial stage.

When phosphating was introduced after the Second World War, extravagant claims were made for its rust-proofing properties on the basis of accelerated weathering tests, which showed that if a phosphated panel were scratched, rust did not spread under the paint to the same extent as on an unphosphated panel. Unfortunately this demonstration is not relevant to corrosion starting on the unphosphated side.

Hot-dip galvanising:

The use of hot-dip galvanised steel, which has a coating of zinc on both sides, would extend the life of car bodies considerably. A car underbody with .005 inch of zinc, properly painted, should last between 15 and 20 years – three times longer than existing car bodies. Painting is necessary because zinc itself corrodes away if exposed to the atmosphere. To meet the car manufacturer's objection that zinc-coated steel is more expensive to spot-weld, the British Steel Corporation produced a differentially-coated hot-dip galvanised steel, which has more zinc on one side than on the other, to facilitate spot welding, but the motor manufacturers seem reluctant to use it. Hot-dip galvanised steel has been used successfully in America, Germany and by Rolls-Royce and Volvo.

Exhaust systems:

Mild steel exhaust systems often rust out in a year or two. Some have failed just within the manufacturer's 12,000 mile warranty instead of just beyond, and this may lead to some improvement. A promising alternative is aluminised steel, which has a protective coating of aluminium on either side. It offers strong resistance to most of the forms of corrosive attack to which the exhaust is prone, and the extra retail cost on a new car would be between £1 and £2.50. Aluminium paint, which is seen on the outside of replacement silencers, is useless.

Stainless steel offers even more substantial improvement, but at considerably higher cost. However, a motorist specifying a stainless steel exhaust on a new car will recoup the additional outlay when the first mild steel replacement would have been due, and show a profit on the second occasion.

Undersealing:

Undersealing of the black rubber or bitumastic type is only a temporary rust inhibitor; even the best can do more harm than good after two or three years by concealing rust that is slowly destroying the structural steel members beneath it. Underbody sealing on new cars is not always carried out carefully, and temperature changes in the bodywork can cause cracking of the sealant. If water gets under the compound, rust will spread under the seal, which is nothing more than a poultice, locking the moisture in and aggravating the trouble.

1:3 The manufacturer's point of view

While it is easy to criticise production methods which lead to cars rusting away in a few years, it has to be remembered that the motor industry also has a case. Although car bodies could be made to last twenty years with the use of more expensive materials such as zinc-coated steel, how many motorists would want to keep the same car for that length of time? Other consumer 'durables' are discarded before they are worn out, simply because they look old-fashioned, and the car market is as fashion conscious as any.

Up to the present, motorists appear to be more interested in low first cost, reliability and performance than in corrosion resistance, and the car manufacturers maintain that they are giving the motorist the best possible cost benefit based on his own preferences. It might be said that the basic cause of rust is apathy on the part of motorists.

The industry is competitive and the maker with the keenest prices tends to get the business. So the manufacturer's criterion in selecting materials is cheapness, not corrosion resistance, and the conservation lobby has a long way to go before it can enforce the use of longer lasting materials for car bodies. A 1971 Government report suggested several ways in which cars could inexpensively be made to last up to three years longer, but action is unlikely to follow such suggestions without some compulsion. Where better standards have been adopted – the use of galvanising by Volvo and Porsche for example – it is usually on cars selling in a high enough price bracket for the extra cost to be acceptable.

There are some signs that the situation may be changing. Growing awareness of the problem has resulted from increased publicity. It has been estimated that corrosion of an unprotected car body costs the owner something like £1 a week in depreciation, and the increasing number of people willing to pay to have their cars rust-proofed by one of the commercially available processes indicates that the potential cost of rust no longer goes unnoticed. This growth of public opinion may in time influence the manufacturers. The publicity given by some firms, Fiat for example, to recent improvements in their production rust-proofing processes may be the first sign of this movement. Another example is the use by British Leyland of wax injection to protect the sills of some of their recent models.

1:4 Buying a used car

Rust must obviously be a major factor to be taken into account when looking for a secondhand car. Take a stroll around a large car park and examine some older examples of the model you are thinking of buying. The age is usually indicated by the suffix of the registration number ('C' for 1965, 'D' for 1966 and so on through the alphabet; 'I' was omitted).

Most cars are affected by rust in some or all of the following spots: top of wing behind headlamp; rear of front wheel arch; bottoms of doors; sills under doors; front and back of rear wheelarch; around jacking points; bottom of boot lid; either side of wing panel joints; around trim strip attachment points; and in horizontal channels where water can lie. At the used car dealer's premises there is not usually a fleck of rust to be seen, but you will know where to look for body stopper under that new coat of paint. Resprayed or touched-up panels may very well conceal rust. Remember that if the paint is actually bubbling and lifting at any point the rust has almost certainly come right through the metal from the other side. Without very thorough preparation corrosion will continue under the new paint, and within a year the first brown lumps will push their way to the surface.

Rust is no respector of price tags. The Automobile Association's statistics, published in the autumn of 1974, show that advanced corrosion was found on 3 per cent of the 4500 one to two year old cars examined, on 10 per cent of four to five year old cars and on 24 per cent of those over five years old.

Inadequate ventilation and drainage of box sections appears from this survey to be a major cause of trouble, particularly in sills.

Underfloor inspection:

One problem involved in buying a secondhand car is that although superficial rusting is often fairly easily detected, dangerous structural corrosion is often not visible without a thorough examination of the underside.

A dealer cannot reasonably refuse permission for an intending purchaser to examine the underside of a car, but he may try to talk his way out of it. Arrange for the use of the hoist at a nearby garage or, better still, at a garage you use regularly. If they value your custom they will soon tell you whether the car is worth buying. Alternatively, an AA or RAC inspector will examine the car for a moderate fee.

If you decide to make the inspection yourself, you must identify the main stress-bearing members. In the case of a car with the older kind of separate chassis made up of two channel section sidemembers this is not difficult. Look for cracks around the spring shackle bolts, steering box mounting and at all other bolt holes, joints and welds. Make sure that there are no notches or breaks in the upper or lower edges of the main channel sections. Damage to these flanges can lead to chassis breakage.

With more modern designs it may be less easy to decide which parts of the structure are vital. If in doubt refer to the next section of this chapter, **Section 1:5**, which describes the principal types of construction likely to be encountered. Ideally, of course, the car should be entirely free from rust. But circumstances may well dictate that you settle for less. Common sense suggests that corrosion of structural members must be rectified by replacement which is often not easy and this may well constitute a reason for not buying the car. Corrosion of non-structural parts such as doors, bonnet, boot lid and bolted-on wings is less important.

A methodical way of checking for structural weakness caused by corrosion is to start at the suspension or shock absorber mountings at the front end and follow the main flitch plates and sills back to the rear mountings. If none of this metal is rotten, the car body probably has some mileage left in it.

If time permits, take out the headlamps and see whether the headlamp housing is corroded. Complete front end outer skin assemblies in steel or GRP (glassfibre) are available for popular models but it is a waste of money to fit these if the main structure is beyond repair. Tidying up the exterior appearance will not offset the dangers of a weakened structure.

Trouble spots:

It has already been indicated that box sections and enclosed cavities are the biggest danger areas where rust is concerned. Places in the wheelarches where mud can accumulate must be investigated as well. Individual models have their own weak spots but a number of other general warnings can be given.

Seat mountings:

Remember that the floor below a seat carries the weight of the occupant, a load magnified by up and down movement over rough road surfaces. Any failure here is potentially very dangerous. Look carefully for any sign of distortion in the seat frames, mountings and slides, and check that the slides are firmly anchored to the floor. Inspect the floor to ensure that it is not weakened by corrosion around the seat mountings.

Steering box mounting:

Another fruitful source of trouble is loose or rusted steering box or rack mountings. Get an assistant to turn the steering wheel while the car is stationary and watch for any movement of the unit against the bodyshell.

Doors and windows:

Check the operation of all window winders and ventilators and see whether the felt or rubber seals are worn or rotten. Make sure that all the door catches work properly (from inside as well as outside), that the door locks are not stiff and that the catches on the ventilators are not broken. Look all round the inside of the windscreen glazing strip and door seals for signs of leaking. If possible, run the car through an automatic car wash to test for leaks.

Persistent leaking can cause severe floor pan rusting over a period of time. The dealer may be willing to rectify small faults if you point them out before you buy.

When purchasing a vehicle with any wooden framing – some estate cars retained structural woodwork until quite recently – check the timber for rot and woodworm. The fit of doors and sliding windows may be affected by deterioration of the woodwork too.

Vehicle test certificates:

Strange as it may seem, a corrosion-free underframe is not one of the statutory requirements of the annual safety test of cars, which is carried out by garages for the Department of the Environment, and still often called the MoT test after the old Ministry of Transport. The test concerns only brakes, steering gear, tyres, lights, reflectors and seat belts.

On the other hand an authorised examiner may, and usually does, refuse to carry out the brake test if the chassis (or its equivalent in unit construction vehicles) is so weakened by corrosion that it could not be driven and the brakes applied without risk of an accident or damage to the vehicle. Similarly, an insecure driver's seat, or a corroded steering box mounting, will cause him to refuse to carry out the steering test. A corroded engine subframe is another common ground for refusal to complete the test.

Details of the DoE test are published in **Vehicle Testing: The Tester's Manual**, which is available to the public from the Stationery Office or through any bookseller. It gives details of what to look for when testing the brakes, steering, tyres and lights, but 'dangerous corrosion' is not defined. This is left to the examiner's discretion. There is provision for appeal against the refusal of a test certificate, but this is rarely invoked.

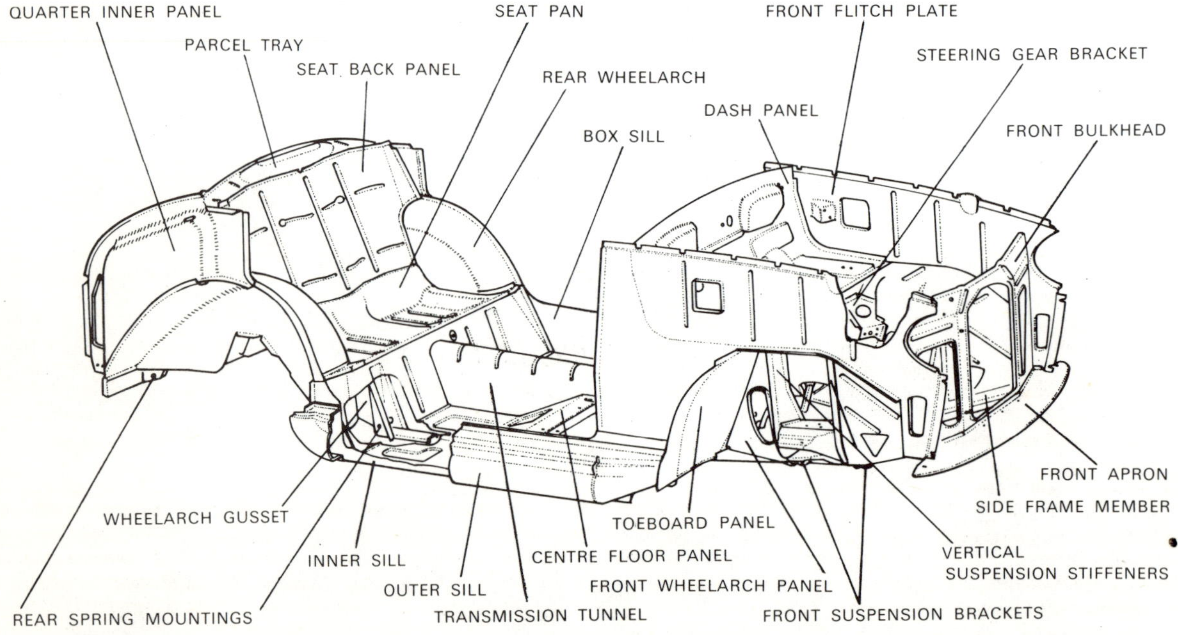

FIG 1:1   **Unit construction: Austin A30 inner shell structure**

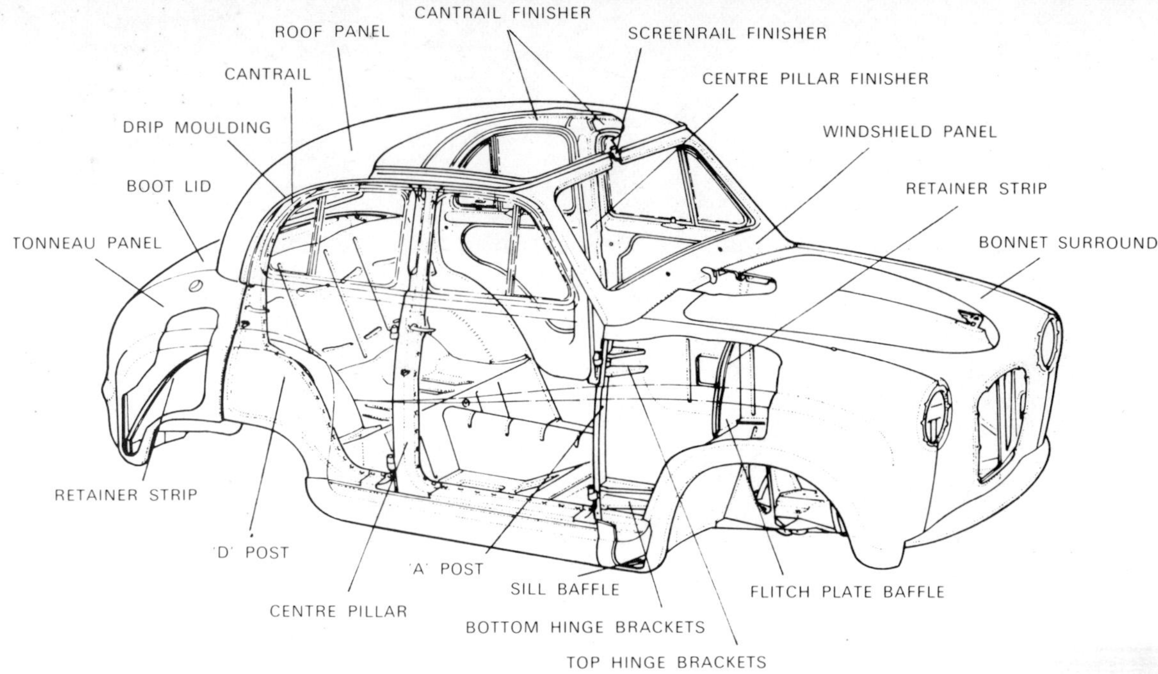

FIG 1:2   Unit construction: cutaway view of complete A30 bodyshell

1:5 The structure of the car

The majority of modern cars are built on the unit construction principle, in which the old distinction between body and chassis has disappeared and the bodyshell, an assembly of sheet steel pressings, combines both the external panelwork and the load-bearing structure of the vehicle. There are many detail variations in the design of unit construction cars, but they all consist of inner and outer skins forming boxes to give the rigidity formerly provided by heavy channel-section chassis. Despite the changes in outward appearance, the underlying techniques have remained the same since unit construction began to be used.

One of the first post-war British cars made in this way was the Austin A30. The A30 shell (FIG 1:1) is made mostly of 20 swg sheet steel, and the outer and inner skins are readily recognisable. The main vertical loads run from the suspension points into two side beams, which are made up of the front flitch plate, box sills and rear wheelarches. At the rear end of the sills the vertical loads are carried through a torsion box into the rear wheelarch. The box is formed by the heelboard, inner sill, rear wheelarch and wheelarch gusset.

Transverse beams, which provide torsional rigidity, run between the side beams. They consist of the front apron, front bulkhead, dash panel, toeboard panel, centre floor, heelboard, seat-back and seat-pan, and the spare wheel floor panel.

On top of the rear wheelarches are spot-welded the quarter inner panels which run back from the seat-back to the rear of the car. These are tied together by the parcel tray, and by the spare wheel floor extension.

Spot-welded to the underside of the front apron and running to the toeboard are two side frame members, which are made up of two parts forming an L-section with flanged sides. The front wheelarch panel is welded to a flanged opening in the flitch plate, also to the toeboard panel and front bulkhead. Inside the front wheelarch, sitting on top of the side frames, are the vertical suspension stiffeners, bridged by the front shock absorber mounting bracket.

Severe corrosion of any part of this inner structure could lead to refusal of a test certificate.

The outer shell (FIG 1:2) consists of the 'A' posts, centre pillars and 'D' posts, U-section cant rails running across the tops of the pillars, roof panel, windshield panel, tonneau panel and bonnet surround. There is a rubber seal between the inner structure and the outer panels. Detachable front wings are bolted to the front flitch plates, bonnet surround and 'A' posts.

Unit construction with subframes:

The commonest variation on the completely integral unit construction just described involves the use of subframes, exemplified in the BLMC Mini and 1100/1300 ranges. The bodyshell is of the same basic type, with load-bearing sills and crossmembers. But the power unit and suspension components, instead of being mounted directly on the shell, are carried on front and rear subframes, separate pressed steel structures which initially accept all the running stresses. The subframes in turn are attached to the main body by rubber insulated mountings.

Advantages of this type of construction include ease of assembly during manufacture, the fact that the operating stresses can be fed into the bodyshell over a wide area rather than at concentrated high stress points, and the

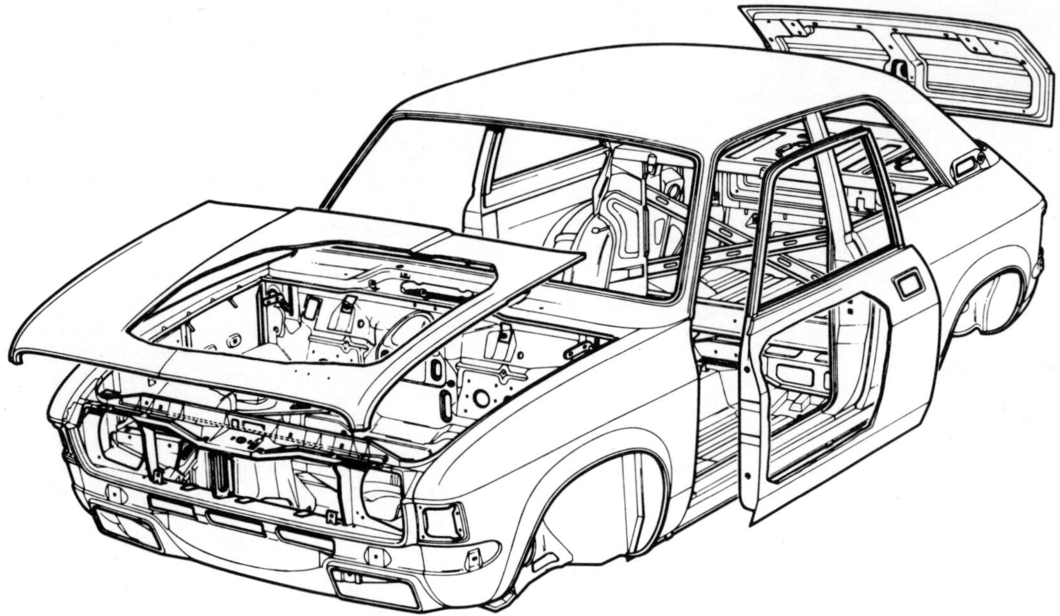

FIG 1:3   Unit construction: the same principles apply to the Austin Allegro bodyshell

possibility of insulating the passenger compartment more effectively from noise and vibration. Disadvantages can include higher cost and weight, problems of servicing accessibility and the vulnerability of some subframe designs to corrosion.

Some unit construction cars have a removable front crossmember carrying part or all of the front suspension components, and in some cases this has been developed to carry the engine mountings as well so that it becomes a kind of abbreviated subframe. Similarly, some cars with independent rear suspension have the differential unit mounted on a small subframe.

Subframes are almost always pressed steel assemblies like the main shell, and so are no more or less corrosion resistant. They are, however, usually replaceable. What can be more of a problem are the areas of the bodyshell to which the subframes are attached; severe rusting there can render the car irreparable.

Separate chassis construction:

The type of construction which utilises a separate chassis frame is still to be found on some vehicles. It is not common among recent mass production cars – some Triumph models including the Herald and Spitfire are exceptions – but is widely employed by the smaller production specialist manufacturers, often in conjunction with GRP (glassfibre) bodywork, and it is still almost universal for larger commercial vehicles.

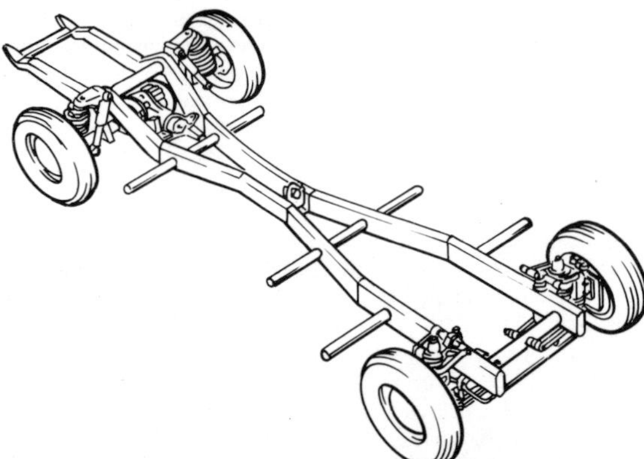

FIG 1:5   Example of separate chassis construction

Open channel sections, boxes, square tubes or round tubes may be used, and different designs vary in the disposition of the major members. The Triumphs already referred to, for example, have two main longerons close together in the centre of the car, forming a rigid backbone, with a rectangle of lighter section outriggers to carry the floor and body.

All the major mechanical and running loads are absorbed by the chassis, leaving the body panels largely unstressed. The floor is still important, of course, as it carries the weight of the passengers, and the body

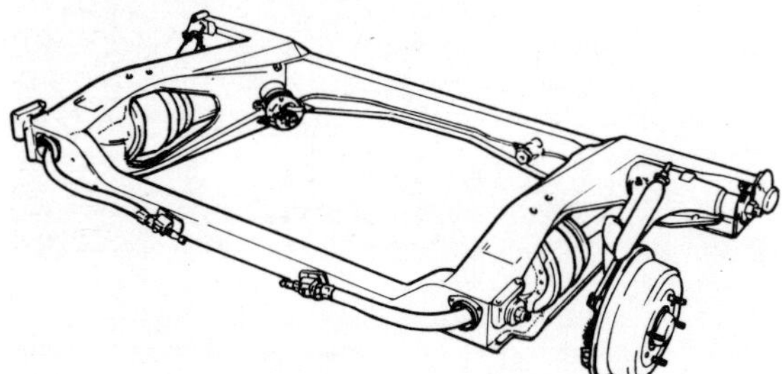

FIG 1:4   Mini rear subframe and suspension

14

framing must be able to accept some strain, for example from door hinges and locks. In some cases, too, the body contributes to the stiffness of the whole car, providing additional bracing. But it is the chassis frame which bears the principal strain.

Compared with unit construction, the separate chassis design has the advantage that the important components are usually of thicker steel and thus able to withstand rust for longer before becoming dangerously weakened. But they are not immune and the same careful check for mud-filled cavities and corrosion traps is required. Where rust already has a hold, the chassis can be easier to repair than an integral bodyshell because the structure is simpler and the metal thicker. For the restorer of old cars separate chassis construction facilitates the process of completely dismantling, reconditioning and rebuilding; the principal requirements are almost limitless time and patience.

Alternative structures:

A number of other types of car construction have been employed. The Rover 2000/2200/3500 models are built round an endoskeleton or base unit which is somewhere between a separate chassis and the inner skin of a unit construction car; all the visible body panels are unstressed and bolted on. The VW Beetle has a flat floor pan, braced by a central tunnel, which forms a completely self-supporting chassis – hence its use as the basis for Buggies and other specials – but is stiffened when the body is bolted on. Recent Lotus road cars (Elan, Europa, Elite) have a backbone of sheet metal which forks at each end to carry the suspension and power unit; the GRP bodyshell sits over this backbone and itself carries the driver and passengers.

Other possible structures which have been tried in small numbers include multi-tube spaceframes and unitary shells entirely made of GRP and marine plywood.

1:6 What can the motorist do about rust?

The problems of rust can be avoided by purchasing a car with a body made of GRP (glassfibre) but the choice is very limited. And it should be remembered that most GRP cars have a steel chassis to compensate for the material's natural lack of rigidity. GRP itself is not perfect, either, and the owner may find that he has exchanged one set of problems for another. So for most motorists the rust bogey remains.

New cars, or those less than three months old, can be protected by spraying the underside and the inside surfaces of all closed cavities such as front wings, doors and sills with a non-hardening sealing compound. Firms such as Ziebart, Endrust, Dinitrol and Cadulac offer this service. None of these protection systems has been in use long enough in the humid British climate to enable anyone to say with certainty how far the life span of a steel car body will be extended, but experience in America, Sweden and Japan indicates that the treatment is well worthwhile on a new car.

Ziebart, for example, whose process is specified by top quality car manufacturers and was chosen by the US Defense Department, are confident enough to offer a ten year guarantee. They use a petroleum-based waxy sealant with a bonding agent to ensure that it adheres

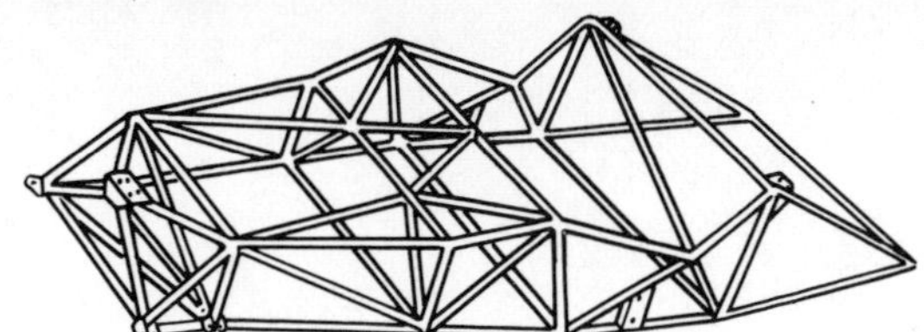

FIG 1:6   Multi-tube spaceframe chassis

to the metal. The sealant remains soft enough to be self-healing in the event of small scratches and slight distortion of panels. The cost of treatment varies with the size of the car from around £50 to £70, not a large sum to add to the price of a new car.

To be effective, such treatments need inspection and partial renewal from time to time. To comply with the Ziebart guarantee against rusting through from the inside in 10 years (or 100,000 miles) owners should take their cars to the service station every two years, where they will be charged an inspection fee (at present £2) and the current cost of a preliminary power wash. Other rust-protection companies offer guarantees, but not all in the same terms, so it is advisable to read the small print carefully, before deciding where to have the work done.

Some new cars arrive at the rust-protection station with advanced rusting on them, and this needs sand-blasting before the protective wax is applied. It is impossible to lay down any hard-and-fast rules because rusting is a haphazard effect, depending on weather, locality and workmanship. All that Ziebart can say about older cars is that they will make an inspection and decide whether they can offer a guaranteed treatment.

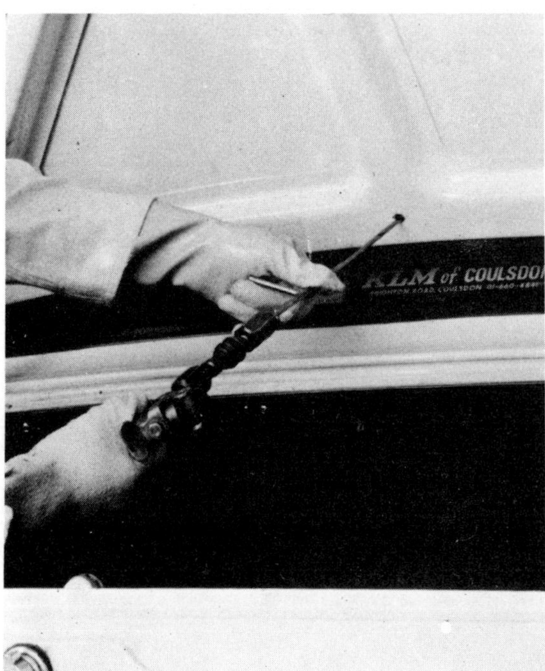

FIG 1:7   Injecting Ziebart sealant

Can I do it myself?

Spraying the underside of a car with sealant is an extremely messy process. The proprietary solution is not readily available, and the special nozzles and guns will be useless for anything else. An industrial air compressor and a car lift are necessary, also some heavy protective clothing. In short, the private owner should have this work done by a properly-equipped service station. For home use, undersealant applied by brush is the stuff to use, but of course one cannot get into closed sections with this.

The alternative to professional waxing of closed sections is to use a syringe filled with one of the lighter proprietary mixtures sold for the purpose. Suitable compounds are advertised in the motoring press. In some instances, the syringe can be inserted through a screw hole to save drilling. If it is necessary to drill a hole, this should be plugged afterwards, if there is any possibility of rain or road splashes entering it. If it is in a sheltered position inside the car it may be left open to provide ventilation. Needless to say, there is no guarantee attached to the use of these syringes, and one must repeat the process fairly frequently.

Before applying any kind of undersealant, the under-side of the car must be thoroughly cleaned. Steam cleaning is best, and your garage will tell you where to have this done. It takes about two hours, including the engine bay. Alternatively, you can do it yourself with a proprietary solution called 'Gunk', which is very effective. Have a good look round for patches of rust, and investigate any stains suggesting that water is seeping through from the other side of the panel. Corrosion spreading from such places will lift the undersealant off the metal it is supposed to protect. The car should be left overnight to dry out thoroughly after cleaning.

Do not apply undersealant to the propeller shaft, sump, rear axle casing, silencer, exhaust pipe, brake gear or any of the lubrication points. An even coat should be applied to the wings, wing skirts, gravel deflectors, petrol tank, rocker panels, floor and the inner face of the bumpers.

The brushed-on sealers of the rubberised or bitumastic kind which dry hard are very resistant to water and grit thrown up by the wheels. The danger with them is always that the adhesion to the paint underneath may be less than perfect so that water penetrates between the two; in that case the rust is merely concealed, not prevented. This is why it is important to clean the surface thoroughly

FIG 1:8   Surfaces to be treated with undersealant must first be thoroughly cleaned

FIG 1:10   Exhaust pipe and propeller shaft are kept free of sealant by masking

FIG 1:9   Remove surface rust with a wire brush

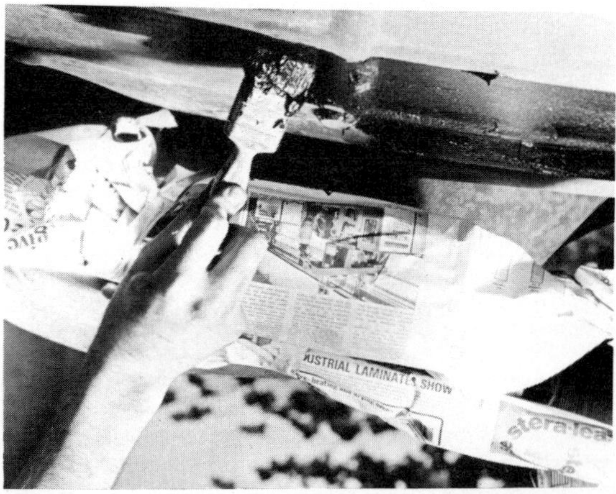

FIG 1:11   Brushing undersealant on flat surfaces

before application. It also means that these compounds are not ideal for use over panel joints or crevices, and the non-hardening, waxy sealants are better for such applications. For most cars the best compromise may well be a combination of both types, with wax in the enclosed cavities and crevices and a rubbery sealer on flat exposed areas.

Rust removers and rust inhibitors:

The processes described so far are aimed at preventing the onset of rust. What is to be done when rust is already in evidence? The use of acids to remove mill scale and rust from steel is not a new technique. Since the advent of the high-street motor shop, competing brands of rust remover and rust inhibitor have proliferated, and the claims made for some of them owe more to the advertisement copy writer's imagination than to chemistry. In an attempt to divide the sheep from the goats the Automobile Association commissioned Yarsley Testing Laboratories to measure the performance of the ten best-selling rust removers and inhibitors. The results were published in the AA magazine DRIVE. The form of test, known as an accelerated weathering test, is equivalent to five years in the life of a car, packed into 400 hours. It may be objected that 400 hours is not the same as five years on the road, but many years' experience has shown that such accelerated tests are 'qualitatively' accurate, meaning that if one material is better than another in the tests, it will be better in long-term service.

Most rust removers are solutions of hydrochloric or phosphoric acid. If they are not completely cleaned away after use they will eat into the subsequent paint film.

Rust inhibitors are really primers containing lead or zinc, which forms a protective coat. The AA tests did not support any of the claims that some rust removers gave subsequent protection, or that some inhibitors also acted as removers.

There are also a few 'half and half' products known as rust killers, which are a mixture of acid and chemicals that react with rust to form a coating. They are designed to make rust inert and to form a protective coat. Kurust is claimed to be the first in this field and it performed well in the AA test, giving a few months' protection without a primer.

Motor body repair firms do not use any of these high-priced products. They use wet-or-dry sanding paper and 'elbow grease', except in inaccessible situations, where raw spirits of salts (hydrochloric acid) may be applied, then flushed away with plenty of water, followed by drying with a compressed air line.

It is worth examining the AA test in greater detail, in order to remove some of the misunderstandings fostered by advertising. Test panels cut from mild sheet steel were uniformly rusted for a fortnight by being placed in a cabinet and subjected to a fine spray of 5 per cent salt solution for eight hours daily. They were put out of doors for the remainder of the day, and at weekends.

At the end of the fortnight each of the proprietary inhibitors or removers was used, strictly in accordance with the instructions, to treat four panels. Each rust remover was tested with and without a further coat of red oxide primer. The conclusions and the strength and appearance tests published in DRIVE were based on the performance of the primed panels. As a control, four rusted panels were painted with red oxide primer only.

All the panels were re-subjected to the salt spray and checked every 48 hours. After 400 hours, equivalent to five years in service in the British climate, the panels were checked for appearance and for the adhesion strength of each product. This was measured by scratching with a scriber loaded with different weights until the surface broke.

The red oxide primer on the control panels survived for the equivalent of two years before any rust appeared on the surface. By the end of the test, after 400 hours, there was no sign of the surface lifting. The panel had a strong, scratch-resistant bond, but looked rough.

Holts Zinc Plate inhibitor emerged as clearly the best of all the products tested, reports the AA. The instructions on the container call for the addition of two coats of Holts Universal Primer, which were sprayed on from the aerosol in which it is sold. Holts Zinc Plate was easy to apply, its failure time was much longer than any other product and in the long term it was durable and looked good.

Two other inhibitors claimed to be complete primers in themselves and so these were tested without any further primer. The results were poor.

All the rust removers helped to clean off rust, but their other properties were strictly limited. Plus Gas Formula E was the best of the removers for strength and was safe to handle with bare hands. It also looked good. Only two others were better than ordinary red oxide primer in the short term, and remainder could do no better than red oxide.

Painting red oxide over a rust patch will give a motorist two years of blemish-free bodywork says the report, but it would be a false economy. When rust first appeared on the control sample it came in a rush. For all their claims like 'retards re-rusting' or 'primes and protects', none of the conventional removers inhibited rust. On the panels tested without primer, rust appeared just as quickly as if there were no preventer there at all.

The lesson of this, as Marcus Jacobson, the AA's chief engineer insists, is that whatever product is used for cleaning off rust, an additional coat of primer is needed before the colour coat is applied, no matter what the instructions on the colour-coat tin may say. Very few of the rust removers tested included this advice in their instructions.

With so much emphasis on 'quick and easy' repairs, the time required for rust removers and inhibitors to do their work is often overlooked. Holts Zinc Plate inhibitor, for instance, should be left for 24 hours before their grey primer is applied, and this primer needs two hours to dry before a second coat or a colour coat is sprayed. The other inhibitors tested for the AA by Yarsley needed at least 24 hours. One required at least 48 hours.

Kurust needs one hour. The Plus Gas Formula E treatment needs drying time for the first coat and 24 hours for the second. The rust removers are acids and need only 10 or 15 minutes. They must be cleaned off thoroughly before any paint is applied.

The need for this educational effort on the part of the AA is illustrated by the fact that a well-known maker of rust remover was fined £100 under the Trade Descriptions Act in the autumn of 1974 for publishing an advertisement claiming that their brand converted rust back into metal.

The defence said it was a mistake, but the chairman of the bench called it flagrant misrepresentation.

1:7 Maintenance

Regular washing:

Having protected the inner surfaces and underside, and made good any break in the paint film, all that the owner can do is to prevent the build-up of acid on the body by regular washing. The car should be washed at least once a fortnight, rinsing with plenty of water. This dilutes the acid to the point where it is harmless, and flushes it away. Dry off with a chamois leather, paying special attention to hollows where water can lie. Crevices are best dried out with an air line, if this is available. Ascertain that there are drain holes in the bottoms of the doors and sills and that these are clear. After a wash, leave boot, bonnet and doors open until the car is dry.

Because warmth speeds up chemical reactions, it is better to leave a wet car outside a heated garage. This does not mean that garages are unnecessary. They should be used whenever possible to protect dry cars from the weather.

Ideally, a car should be washed every time it has been out in the rain, and 100 years ago a groom would be standing by to wash the carriage directly it arrived on a wet day. This is impracticable today, but the more frequently a car is washed, the longer it is likely to last.

A much-needed improvement to car-washing machines is a high-pressure jet of water to scour the wheelarches and underside, but in the present state of apathy on the part of car owners, there is little incentive for the garage owner to spend money on such an improvement.

The car owner must usually do it himself, and the work is made much easier by investing in a pair of ramps. Choose a well-made pair and they will last indefinitely. **Do not use makeshift supports like piles of bricks.** Too many people have sentenced themselves to a painful death in this way.

Polishing:

Cars, like carriages before them, are traditionally glossy. Polishing makes the car look attractive but it is useless for the prevention of corrosion. Modern paints do not need surface protection; it is the metal underneath that is the cause of the trouble.

Avoid the use of polishes containing silicones; all they have in their favour is a quick shine. The snag is that they repel paint as well as water, and cause a great deal of trouble when any touching-in or repainting has to be done. Always wash a car well before polishing, otherwise the loose dust picked up by the polishing rag will erode the paint just as effectively as sandpaper.

Cleaning leathercloth:

Leathercloth seats, hoods and hard tops may be cleaned with soap and water and a nail-brush, or with one of the proprietary solutions sold for the purpose. If soap and water is not effective against longstanding grime, try methylated spirit and a nail-brush. As explained in the chapter on Trimming, leathercloth can be resurfaced with special paint.

Care of leather seats:

Cowhide seats should not be cleaned with the detergents used on leathercloth and other synthetics. They should be washed occasionally with toilet soap and warm water, and given a rub over with 'leather food' to maintain their softness. Old, neglected leather seats sometimes found in vintage cars can be restored by the curriers if the covers are taken off and returned to them.

Cleaning carpets:

Carpets should be cleaned with a stiff brush or a vacuum cleaner. It will be found that some of the American-style car vacuum cleaners which plug into the cigar lighter are too long to be useful in British cars, and that a domestic vacuum cleaner with a flexible extension hose is more effective. The carpet can then be cleaned with a domestic carpet cleaning solution. It is not advisable to subject car carpets to the dry cleaning process.

Squashed flies:

Squashed flies and bird's droppings should be washed off paintwork as soon as possible, because they contain acids which will eat into the paint, forming a pit which will become a rust spot. Special solvents are sold for the purpose, but human spittle costs nothing and is equally effective!

Tarspots:

Tar spots can be removed with a rag moistened in petrol or eucalyptus oil. Give the solvent time to loosen the tar. Do not use cellulose thinners for cleaning; keep it for its proper purpose, which is the dilution of cellulose lacquer. It may appear to be cleaning paint, but in fact it is dissolving it and taking it off.

Cleaning chromium plate:

Chromium plate is a 'flash' coating, less than a thousandth of an inch thick, on a substrate of nickel. Abrasives should never be used on chromium plate because they will rub it off the nickel completely. Metal polishes should not be used either, for the same reason. Grease and tar spots should be removed with petrol, eucalyptus oil or white spirit, and the remainder washed with water containing a mild detergent, as used on the paintwork. Chromium should be polished with a clean, dry cotton cloth or chamois leather. The slight tarnish found on neglected chromium may be removed with one of the harmless chrome cleaning fluids on the market. Some manufacturers recommend an application of light mineral oil or grease on chromium plate during the winter months, when there is salt on the roads, but grease should not be used on bright plastics trim.

Cleaning glass:

A little domestic detergent added to the windscreen washer water will help to prevent smears on the screen, and the greasy traffic film which builds up on the glass in dry weather can be removed with a domestic window cleaning solution or one of the screen cleaners sold in motor shops.

CHAPTER 2

Repair techniques

2:1 Panel materials

The panels of early cars were made of Honduras mahogany, which paints well and is not given to warping. To save weight it was sometimes cut thin and reinforced with canvas. The demand for cheaper cars and greater curvature led to experiments with plywood, papier maché and radiating segments of softwood glued together and covered with canvas. None of these was successful, mainly because there were no waterproof glues. The Weymann fabric-covered body was successful but did not lend itself to mass production.

The ductility of aluminium was recognised, and at first aluminium was used for curved panels and steel for flat surfaces. Hard-temper aluminium was used for plain bending and half-hard for panel beating. The objections to aluminium were its high price compared with steel and the impossibility of soldering over screw heads which had to be hidden under stopper or a moulding.

Steel panels suffered badly from rust, and the answer to this was terneplate (lead-coated steel) which was difficult to paint, or tinplate (tin-coated steel) which was too expensive for general use. And neither of these coatings is suitable for welding. Zinc-coated steel is one of the best materials for corrosion resistance, but paints do not adhere to it well unless it has been well weathered. Adhesion may be improved by weak acids, by phosphating, or by the ICI Lithoform process. But zinc coating raises costs and can lead to welding difficulties. So most firms settled for plain steel, with a phosphate primer.

In a letter to THE AUTOCAR of April 30, 1954, a reader ruefully compared a galvanised bucket bought in 1938, and still serviceable although it had no maintenance since new, with his post-war car which was falling to pieces through rust. Could not the directors of the motor companies galvanise their car bodies, he asked.

Twenty years have passed since that letter was written and only now is there some sign of progress, thanks to the public attention drawn to the problem by the AA and the motoring press.

But whatever its qualities of resistance or lack of resistance to rust, the use of steel for car bodies necessitates the employment of pressing and panel beating techniques. For mass production huge power presses are used. The deep-drawing sheet steel used by the motor industry is stretched thin and sometimes even pinholed in the press, which is one reason why it often rusts through so easily. For one-off jobs and the repair of damaged panels, less complicated equipment is needed. Slight damage can be made good with polyester filler (see **Section 2:9**) but anything more will require panel beating.

2:2 Principles of panel beating

Panel beating depends on the ductility of the metal and the skill of the beater. It is impossible to teach manual skill by means of the written word, but the principles can be explained. Manual skill is best acquired by standing next to George while he works, and then by having George stand next to you while you try.

Curvature of sheet metal is achieved by reducing the thickness of the centre part of the sheet, either by hammering or by squeezing between crowned rollers. These processes have the effect of stretching the metal. Conversely, metal which has been stretched, as in a dent caused by accident, can be thickened by hammering, which takes up the slack. The equivalent of 'darts' in needlework are puckers in sheet metal, which are drawn together by hammering to form a thicker section. This is called gathering. A moderate amount of heat increases the ductility of sheet metal. Prolonged hammering leads to embrittlement or 'work hardening' and this can be corrected by heating the metal and allowing it to cool slowly (annealing). Another way of shrinking sheet metal, particularly aluminium, is to heat it and then cool it suddenly with a wet rag (quenching).

2:3 Tools for panel beating

The minimum plant required for a sheet metalworking shop consists of a guillotine for cutting sheets, a folder for preparing long joggled joints, rolls for making stiffening ribs or swages, a wheeling machine for producing compound curvature, a hollowed-out elm bole and a sandbag made of leather. But for jobs within the scope of the amateur much simpler hand tools are adequate.

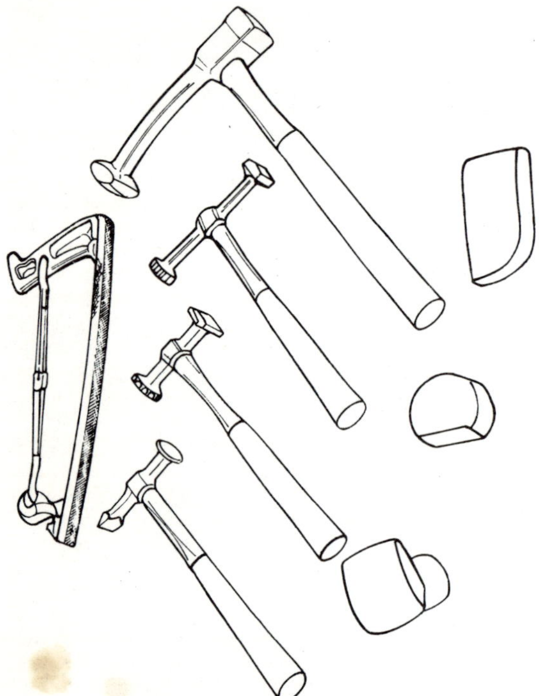

FIG 2:1   A selection of panel beating tools

Hammers:

The difference between a panel beater's hammer and others is the polished and slightly crowned surface. No panel can be smoother than the hammer used in shaping it, so the panel-beating hammer should not be used for any other purpose. There are half a dozen types, mainly differing in the length of neck. They can be obtained in sets, but there is no need to buy a full set to do one job. The long necks are intended to give clearance for working under high-crowned wings.

The basic type of panel-beating hammer is the finishing hammer, which has $1\frac{1}{2}$ inch clearance (meaning the distance from the shaft to the underside of the head). This hammer has a slightly crowned round face $1\frac{3}{8}$ inch in diameter at one end, and a wedge-shaped cross-pein

1 inch wide with a 2 inch clearance at the other. The weight of this hammer is about 12 oz.

A second type of finishing hammer has a $1\frac{1}{2}$ inch diameter round face, slightly crowned, and a $1\frac{1}{4}$ inch square face. The next in the series is the long-head 'dinging' hammer for use where clearance is needed. This has a $1\frac{1}{4}$ inch round face and a $1\frac{1}{8}$ inch square face, and weighs 24 oz. The long-head bumping hammer, for getting under high crowns, has one crowned head with $6\frac{3}{4}$ inch clearance and weighs 24 oz. The heads are carbon steel drop forgings and set on hickory shafts.

Spoons:

As the name implies, spoons are spoon-shaped hammers with either smooth or serrated working surfaces. They can be bought ready-made, or made in the workshop by bending old files after local annealing.

Dollies:

The general-purpose dolly block, or hand anvil, has a variety of radii and a good hand fit. There is about $7\frac{1}{2}$ sq inch of working area on the large face, and there is a thin beading edge. The weight of the block is $3\frac{1}{2}$ lb. The lozenge dolly, another general-purpose type, has many radii. The bottom and one side are flat, and both ends have high crowns. This type of dolly may measure 5 inch x $1\frac{3}{16}$ inch x $2\frac{9}{16}$ inch and weigh just over 3 lb. The heel dolly is semi-elliptical, with two flat and two crowned working surfaces, and is particularly useful in restricted places. Many other dollies are made to suit particular jobs.

Minimum tool kit:

The minimum kit of hand tools for car bodywork should contain a selection of dolly blocks; four planishing spoons (smooth, medium smooth, medium and extra heavy); an adjustable body file, which can be set concave, convex or flat; a hide mallet; a wooden mallet; and a planishing hammer.

2:4 Repairing steel panels

Badly crumpled panels of the thin gauge used in modern cars are not economically repairable on a commercial basis, but some of them may be uneconomically repaired as a labour of love, if the owner is prepared to keep the car off the road for long enough. It is best to straighten up the assembly as far as possible with a jack and to return the straightened part to its original position on the body before deciding whether to scrap a panel or not.

Repairable damage is knocked out with a hammer and dolly block, and then a good surface has to be restored by planishing. This is the most difficult part and it takes time and patience. The alternative is 'lead bodging' which means tinning the surface and then paddling on plumber's solder to hide the damage, or cold bodging with filled epoxy or polyester resin.

Planishing:

To planish a panel, the body file, which has a flexible cutting base, is set to the same curve as the panel, and worked over the surface lightly to remove any remaining paint and show up the high spots as bright scratched areas. Now for the spooning-up. Select a dolly block as near to the curvature of the panel as possible and hold it at the back, under each low spot, and hammer the top surface with the face of the spoon. The spoon blows should raise the low spots to the level of the high spots. The serrations on the face of the spoon will mark the surface of the metal over the head of the dolly, and act as a guide to its position underneath. They also show which areas have been spooned.

Now use the file again to reveal the new contours, which should show fewer and smaller hollows. These are spooned again and the process is repeated until there are no low spots. Hollows and ripples are more noticeable when a panel has been painted and polished, so good planishing is essential to obtain a professional finish.

The main point to understand is that the body file is only a guide. It must not be used to file off the high spots; this is a recipe for disaster. The whole process will take several hours, and is finished by sanding off the dolly marks and stopping those that remain with paintshop stopper.

Sometimes it is not possible to get a dolly behind the panel, but it may be possible to reverse the process and insert a flat or curved spoon and use the dolly on the outside. Concave surfaces require a convex spoon, which can be made out of a half-round file by local annealing and bending.

Shrinking:

The second basic process is shrinking, which involves the use of heat unless the damage is slight. When a car body panel is dented, the dent may be sprung out, but it will be found that the metal has been stretched and consequently thinned. The bulge can be removed by a sequence of local heating and hammering operations. Using a small nozzle on the welding torch, bring a small area about the size of a new penny ($\frac{3}{4}$ inch) to cherry-red heat. Hold a dolly behind the hot spot and with a mallet work the surrounding metal in towards the centre of the spot, using glancing blows to drive the metal from an area of about 6 inch surrounding the spot. Continue until the metal is cool. It will probably be necessary to repeat the operation several times, working further hot spots around the original, either in a circle or a spiral. When the shrinking is complete the whole area should be slightly below the original curvature, and it is restored to the correct shape by planishing.

Another method of shrinking is to heat the centre of the dent and hammer the bulge with a steel hammer against a dolly at the back, working spirally inwards, and quenching the metal with a wet rag to shrink it. Heavy blows are not required, but quick, light working. Several workings and shrinkings may be necessary.

Sometimes panels are stretched or bulged by distortion of the heavier sections to which they are attached, such as a door frame. In such cases the frame should be pulled or pushed back to correct shape with a body jack, which may take most of the slack out of the panel. Sometimes a slightly stretched panel can be tightened by hammering at the edges without the use of heat. This draws metal away from the centre by thickening it at the sides. Likewise, thickening the centre will draw away slack metal from the edges.

2:5 Repairing light alloy panels

Aluminium alloy panels require different treatment. Strip out the trim if any heat is to be used and clean off the paint mechanically or with a chemical stripper. Do not use a blow lamp for removing paint because of the danger of distorting the sheet metal. Whenever possible cold working should be used, particularly in deeply curved areas which are easier than flat surfaces. A dent should be bumped out with blows of a boxwood mallet on the convex or back surface, working outwards from the centre. If the damage did not cause much stretching the sheet will return almost to its original curvature.

If it is badly stretched, cold working would take far too long. The best way is to heat it with a welding pipe played on the back of the metal, raising the temperature to about 300 deg. C. This metal does not show red when hot but melts suddenly if overheated. The safe working temperature may be gauged by a piece of tallow, which turns brown when the metal is ready, or by a sliver of pinewood which scorches at the same temperature.

Hot shrinking of light alloy sheet differs from the method of hot-shrinking steel. Instead of the two stages of local heating and quenching, three stages must be performed in quick succession. First, heat the highest spot of the damaged area applying the tallow test. Second, tap the heated spot with a mallet backed up with a dolly. Third, quench rapidly with a wet rag. These processes should be repeated on the high spots of a panel until they have disappeared. The sheet will become rigid and slightly below the original level. A final light working with the hammer will bring it up.

2:6 Carbon-arc welding

Oxy-acetylene welding equipment is found in motor body shops because it can be fitted quickly with a cutting nozzle and used to cut through sheet metal. For welding alone the carbon-arc method is preferable, because it does not generate so much heat and leaves a softer bead, which is easier to file down.

Beware of some of the small electric welding sets sold in do-it-yourself shops. For car body welding it is essential to have direct current with uniformly straight polarity and independent control of both current and voltage. The filler metal used is a copper-silicon-manganese alloy, 95 to 98 per cent copper, 1.5 to 4 per cent silicon, and 0.25 to 1.10 manganese, such as 'Everdur' or 'Herculoy'. A $\frac{3}{32}$ inch rod is used for 16 and 18 gauge, and $\frac{1}{16}$ inch rod for 20 and 22 gauge. Use a standard $\frac{5}{32}$ inch carbon with a very small point, and extend it $1\frac{1}{2}$ inch from the holder. The current should be 50 amps for 16 gauge, down to 20 amps for lighter metal.

Strike the arc on the metal in the vicinity of the joint and hold it there until the carbon becomes incandescent, then slide it along without striking an arc until it touches the filler rod. Hold a very short arc, and always play the arc on the filler rod, not on the sheet metal. Long joints should be tack-welded every two or three inches and then filled in. Lay the filler metal at a 10 deg. angle, and keep the heat low to avoid warpage. The Lincoln dual continuous control equipment is ideal for this work.

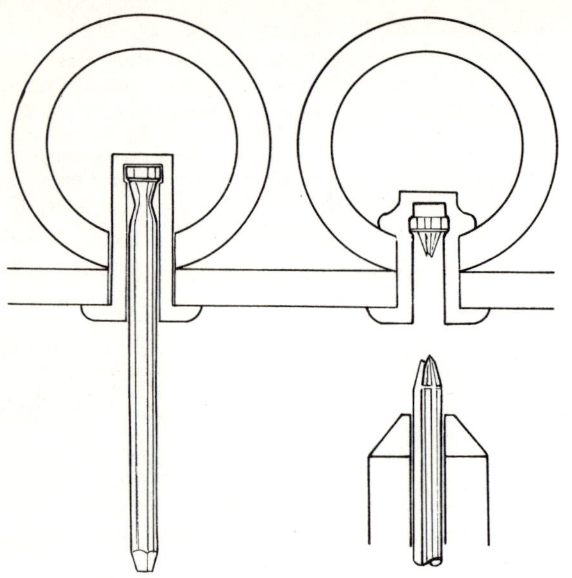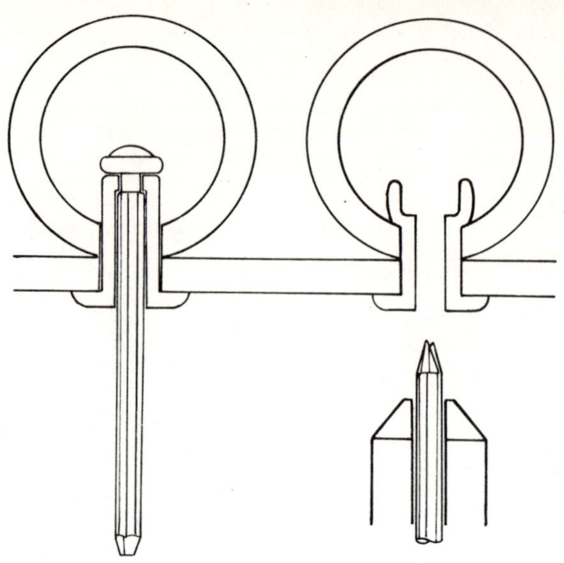

FIG 2:2   Pop rivets: sealed (left) and open (right)

When welding operations are to be undertaken on a car fitted with an alternator, as distinct from the older dynamo, it is essential to disconnect the battery and alternator before commencing, otherwise irreparable damage to the alternator may result.

2:7 Using rivets

Blind rivets and a heavy stopper such as Cataloy can be used as an alternative to welding for some body repairs, but this method should not be attempted on structural members of the underframe. A major attraction is that no heat is applied, which saves damage to paint and avoids

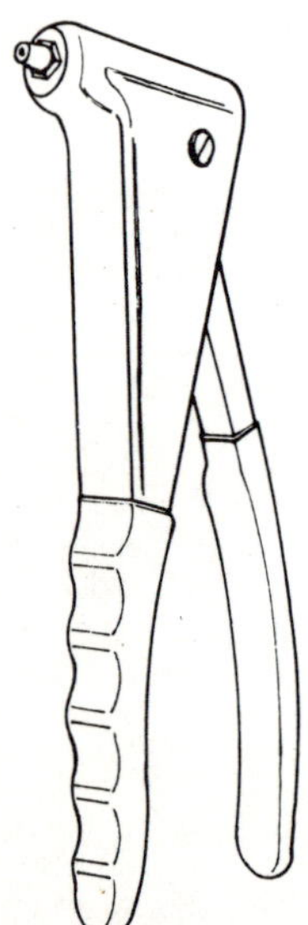

FIG 2:3   Hand pop rivet gun

the need to remove internal trim which would be scorched by welding heat. Another advantage is that access to the back of the panel is not required. No time needs to be spent in rectifying welding distortion before re-painting.

A typical example is the fixing of a patch panel to the lower part of a corroded door. To weld in a patch of sheet steel flush with the upper part of the door is a complex and difficult job. Although the riveted patch overlaps the original metal, the joint can be faired off and made presentable. If an aluminium patch is to be used the interface between the aluminium and the steel should be well primed, preferably with zinc chromate primer. If this is omitted the two sheets will form an electric cell and destroy one another.

There are a number of makes and types of blind rivet. The heavier ones need a hydraulic gun to drive them properly but pop rivets, for example, are set with an inexpensive hand gun. Another well known type is the break-stem; the mandrel remains in the rivet after driving and serves as a sealing pin after it has been ground flush. A third type, the Chobert, is sealed with a separate pin driven in with a hammer.

The advantage of the break-stem rivet in both snap-head and countersunk forms is the self plugging action of the mandrel. This avoids the distortion of the panel and damage to paint which can occur when pins are hammered in to rivets.

Cut countersinks in the outer surface, which is usually the patch, will give adequate strength even in 20 gauge sheet, if a good tool is used. The alternative is to punch countersink or dimple both surfaces so that the dimple of the outer sheet sits in the dimple of the inner.

If a thin sheet is to be attached to a much thicker section, the inner surface may be cut countersunk and the thin outer sheet punched into the depression or squeezed in during the driving of the rivet. Two thin sheets may be dimpled by the Caudron method. A clearance hole is drilled through both sheets and the countersink is formed by a specially-shaped punch and a dolly, with a countersunk cavity held at the back of the inner sheet. Unfortunately there is no method of blind dimpling from one side only.

In most instances, the patch plate will be marked out and drilled on the bench, then offered up to the job. Two or three holes are drilled to position the patch accurately before the remainder of the holes are drilled. Remember that a blind rivet can hold more than two sheets, so if a flange has corroded away an L section can be included in the joint to support a second panel.

The type of blind rivet employed depends on the position of the joint. Where the joint is out of normal sight, snap-heads, which are raised heads with flattened crowns, are good enough. They will need plugging, either with pins or stopping paste. The smallest rivets have ample strength for this class of work, but the larger sizes give a better hold on corroded or very thin metal. If they are put in at close centres it is to tighten the joint and prevent paint cracking rather than to take a heavy load.

The best finish on visible panels is achieved with countersunk blind rivets, either pinned or break-stem. Having fixed the patch, crop and grind the mandrels flush on the heads of the rivets. Where countersunk rivets are used the whole joint can be ground in one operation then cleaned up with abrasive paper ready for body solder or paste.

As joints become more difficult to get at the more attractive blind riveting becomes. For example, blind rivets have been used for fitting replacement window reveals.

Another use for rivets is for replacing drip mouldings. These are not easy to repair when welded to the roof panel. One method is to cut them away and then grind the remaining edge flush. A replacement can then be riveted on the line of the old channel without spoiling all the paint on the roof or having to remove the headlining inside.

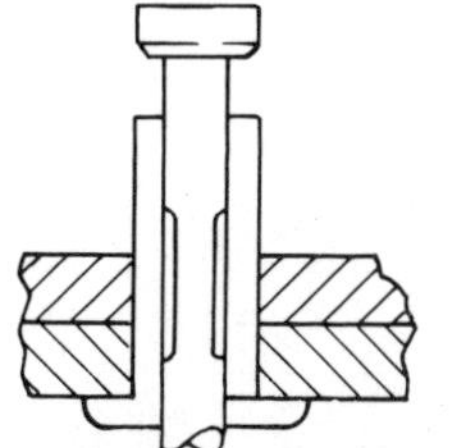
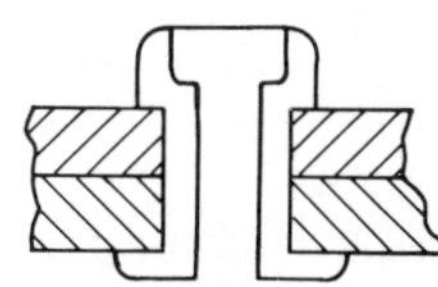

FIG 2:4   Snap head pop rivet

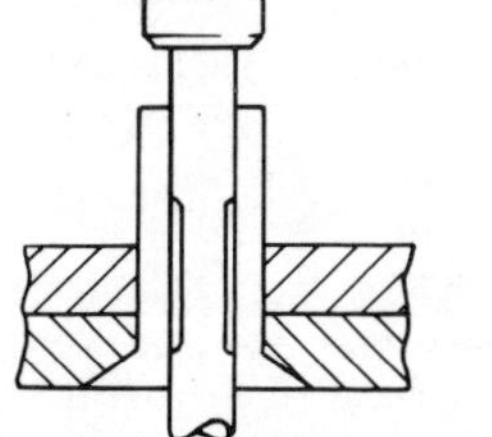
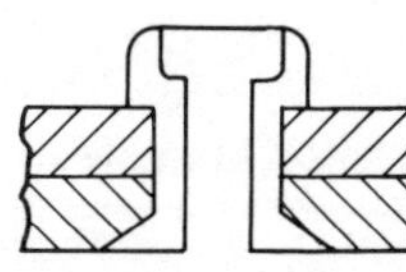

FIG 2:5   Countersunk pop rivet

2:8 Body solder

The professional bodybuilder or repairer often uses body solder in applications where the amateur thinks in terms of polyester or cellulose putty. Body solder is used, for example, to obtain a smooth curve at the scuttle and below the rear window and sometimes on wing valances of the older style of large car. It is cheaper than tinman's solder but will not adhere to steel direct, so an interlayer of tinman's solder is used. The solder is spread with a wooden block.

Cracks and blisters are sometimes found in the paint above these soldered areas. This may be due to inclusions of tinning flux, or rust, or unreacted phosphating solution. The body solder may have been worked out beyond the tinned area, so forming a crevice, or the heat may have been too concentrated so that hot solder was spread over a cold part, causing a void. Sometimes the solder bond fails because of vibration of the panels.

To paint a soldered area, wash it well with petrol or methylated spirits, allow to dry, then treat the surface with a phosphating solution such as Deoxidine. Make sure that there is no fresh contamination before applying the first primer coat. The phosphate coat is the key which holds the entire paint system. For this reason it is better not to rub down the first coat of primer. There is a risk of rubbing through the phosphate and destroying the key, as so often happens on the rectification line in car factories.

2:9 Filling dents and holes

There are a number of body repair pastes based on polyester resin on the market. One of the best known is Holt's Cataloy, available in two forms. One is a three part material consisting of pre-accelerated resin, an inert filler and a catalyst in paste form. The repair kit also contains glassfibre mat for bridging holes and reinforcing badly corroded metal, glass surfacing tissue for small holes and glass tape for edging and awkward shapes. The other form is a ready-mixed paste to which a hardener is added just before use, and this form is better suited to dent filling.

Holes:

To cover a hole, clean the surrounding metal up to 2 inch beyond the edge and if possible bend it in by hammering to make the repair flush (**FIGS 2:11** and **2:12**). Score and drill the surface to improve adhesion. Cut a piece of glass mat one inch larger than the hole all round.

Mix some resin in a bowl, adding 1 inch of blue hardener squeezed from the tube for every tablespoonful (25 cc) of resin. Do not add any filler. Brush this mixture all around the hole, working it well into pits and scores. Apply the glass mat immediately and stipple more resin into it until it becomes almost transparent; this indicates that it is thoroughly impregnated. Apply a second or even a third layer of glass mat if strength and rigidity are required (**FIG 2:13**).

After 20 minutes setting time, mix up some more resin in the proportion of two spoonfuls of powder to one of resin and stir to make a paste. Add $1\frac{1}{2}$ inch of catalyst squeezed from the tube for each spoonful of paste and spread this over the hardened glass mat. Build up the surface to the correct level and finish as for a dent (**FIGS 2:14, 2:15** and **2:16**).

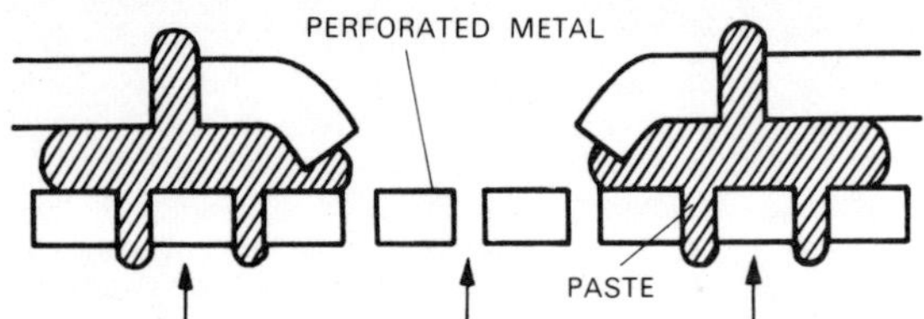

FIG 2:6   Using paste and perforated metal

Do not add any more resin to the mix once it has started to gel and do not pour unused catalysed resin back into the resin can, because this would cause the whole can to solidify. Stirring sticks and spatulas covered with catalysed resin should be kept out of uncatalysed resin. This starts to gel seven minutes after the catalyst has been added, so do not mix more than can be used in this time.

Cataloy in either form can also be used with perforated metal to cover a hole from the back. Cut the metal about ½ inch larger than the hole. Apply a layer of paste around the reverse side of the repair and press the perforated metal into it. If the reverse side cannot be reached, for example in a box section, the perforated metal should be inserted from the front and pulled back into place with one or two pieces of bent wire. Some other ways of

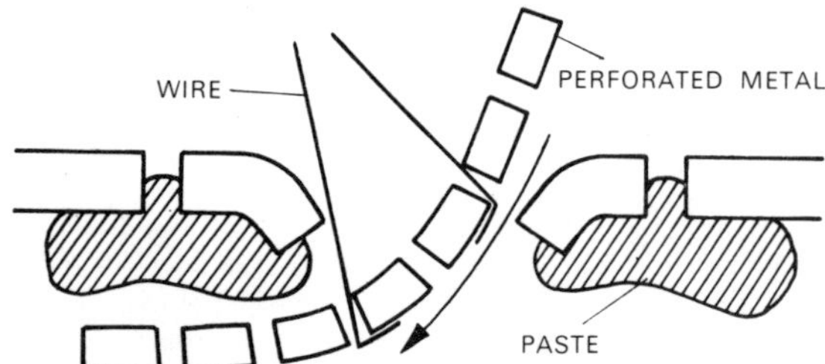

FIG 2:7   Perforated backing slid through hole

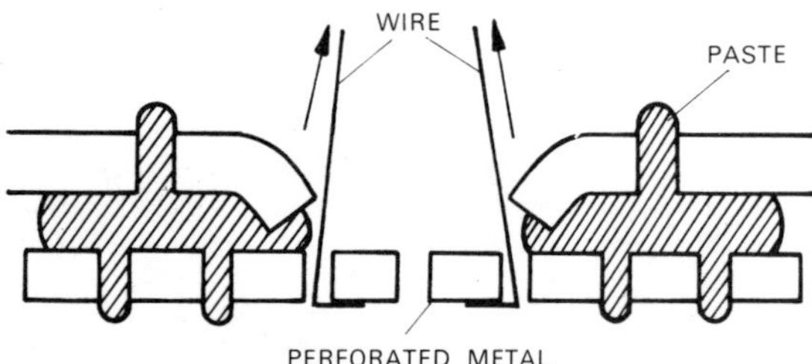

FIG 2:8   Backing held by wire while paste gels

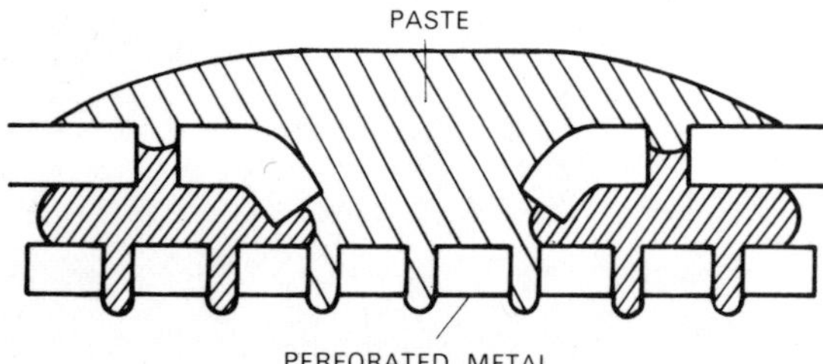

FIG 2:9   Wire removed, final filling added

FIG 2:10   Paint bubbles reveal rust underneath

FIG 2:11   Clean right back to bare metal

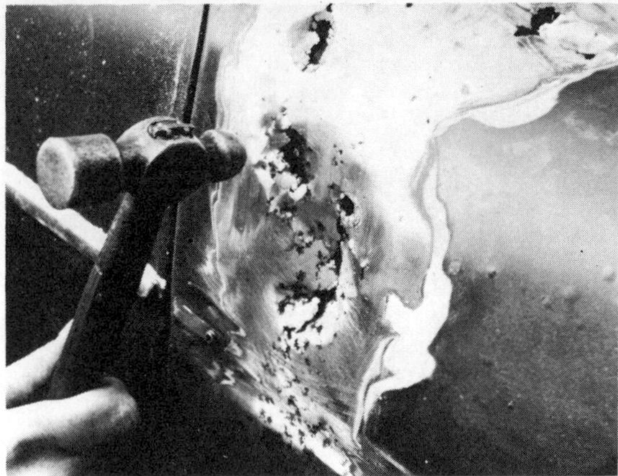

FIG 2:12 Turn the edges of holes inwards

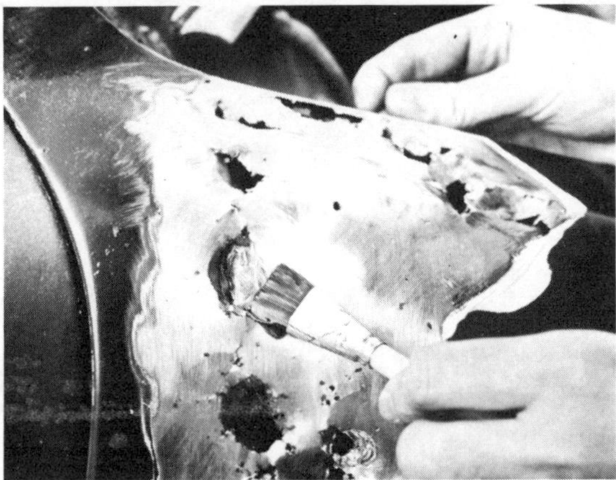

FIG 2:13 Resin and glass mat to back the repair

FIG 2:14 Paste filler built up proud of surface

FIG 2:15 Initial smoothing of filler

FIG 2:16 Finish with abrasive paper

obtaining temporary support for patches as well as more elaborate repairs using glassfibre are described in **Chapter 4**.

Allow the first layer of paste to gel for 10 minutes, then add further paste, knifing it in well to cover the entire repair, standing slightly proud. Allow up to 20 minutes for hardening then rub down to contour. Check that the paste has not shrunk below the required contour at any point. If this has occurred add another layer. Cataloy is formulated to make rasping and sanding easy.

Dents:

If there is access to the back of the panel, hold a dolly or wooden block against the dent and flatten the metal with gentle blows with a rubber or rawhide mallet. Do not use a hammer. Fill the remaining dent with Cataloy paste after removing all rust, grease and paint from the dent and an area about an inch wide all round the damage. Score the surface with a sharp tool to improve adhesion. Heavy rust may be removed with a rust remover, but it is not advisable to use a rust inhibiting paint under Cataloy as it will prevent a good bond between metal and filler.

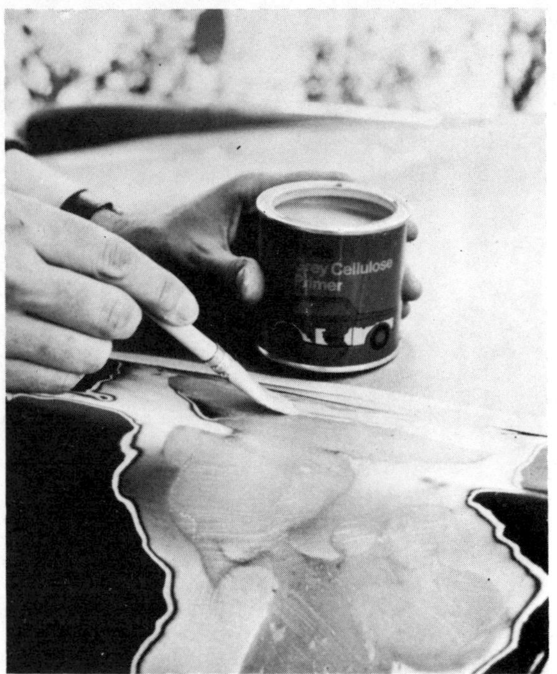

FIG 2:17   Applying primer

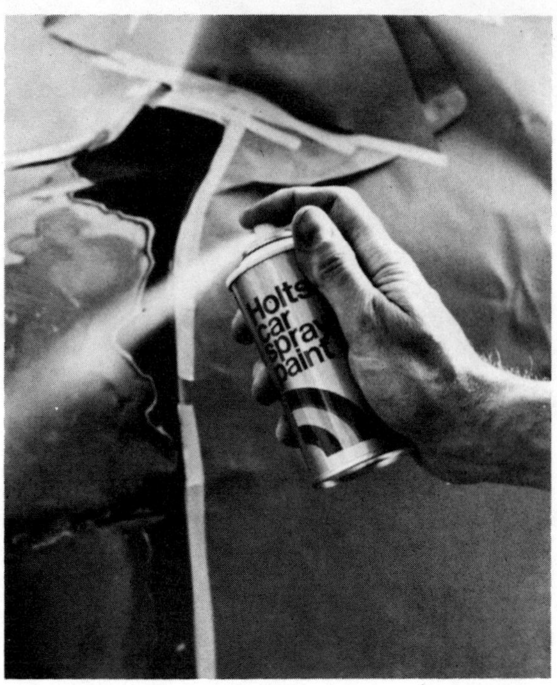

FIG 2:18   Finishing coats can be applied by aerosol

Mix the required amount of paste with the correct proportion of white hardener on an old tin lid or a piece of stiff card, folding the hardener in until the colour is even and no white streaks are visible. The mixture quickly becomes unworkable when it gels, so do not mix more than necessary or use too much hardener.

Knife the paste into the dent, leaving it slightly above the surrounding surface. The paste will shrink as it hardens, so a second application may be necessary. It will become hard in 20 to 30 minutes and then it should be filed flat with a rasp or rubbed down with coarse abrasive paper. Smooth it with 320 paper used with water, then wash off any dust and dry thoroughly. Follow with two coats of Holt's Universal aerosol spray primer and two coats of aerosol finishing paint. Rub this down with fine cutting compound, which will also take the overspray off the adjacent paint. Polishing the whole panel with wax polish will make the repair less noticeable.

CHAPTER 3

Major repairs

3:1 Repairing body damage

Without a gas welding set and the skill to use it, and at least one body jack, the private owner unfortunately cannot go very far in repairing an all steel car suffering from body damage due to accident or corrosion. Some cars have bolted-on wings which can be replaced by the owner and cover panels are available for some non-structural parts (see **Section 3:2**). But beyond that, welding and cutting techniques begin to be necessary. One thing the amateur may be able to do is to establish friendly relations with a body repairer and save himself a considerable amount of money by doing all the semi-skilled work of preliminary stripping down and the subsequent finishing and painting.

Spot-welding:

The bodyshell is usually built up from pressings with flanges which are spot-welded together. The manufacturers' drawings, not normally available to the public, show where the joints are. Do not try to prise them apart as this will only damage the adjoining section. The spot-welds can be found by rubbing the flange with paint remover, or by light sanding. If a drill can be brought to bear, the spot-weld in the outer flange is drilled away, stopping before the drill cuts into the inner flange. The joint can now be broken with a sharp cold chisel. If the spot-welds are inaccessible it may be necessary to cut an access hole, which is filled in again later. Such items as boot lids, doors and front wings usually consist of inner and outer pressings and sometimes only the outer pressing is damaged. Some money can be saved if the two pressings can be separated and the undamaged part welded to a new outer. The tendency is for manufacturers to supply complete sub-assemblies

only, although the Motor Insurance Repair Research Centre at Thatcham has done some good work recently in persuading them to make more outer skins available separately. Trade repairers may order a new assembly and use only half of it, knowing that they will soon have a use for the other piece, but this is not economical for the private owner.

Anyone contemplating major repairs to a modern body should obtain a copy of the relevant bodywork service manual and a parts price list, which shows the prices of the panels and sub-assemblies available as replacements. The drawings will show where the makers' joints lie under the body solder, which must be melted out to give access to them.

To sum up, the amateur must decide whether he is a welder or not. If not, let someone in the trade do the job.

3:2 Non-structural repairs

Cover panels:

Non-structural parts such as doors and some outer sills can be covered with replacement panels sold for the purpose, leaving the original damaged skin in situ, but this is 'bodging' rather than repair. It is a waste of time and money to cover corroded structural members with light gauge panels, GRP mouldings or filler paste. Such repairs have no structural strength, and they will not deceive the DoE examiner.

Removing bolted-on wings:

Removing bolted wings is easier said than done, because very often the bolts are rusted into the anchor nuts. Penetrating oil is effective in some instances, if given time to do its work. A quicker way is to heat the heads of the bolts to a red heat, using a very narrow flame to avoid heating the surrounding metal. Wait until the head is cold before trying to turn the bolt with a box spanner. The expansion and contraction of the bolt caused by the heat running up from the head usually breaks up the rust in the threads of the nut.

As a last resort, the bolt-head can be burnt off with an oxy-acetylene cutting flame, or drilled out if a drill can be brought to bear. Centre-pop the head of the bolt carefully and drill right through the bolt with the corresponding tapping size drill, or one slightly smaller. This will leave just a thin shell which can be broken out. The threads of the anchor nut should be cleared with a tap.

Bolts which have broken off flush can be shifted with a stud extractor. This is a conical plug with cutting edges on a very quick lefthand thread. It is wound anticlockwise into a hole drilled down the centre of the bolt. The cutting edges of the plug bite into the bolt, gripping it so that the two can be unscrewed together.

Repairs to doors:

Car doors usually consist of an inner pressing with an outer pressing clenched over the flange of the inner. If the outer sheet, or part of it, is to be discarded, a quick way to get it off is to grind the turned edge away, being careful not to cut into the inner pressing. The sheets may be held together by some spot-welds as well but these can be drilled out, taking care not to go deeply into the inner flange, and the sheets parted with a chisel. The horizontal cut across the outer panel is made with a metal-cutting padsaw.

To restore a dented or creased outer door panel to shape, it will be necessary to get access to the back of the panel and this is done by cutting away part of the inner panel and welding it in again later. Make the cuts in places which will need the minimum amount of welding or brazing. Brazing with bronze filler-rod is preferable to welding for this job, because less heat is generated and, consequently, there is less risk of panel distortion.

The clenched edge of the outer panel is turned up carefully to permit removal of the inner cut-out. The outer panel can now be bumped back into shape with a hide mallet, resting the door on a sandbag. The use of these soft tools avoids stretching the sheet metal. A cardboard template taken off the edge of the corresponding undamaged door will serve as a guide to the curvature required. The panel is brought up to shape with panel hammer and dolly, then planished as necessary. The cut-out is brazed back in place, filling in the spot-welds with the same rod, then the flange is re-clenched with a hammer.

Cracked wing flanges:

There are still some old cars on the road which have wired-edge wings, which means that the edge of the wing was rolled around a piece of wire during manufacture. If the wire is corroded away, welding the cracks in the wing is a waste of time. If the wing is detachable, unbolt it, and weld an inward flange around the inside just above the original rolled edge. This should be cut from 18 gauge steel, about 1 inch wide, with a $\frac{1}{4}$ inch flange turned over

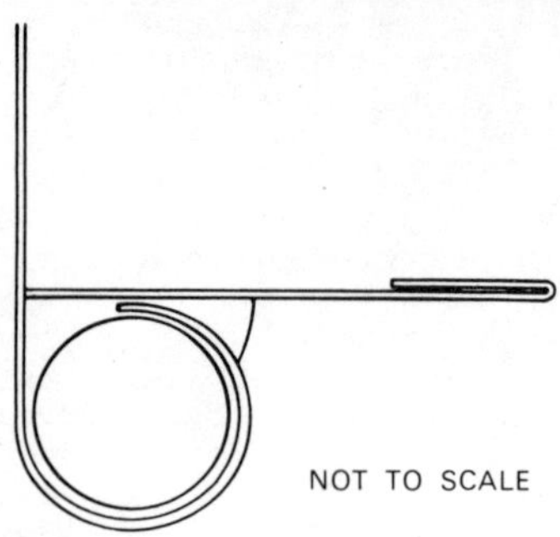

FIG 3:1   Repairing a wired-edge wing

along the inner edge, to make a smooth finish which will not cut the wrists of anyone changing a wheel. The strip is bent to the curve of the wing and brazed in place. The inside of the wing should be cleaned out with a wire brush followed by spirits of salts (see **FIG 3:1**).

Modern cars have an inward flange instead of a wire. If this flange is badly corroded it is possible to replace it without access to the inside of the wheelarch and without attempting overhead brazing. In such cases, make a similar strip about 2 inches wide with the same $\frac{1}{4}$ inch flange turned over to make a safe edge on the inside of the wheelarch. A strip 1 inch from the other edge is then turned up at right angles to make a flange which runs around outside the wheelarch. If it is considered worthwhile the outside edge of the wheelarch can be joggled to form a seating for the flange, but the flange will not look too unsightly if neatly finished and left standing proud especially if all four arches are treated in the same way (see **FIG 3:2**).

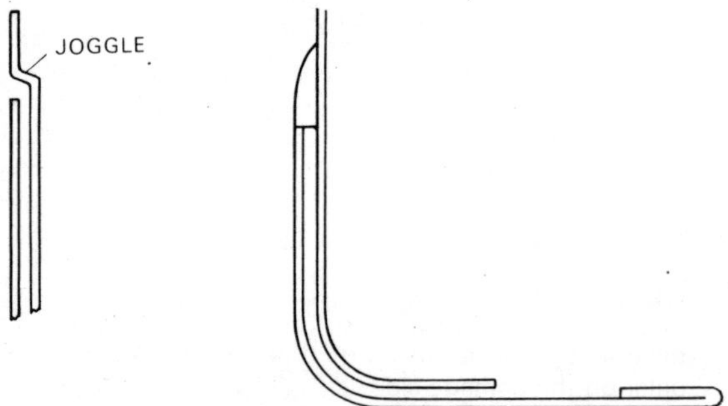

FIG 3:2   Fitting a new wing flange

Now the right angled strip has to be curved to fit the wheelarch. This is done by hammering the wider, unfolded edge on an anvil, spreading the outer part of the metal so that the whole strip gradually curves. The hammering will make the edge ragged, but this can be trimmed off with shears when the durve is correct. Slight sweeps can be obtained by bending while the metal is hot and very sharp curves can be helped by nicks in the flange, which are welded-up when the correct shape is obtained. Finish the upstanding flange with a planishing hammer to take out the dents, then offer up the flange to the body and run a scriber round the outside to mark the rebate if this is to be made.

The new flange is clamped in place and tack-welded. If rebated, the whole joint will need planishing. Sand and clean up the whole area to prepare for filling and finishing in the usual way.

The under-wing clearance on some modern cars is rather limited and consequently it is important before re-flanging a wing in the way just described to check that the tyre will not foul on the flange. This is particularly likely to occur at the front with a combination of steering movement and suspension compression. The resultant tyre damage could lead to a dangerous blow-out.

3:3 Structural damage

Any unit construction car which has suffered more than superficial damage is likely to show some distortion of the structural members, because of the way in which the loads are widely spread over much of the shell (as outlined in **Chapter 1**). Where any such damage is suspected, the car must be submitted to an alignment check (see **Section 3:4**).

No two body repairs are exactly alike but it is possible to divide accident damage into six main categories; three-quarter front, three-quarter rear, full front, full rear, side impact, and roll-over. The commonest is three-quarter front.

Three-quarter front impact:

In this case the wing assembly absorbs most of the energy, dragging back with it the front end panels, and perhaps buckling the bonnet lid. The front bumper will be bent backwards and the supporting brackets distorted. The first thing to do is to remove the bonnet and wing assemblies. Separate front wings, as on the Morris Minor and Volkswagen, are bolted to the inner wheelarch panel. Integral front wings may also be bolted, but are often spot-welded in place, so the spots are drilled away. With the wing out of the way it is possible to see what other damage has been done.

If the impact has been severe enough to damage the bulkhead and hinge pillar the windscreen will have to be removed, also the front door which is probably buckled and jammed against the shut pillar. The bulkhead and hinge pillar are pushed back roughly into position with body jacks butted against the bottoms of the centre pillars, one acting diagonally from the opposite centre pillar and the other upwards from the foot of the centre pillar on the damage side.

Alignment checks are now made from the top of the lefthand side centre pillar to the bottom of the righthand centre pillar and vice versa, then diagonally across the windscreen aperture and between pillars at waist level. An adjustable trammel is very useful for making accurate measurements, especially if it has steel points which can leave a small mark in the paint. The front door opening on the damaged side needs checking, and the shape can be taken off the undamaged side with a plywood template. Make sure that the 'undamaged' side has not been repaired before!

Scuttle repairs will probably necessitate cutting out part of the outer panel to get access to the inner, drilling away spot-welds at the edge and melting out the body solder on the top surface. When the damaged parts have been planished or replaced, the door can be tried in

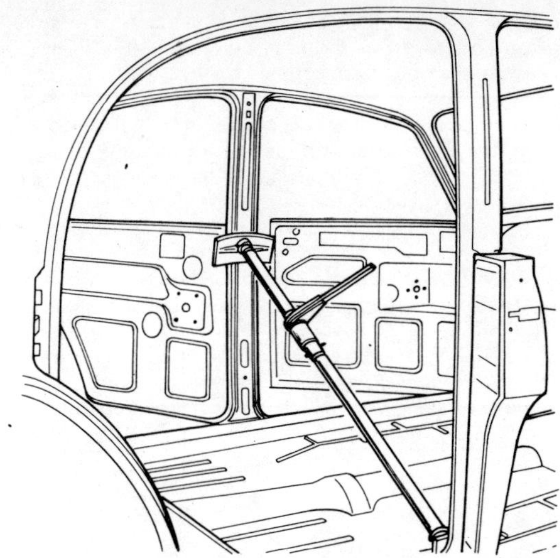

FIG 3:3   Distortion is corrected with body jacks

position. It is better to take the striker plate off the shut pillar, and any draught excluder, so that the fit of the door against the pillar can be seen clearly. A new door or a replacement door from the scrapyard may not have the same curvature, but it is possible to bend a door (or 'break' it, in trade parlance) by clamping a heavy angle iron or rolled steel joist against it and inserting the hydraulic wedge between the steel beam and the inner pressing. The striker plate on the shut pillar is adjustable and the door hinges on some older cars also allow for adjustment.

The position of bolted wings can be checked by sighting two straightedges, one clamped across the tops of the headlamp apertures and the other across the top of the scuttle, resting perhaps on the windscreen wiper bosses. The wing bolt holes are slotted to allow for some adjustment. Further alignment checks and a road test should be carried out before the car is resprayed.

FIG 3:4   A trammel for comparing dimensions

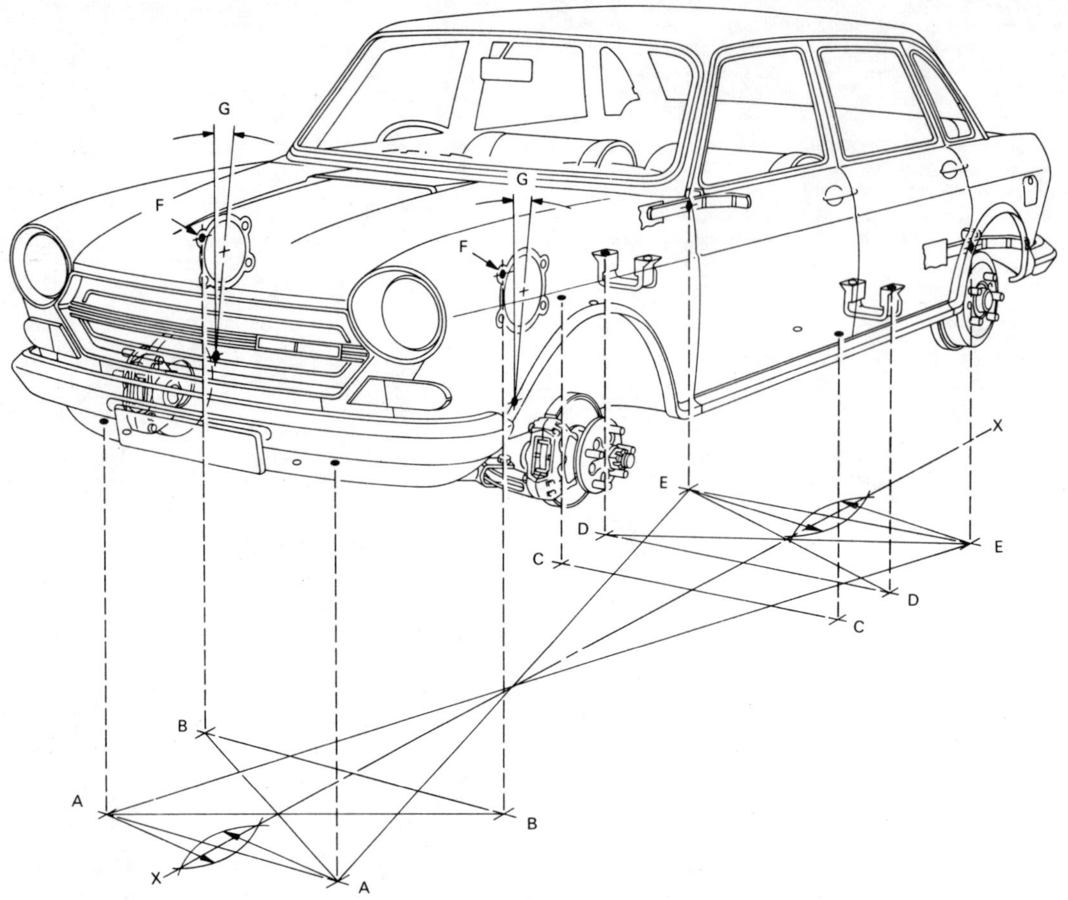

FIG 3:5   BLMC 1800/2200 bodyshell horizontal alignment check

Key to Fig 3:5   A-A Tie-bar mounting holes   B-B Front suspension mounting, front holes (top)   C-C Rear suspension mounting, front holes   D-D Rear suspension mounting, rear holes   E-E Bumper mountings   F Centre of holes (horizontal check)   G-G 4 deg. suspension mounting angle   X-X Centre line

Rear end impact:

The tail panel below the boot lid is pushed in, sometimes springing the boot open, and sometimes jamming it shut. The jammed lid must be freed by driving chasers on either side of the lock, trying to keep any new damage to the pressing which was most damaged in the accident. The tail panel is now pushed back into shape by a hydraulic jack acting on the top flange and butted against a baulk of timber laid against the boot front bulkhead. One must now decide whether to remove the whole tail panel for repairs on the bench, or whether it can be done in position. More often than not these panels have to be taken out, because they extend down below the boot floor and it is impossible to get access to the back of the outer panel for planishing. One or both of the rear wings or rear wheelarch assemblies may have to be taken off also. These jobs are more expensive than appears at first sight.

Boot lids are not easy to repair when they consist of an outer panel clenched and spot-welded to an inner with no apertures in it. The quick way is to cut a hole in the inner, planish the outer, and re-weld the cut-out. Unfortunately the heat of re-welding buckles the inner pressing, if not the outer as well, and nothing can be done to correct it. Therefore it is better to separate the two completely. If there are hand holes, then the space can be stuffed with asbestos cloth to protect the outer and brazing rod used instead of a weld. If the damage to the outer is localised it may be necessary to cut out only a small piece, which can be soldered back into position on false flanges tack-brazed under the edges of the aperture. Wet cloths help to keep the heat down in all such brazing operations. Most rear end damage repair is a matter of access to the inner surfaces of double-skin constructions, cutting away damaged areas as necessary.

Side impact:

Side impact is a common form of damage in urban areas, resulting from crossroads accidents. Old cars often sustain side impact better than more modern ones because their wing and door sections are wider. Usually both doors (on a four-door car) and the outer sill are crushed, the centre pillar is pushed in, and the floor pan is buckled.

If the car has a separate chassis this may be kinked amidships. Bent chassis can be straightened under heat and pressure if the metal has not gone too far beyond the elastic limit. How far is 'too far', is a decision best left to the fully experienced.

The buckle in the floor pan and the sill of a unit construction car can be pushed out with a body jack after drilling away the spot-welds holding the pillar to the sill. It may then be necessary to cut out part of the outer sill to give access to both sides of the inner and weld it back in place after both have been planished. Again, strictly for the experts.

Roll-over damage:

The damage takes the form of large buckles in the roof, which may have assumed the concave counterpart of its original curvature. As many as four body jacks may be needed, but ordinary bottle jacks with timber or metal distance pieces can be pressed into service. The sharp edges of the roof buckles must be taken out by hand and, if they are beyond arm's reach through the door and window apertures, an assistant will be needed to hold up the dolly on the inside. Examine the pillars for kinks and make double diagonal alignment checks before and after rectification.

Structural integrity:

A major problem in repairing accident damaged unit construction cars is that while it may be possible with the right combination of skill, perseverance and brute force to return the structure to its original shape, there is no easy way of knowing how much its strength may remain impaired. Metal which has been bent and straightened loses some of its stiffness and this can mean that while the car performs most of its normal functions quite adequately, its behaviour in abnormal circumstances – resistance to damage in a second accident, for example – may be dangerously substandard. Expert skill, experience and judgement are required to make assessments of this kind. Whatever the pressures of convenience and finance it must always be prudent to err on the side of caution in such matters.

3:4 Alignment checks

Body repairers use a manufacturer's alignment chart to check the whole bodyshell-suspension-wheel assembly before and after major repairs. **FIGS 3:5** and **3:6** show the alignment checks for a BLMC 1800/2200. The procedure is as follows:

Find a clean, level concrete floor on which to park the car and rub chalk over the areas below the suspension mountings. Hold a plumb line against the centres of the points shown in the diagram and mark the position of the tip of the bob-weight on the chalked floor with a pencil cross. Move the car away and find the centre between each pair of crosses with large compasses or by measurement. Connect the centre point by a chalk line. The way to do this is to coat a thin cord with chalk and snap it against the floor while it is held tightly at each end. Alternatively, the line can be drawn with the help of a long straightedge.

Diagonals are drawn in the same way and should

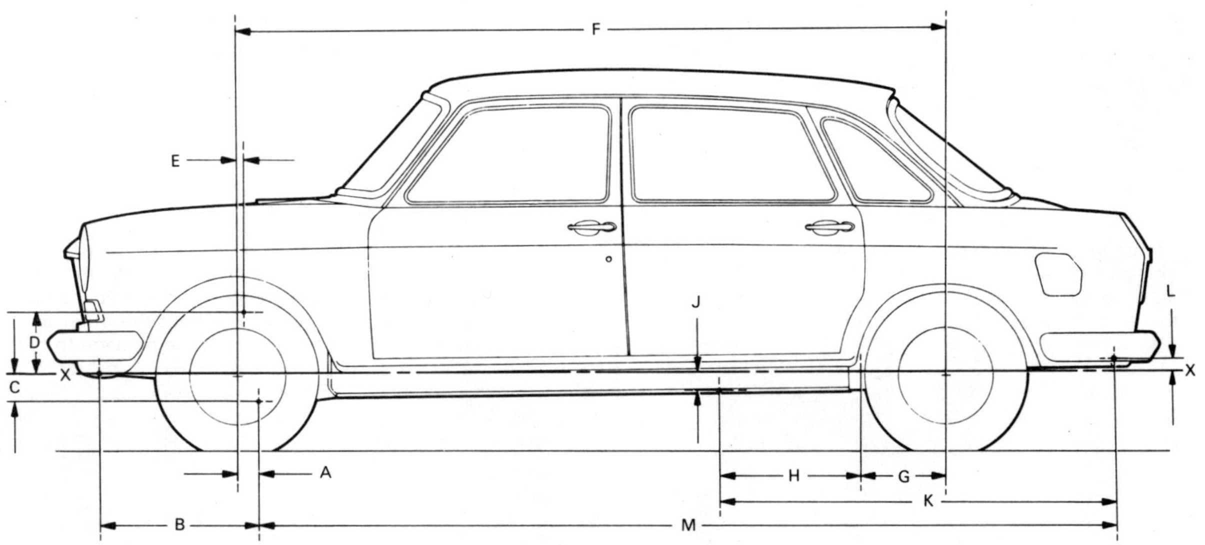

FIG 3:6   BLMC 1800/2200 bodyshell vertical alignment check

Key to Fig 3:6   X-X Datum (body line)   A Hub centre to lower suspension mounting   B Lower suspension mounting to tie-bar mounting   C Lower suspension mounting to datum line   D Suspension mounting front   E Hub centre to suspension mounting front   F Wheelbase   G Hub centre to suspension mounting rear   H Rear suspension rear to front mounting   J Rear suspension rear to front mounting   K Rear suspension front mounting to bumper mounting   L Bumper mounting   M Lower front suspension mounting to bumper mounting cross each other on the centre line, if the underframe assembly is in alignment. Diagonals which do not inter-intersect on the centre line show that the underframe is out of alignment between the pairs of points joined.

The height of datum points above a level floor are shown in **FIG 3 : 6**. These measurements are taken with a full complement of oil, petrol and water and the tyres at recommended pressures, but without any passengers or driver. The measurements obtained may not agree with the manufacturers' figures, but it is the position of the datum points in relation to each other that is important and the height from the ground should be the same all round, whether high or low. Small tolerances of $\frac{1}{32}$ inch or so are allowed as these do not affect road performance. The checking procedure should be followed a second time after major repairs have been completed. Distances can be taken off or compared conveniently with an adjustable trammel and then measured with a steel rule.

Distortion of the bodyshell is corrected by the use of manual or hydraulic body jacks with attachments which will pull or push the body into correct shape. Jacks rigged under a roof truss of the garage can be used to make downward adjustments. One of the most useful accessories fitted to the hydraulic jack is the expanding wedge, which can be inserted between structural members to push them apart.

CHAPTER 4

Glass reinforced plastics

4:1 Introduction to GRP

The only major alternative to metal so far utilised as the material for car bodywork is GRP, and both its properties and the techniques involved in working with it make it a very different proposition from steel. GRP means glass reinforced plastics, commonly called Fibreglass, although Fibreglass is in fact the trade name of one make of glass fibre. GRP is a child of the aircraft industry and has inherited some of its mystique. The technical literature dwells upon the need for perfect working conditions (controlled temperature and humidity) to achieve optimum results, but this need not deter the beginner. The resins are much more manageable than in the early days and technically the material is simple compared with the structure of wood.

GRP car body panels consist of an unreinforced surface coat of polyester resin called the gel coat. This hides the fibre pattern, carries colour, and protects the minute glass fibres, which are attacked by water. Beneath this is the laminating polyester resin, reinforced with one or more layers of glass mat, and possibly a layer of woven glass cloth or woven roving to increase rigidity.

The resin is usually stippled into the glass with a brush or roller, and is transformed from a viscous liquid into a solid by the action of a catalyst such as methyl ethyl ketone peroxide, commonly called MEKP. There is another hardener in the resin called an accelerator, which enables the hardening reaction to take place at room temperature and contact pressure.

There are over 500 different kinds of GRP, which is a generic term for a two-phase material, just as vague in its meaning as 'wood'. Its natural colour is a jaundiced yellow, but colour pastes and metallic particles can be added to the gel coat to give attractive surface effects. Fire-retardant or self-extinguishing grades of resin are available, but their use in motor body panels is far from common and mouldings made of general-purpose polyester will burn readily.

There are several ways of making a GRP moulding, ranging from hot press moulding in matched metal moulds to hand lay-up in an open mould. Hand lay-up needs no expensive plant or tools, but the quality of the moulding depends on the skill of the laminator.

GRP has been in use for sports cars, racing cars and commercial vehicles for over 20 years and there are some GRP boats still in service after 25 years in the water. It has not replaced steel for mass-produced cars because it is a more expensive material, but it is used by motor manufacturers for short runs. There is a break-even point, where the lower cost of sheet steel begins to score over GRP despite the higher cost of press tools for forming sheet metal. One of its first uses in road transport was in front and rear domes of bus bodies, because GRP was cheaper than panel-beaten aluminium.

Reinforced plastics technologists are trying to make GRP more suitable for long-run car production, and moulded front and rear ends (made of GRP sheet moulding compound or dough moulding compound) are coming into use on American cars, but the problems of shrinkage in flat or nearly flat panels have not yet been entirely overcome.

Although GRP is used as a replacement for sheet steel or aluminium, because expensive tooling or panel-beating skills are not required, its physical properties have nothing in common with sheet metal, except that it can be worked with some of the metal-cutting tools. An appreciation of its behaviour will help the amateur to avoid expensive mistakes.

GRP is not ductile, so any forming has to be done

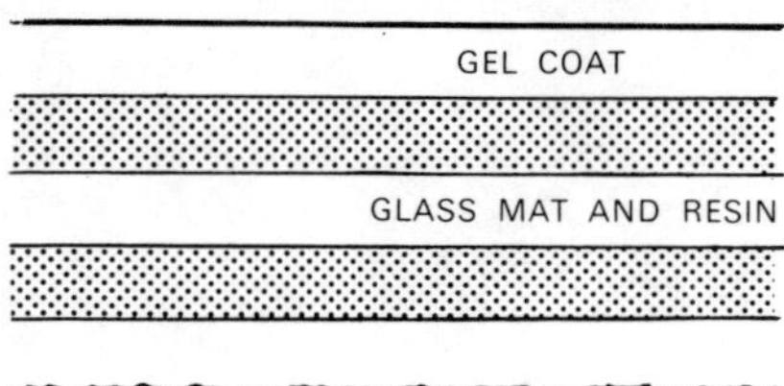

FIG 4:1   Section of typical GRP laminate

before it sets hard in the mould. It is resilient, but if hit hard enough it breaks. Its behaviour under load is different from metal. This complex subject is well documented in the technical literature of GRP, but need not concern the car owner, who will be concerned with light, intermittent stresses. It is in the arrangement of joints and attachments that he is likely to go wrong and find that the moulding has fractured.

GRP mouldings of the type used for car bodies consist of a series of layers which are strong in tension. It is the glass fibre that provides the tensile strength, while the resin provides the shape. The layers can be pulled apart quite easily (delamination), so it is useless to glue the flat base of a mirror, for example, on the surface of the moulding. It will be easily knocked off and will take part of the gelcoat with it. Any such fittings should be bolted through to a load-spreading plate at the back (**FIG 4:2**).

Mouldings may be bonded together, but all joints should be in compression or shear, never in tension. Butt joints should never be used without a backing plate. It is not possible to tie glass fibres together in a butt joint, so a lap joint is used. Where joints may be subjected to tension as well as compression they should be fastened through with bolts. **FIG 4:3** shows the right and wrong

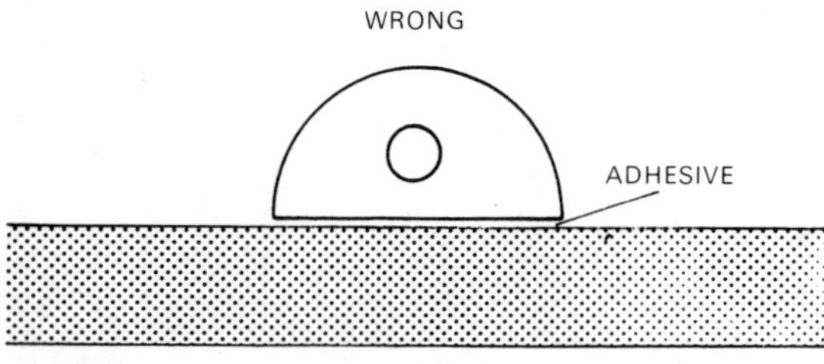

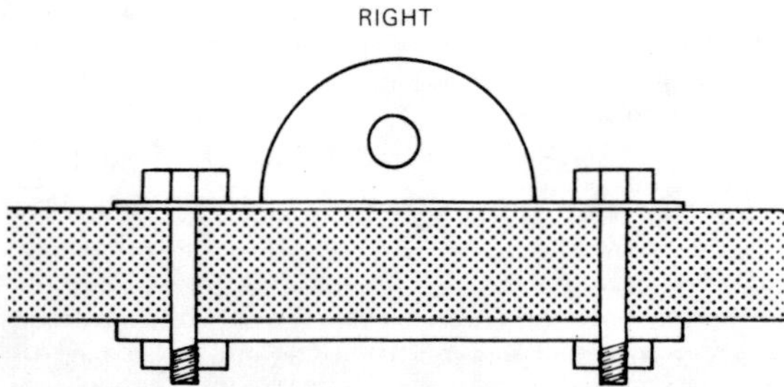

FIG 4:2   **Mountings under tension must be bolted through the laminate, not just glued**

way to make most of the common joints, including flush joints.

GRP may be screwed or bolted to a structure along an edge, but the holes should not be nearer than three diameters from the edge of the moulding, or nearer to one another than three diameters. GRP is not as hard as metal, and screw heads, particularly if countersunk, will soon enlarge their holes by racking.

Stress concentrations:

Due to their inability to 'flow' under load, reinforced plastics are susceptible to stress concentrations or 'hard spots' caused by structural members or attachments. A GRP moulding when loaded should be free to deflect evenly over its entire area. Severe notches or sharp corners should be avoided and the corners of cut apertures should be well rounded. Preferably, structural supports should be joined to one another, but if a support must terminate on a laminate it should be faded in against local reinforcement, as shown in **FIG 4:4**.

In the case of ready-made mouldings, such as hardtops, all likely stresses are, or should have been, allowed for in the factor of safety added by the moulder when he considers the number of laminations needed. He cannot foresee the local modifications which a private owner may make. When in doubt, spread the load over as wide an area as possible with reinforcing layers, and if total rigidity is not essential interpose resilient washers to form a flexible mounting (see **FIG 4:5**).

Joining cured mouldings:

The design rules indicated so far apply to joints between two cured mouldings, or a cured moulding and a new 'wet' one. A wet moulding will usually bond well enough to a cured moulding if the surface of the cured moulding is well roughened. If possible, make some holes in the cured moulding and countersink them on the back face to give a key. The early text books on GRP recommended the use of a layer of glass mat and wet polyester resin to unite two cured mouldings, but to be fully effective the joint needs clamping while the resin sets, and clamps are not always easy to apply over the whole length of the joint. It is better to rely on mechanical fastenings and to regard the polyester resin layer as a sealant. Bedding compounds such as Seelastic are suitable because they remain soft, but ordinary builders' putty should be avoided because it hardens and will not respond to flexing except by cracking and falling away.

The main point to remember is that a GRP moulding should not be forced to fit the structure. The use of hammers and strange oaths is all very well for sheet metal, which will stretch. Trying to stretch GRP only pre-stresses it and reduces the factor of safety to zero. Always modify the structure to fit the moulding, or fill in any gaps with resin/glass putty. 'Green' mouldings, straight from the mould, adapt to one another to some extent while the cure is completed. Any commercial mouldings offered retail will probably be well beyond the green stage before they are delivered.

In short, forget all about sheet metal when working with this unbiddable material. Imagine it is a piece of flexible reinforced concrete or cast iron, and you will not go far wrong.

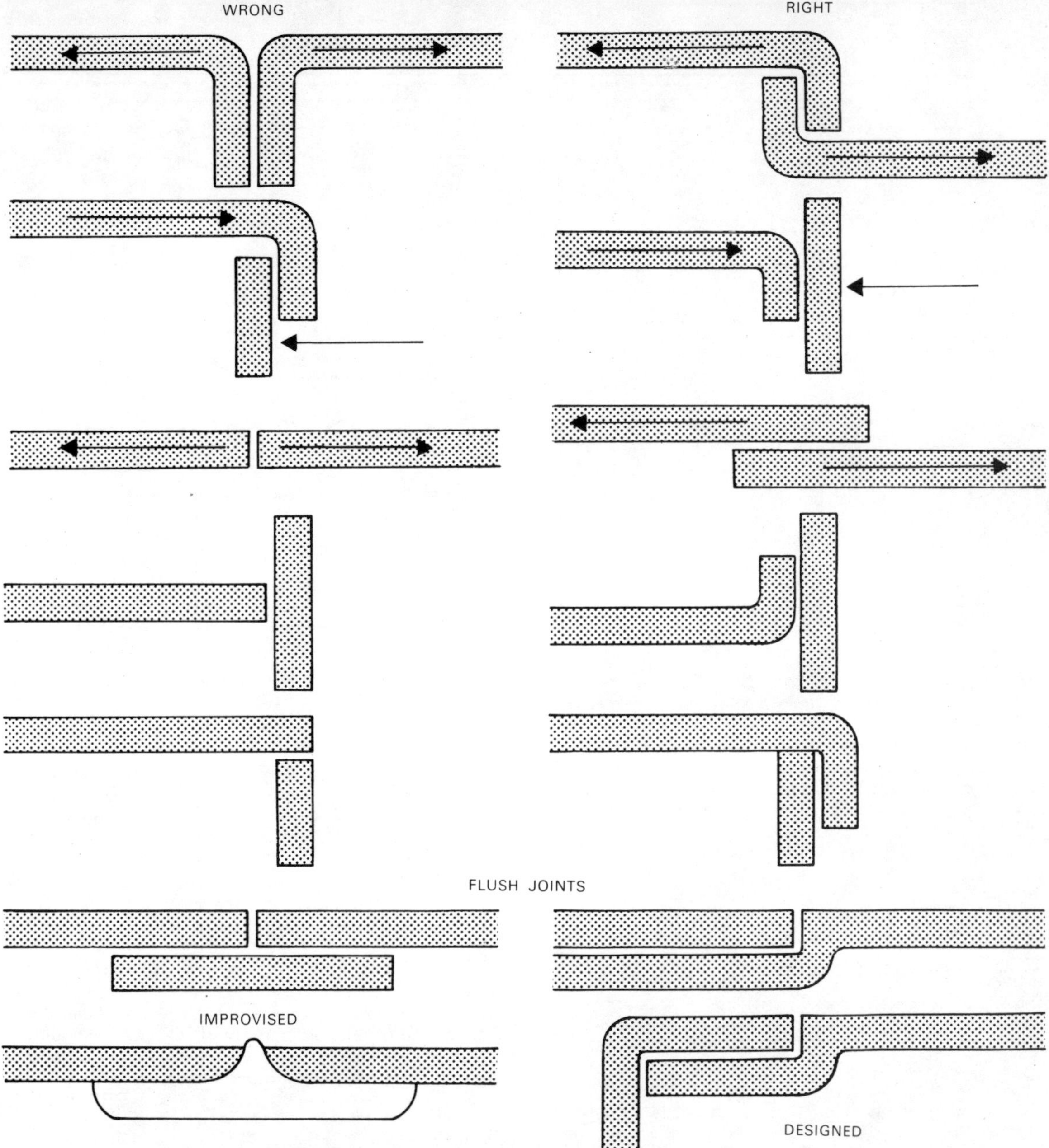

FIG 4:3   The right and wrong ways to make joins between separate GRP mouldings

4:2 Maintenance of GRP bodywork

It is not true that GRP bodywork needs no maintenance. It does not need as much care as steel and will come to little harm if neglected completely. On the other hand that brilliant shiny finish will not last for ever. Production bodies rarely have the high gloss achieved on the Motor Show specimen. Without attention the glossy finish will become dull in 12 months and the colour will start to fade as well.

Badly made GRP bodies, of which there are plenty, have been known to fade out under sunlight coming through between the slats of a crate on the dockside while awaiting export, leaving a striped effect.

No GRP moulding has a better surface than the mould in which it was made. Some GRP manufacturers start off with poor moulds and produce poor mouldings with gel coat defects; they learn at their customers' expense. It takes them a few years to learn all the little tricks of

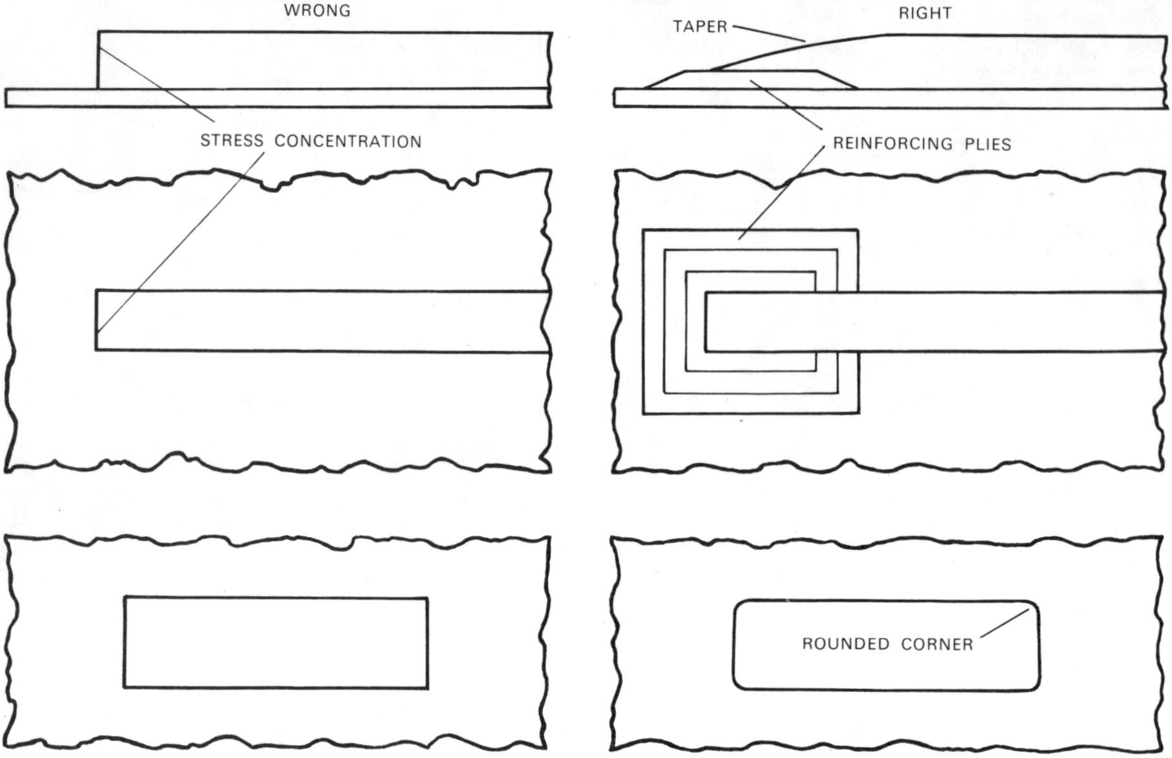

FIG 4:4 Avoid stress-raising reinforcements and sharp cornered apertures in GRP structures

technique and good housekeeping which make the difference between a good moulding and a poor one. It pays to buy from an established company that exercises quality control and has the resources to honour a guarantee.

It is not difficult to keep glossy GRP surfaces bright and polished, but it takes a great deal of hard work to get such a finish on a rough moulding. The gloss can be maintained by a regular wash down with water followed by polishing with wax polish. Where the finish has become dull and the colour has faded, rub over with finest burnishing paste or silver polish. This will take off the faded surface of the gel coat and reveal fresh colour underneath. The burnishing paste must be very fine grade or the result will be a matt finish. Abrasive metal polishes such as Brasso, Bluebell or jewellers' rouge are suitable. Solvent polishes such as Duraglit, Silver Dip and Shipshape, although good for their purpose, are useless for GRP. The solvent will stain the gel coat and may even damage the laminate.

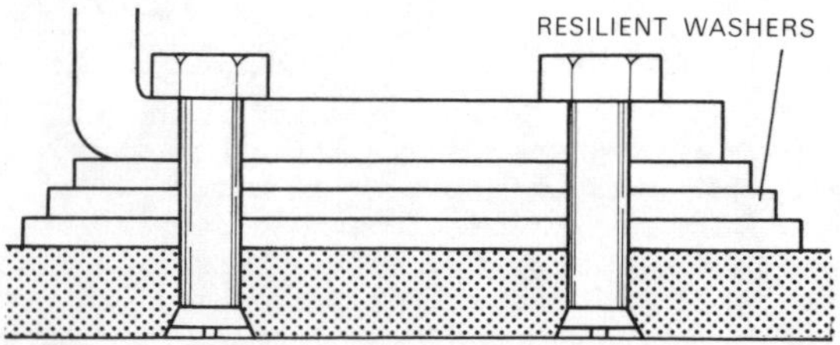

FIG 4:5 Reinforced hinge mounting

The shine can now be restored with a good wax polish. Never use polishes containing silicones; they cause a great deal of trouble when the time comes to paint the body.

One of the disadvantages of GRP is that it marks easily, particularly if it is not polished. Most stains can be removed with water, but if this fails try wiping with detergent. Most cleaning solvents should be avoided because they will attack the resin and take off the gloss. Scouring powder, such as Vim, and steel wool will dull and roughen the surface and a rough surface holds more dirt. Petrol and paraffin are harmless and may be used to remove grease marks and road tar. A wooden scraper will help to get tar off. Do not use a metal scraper, as this will scratch the gel coat. An emulsion hand cleaner, such as Swarfega, is very effective on GRP.

Hand scrubbing may be resorted to, but do not use a stiff-bristled domestic scrubbing brush, which will leave scratches. A soft plastic bristle brush, such as a nylon nail brush, is safer, though the work may take a little longer.

Scratches:

Scratches, such as any car is heir to, are unsightly rather than dangerous unless they go deep into the laminate and expose the glass fibres. Even then deterioration is a slow process compared with the rusting of sheet steel. They show because the walls of the scratch are rough and hold dirt. Filling and painting with resin is the logical method of repair, but it is almost impossible to match the colour and the new area will be more conspicuous than the original scratch. If the surfaces of the scratch can be made smoother, even without filling, it will be much less noticeable. A careful and light treatment with acetone, which dissolves resin, will smooth a light scratch. White spirit or methylated spirit can also be used but are not so powerful. Use a fine watercolour paint brush to keep the acetone in the scratch and wipe off the surplus before it dulls the finish. If left in the scratch it will soften the base resin and do more harm than good.

A scratch so treated will no longer hold dirt and after burnishing and wax polishing it will show only as a glossy hollow, invisible to the casual glance.

Another method is to clean the scratch with water or acetone, remove any loose resin, and varnish with clear polyurethane or polyester varnish. The purpose of the varnish is to smooth the rough sides and bed of the scratch and make them less noticeable. Touching up with clear varnish is much easier than trying to get a colour match. If the moulding has unpigmented laminating resin under the gel coat, or a neutral colour and the scratch has revealed this, clear varnish will not obliterate it, but it can be hidden by coloured resin, paint, or ink, if these can be confined to the scratch and then varnished over.

It is very difficult to match a gel coat, even by using some of the original material, because the colour fades in service and fades unevenly. Try to keep the new material to the crack, and burnish well when dry.

Another method is to fill the scratch with filler and varnish over. Clean out the scratch with acetone, white spirit or water and fill it with clear polyurethane filler or thixotropic polyester paste. Sand·it down when hard, coat with polyurethane or polyester varnish and burnish. Burnishing away the surplus resin outside the scratch will make the repair much less noticeable. A clear polyurethane filler is made by British Paints Ltd., but if this is not available thixotropic polyester resin paste may be substituted.

Coloured polyester resin putty can be home-made by adding talcum powder or french chalk to coloured resin. Unperfumed powder is much cheaper than the cosmetic variety and can be bought by weight from most chemists' shops. The addition of the powder will reduce the strength of the colour, but this can be allowed for after making an experimental mix. The amount of catalyst should be based on the amount of resin not on the weight of the total mix, but double the usual amount will probably be needed because some is absorbed by the filler.

Deep scores which show fibres of the laminate should be filled as soon as possible. It is just as well to do the job properly, because a temporary repair has a way of becoming a permanent one. If such damage is neglected, water will destroy the bond between the glass fibres and the resin as it works its way in by capillary action, leading to local softness and crumbling.

Starring:

Starring is a pattern of radial cracks in the gel coat originating at a point of impact, usually from a stone shot up from under the tyre of a passing car. Examine carefully and if the triangular pieces of gel coat are still attached to the laminate, treat the starring as scratches. If the gel coat has broken away, the only satisfactory treatment is to sand away all the damage and fill and paint the whole panel.

Starring caused by stones thrown up by the tyres against the underside of a GRP wing can be prevented by fitting a stone guard of light alloy sheet.

Crazing:

Crazing is a continuous pattern of hairline cracks over a large area. This is a gel coat fault found on bad mouldings. There is no cure except to use a heavy-bodied paint filler in the cracks and then paint over.

4:3 Repairing GRP bodywork

Because of its nature, GRP cannot be crumpled like sheet metal. It either springs back into shape after an impact, or breaks. The results of a collision are usually splits, cracks or pieces broken off entirely, plus local cracks and gouges. If a piece of the moulding is missing the best way to repair it is to put it back in the original mould and re-build the missing part of the laminate with a scarfed joint to unite it with the remainder. This is not practical for the private owner, but the same result can be achieved by making a part-mould.

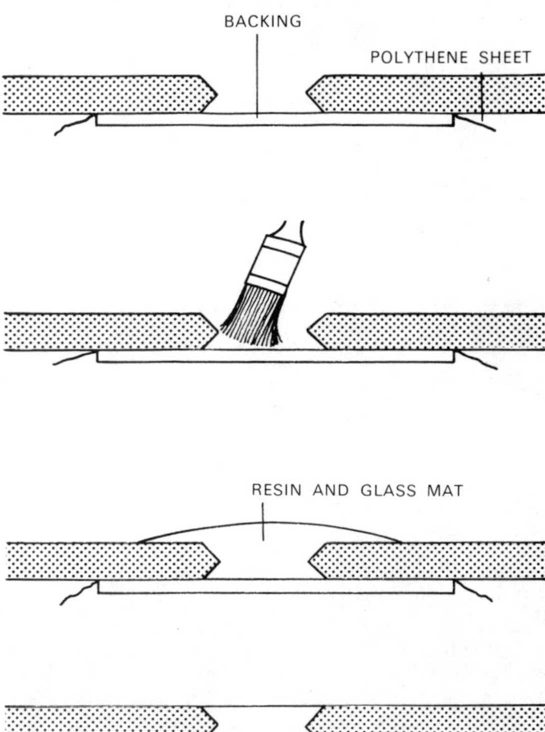

FIG 4:6   Repairing a broken GRP moulding

The procedure for GRP repairs is to cut away all torn laminate and chamfer both sides of the broken edge to form a Vee as shown in **FIG 4:6**. Sand down both surfaces by an inch or more all around the damage to give a good key. Cover the face side of the aperture with sheet metal wrapped in polythene, as a release agent, and lay up glass mat and resin in the hole. Build up subsequent layers until the new laminate stands proud of the old

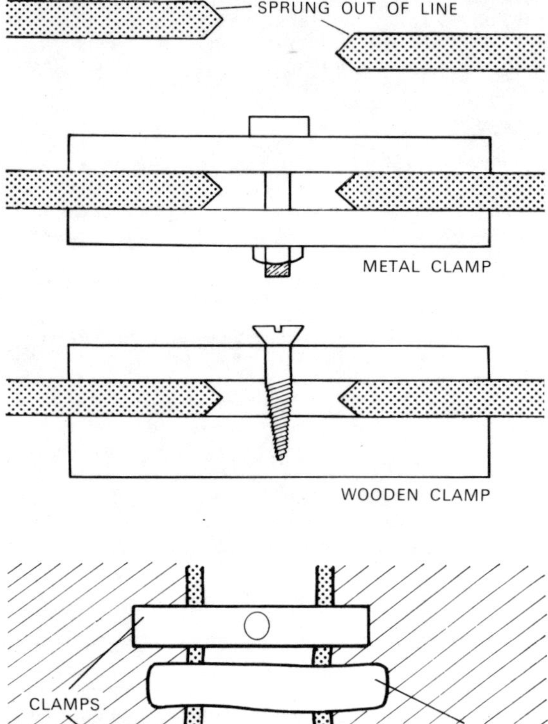

FIG 4:7 Temporary clamps to align a split

inside surface. The first layer should be worked well round behind the back of the Vee in the old laminate and the last should overlap by not less than half an inch. Do not lay up more than $\frac{1}{4}$ inch of resin and glass at a time, but allow the resin to set or 'go off' before applying another layer. Thick polythene (.005 inch) is better than thin, because it does not wrinkle so much. Wrinkles cast into GRP are very difficult to eradicate. Instead of polythene, cellophane or greaseproof paper can be used, or the metal part-mould can be treated with conventional mould release agents if these happen to be on hand.

More often than not, the sides of a split will be out of line and must be held level until the resin has set. Make some clamps out of wood or metal. They should be no wider than necessary, because their presence will prevent parts of the crack being repaired. But sufficient glass and resin can be applied between the clamps to hold the parts together and the remainder can be filled in when the clamps have been removed (see **FIG 4:7**).

Sometimes the back of a moulding is inaccessible and some kind of backing plate is necessary, while the patch is worked in from the front. There are various ingenious ways of doing this. One is to cut a plate from hardboard or plywood and fit a screw-eye as a handle. Wriggle the plate in position and hold it with a piece of wire made fast somewhere while temporary clamps are being

arranged. Another method, suggested by the makers of Cataloy, is to use perforated metal held by wire. Do not use any release agent on these backing plates, otherwise they will fall away and rattle inside the closed section. Perforated metal is ideally suitable for this type of repair because the resin exudes through the holes and locks it in place. If the break occurs in a section with a compound curvature, the backing plate should be shaped to the same curve as far as possible, erring on the thick side of laminate patch. Papier maché, made from wet newspaper and water-soluble paste, can be used for these plates, moulded on an adjoining part of the car.

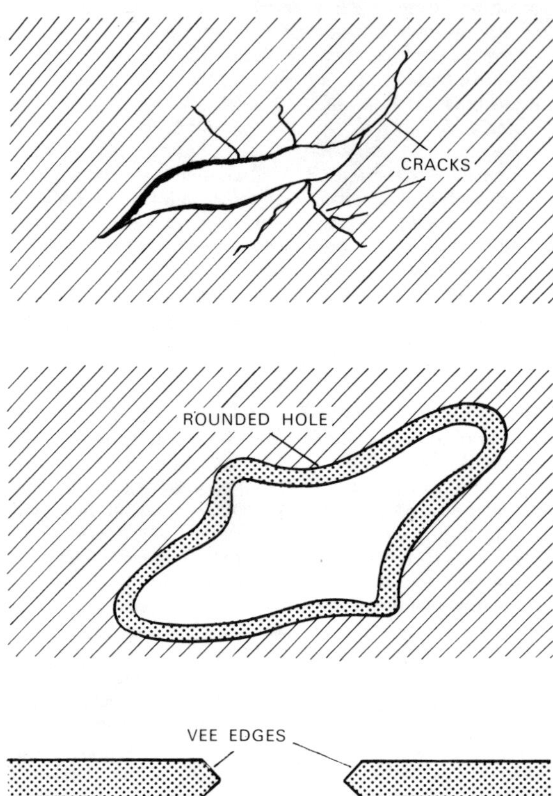

FIG 4:8 Repairing a holed, cracked moulding

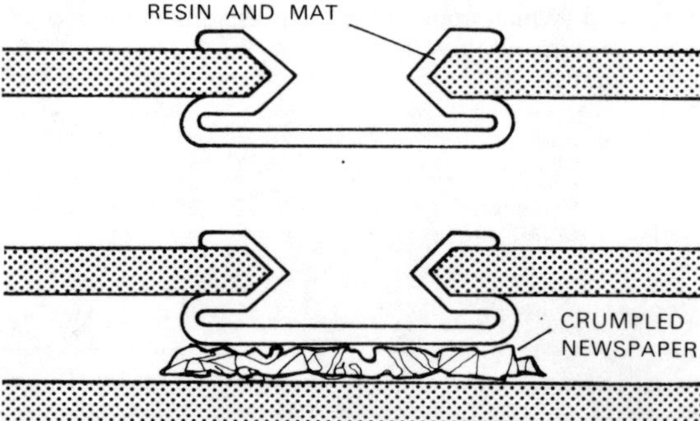

FIG 4:9 Repairs with front access only

A quick, though messy, way of making a backing is to wet-out a piece of glass mat on a piece of window glass and push it into the hole, working it well round the Vee edge. If the hole is very large this mat will need some support such as strips of glass tape or any other fabric that is readily available. If the space behind the damage is not deep it can be filled with a balloon or balls of crumpled paper to hold the mat in position until it hardens. The mat will have nothing to commend it as a moulding, but it will serve as a base for a properly laminated patch. The important point is to leave room for the patch to be worked well round the back of the moulding. As a last resort, part of the inner moulding can be cut away to give access and then glassed back into position.

Very extensive damage to a large moulding is not worth repairing if the original mould is still in existence, but it may be found that the makers are no longer in business or that the mould has been burnt to make room for new models. If the shape is very flat and simple it may be possible to make a mould out of aluminium, plywood or cardboard. If the shape is too complex to be followed by sheet material a pattern can be built up with plaster, or a plaster cast may be taken off the corresponding part of another car. This is a slow business and the plaster will take about three weeks to dry out. For details of mould making on this scale, refer to one of the excellent booklets available from GRP suppliers.

Sometimes a rib or part of a headlamp surround may be knocked off, leaving deep damage too small for a part-mould but too large to be filled and burnished. These parts should be cleaned up and 'Veed' and then built up with glass mat and resin, in layers not exceeding $\frac{1}{4}$ inch at a time. Greater thicknesses of wet resin will cause trouble because of the exotherm or internal heating which occurs during cure. Build the repair well proud of the original surface, then file down to shape, sand and paint. Some moulders add a little french chalk to the outer layers of resin to make sanding easier.

Chipping:

Chips are usually confined to the gel coat and can be dealt with in the same way as scratches, but as they are wider it is more difficult to make the repair inconspicuous. Blisters, cavities and 'worm casts' are common flaws in GRP mouldings; they should have been attended to before the moulding left the factory, but some of them are bridged by a thin skin of unreinforced resin which is broken in service. These are found on ridges on the moulding (which come out of depressions in the mould) and along mould joint lines. Some are caused by nothing more than a drop of sweat from the laminator's forehead. If a cavity is found it is worthwhile to tap the surrounding laminate with a screwdriver to ascertain whether there are any more. The cure is to fill with resin putty, then sand and paint and finally burnish to blend in the repair with the remaining surface.

Recoating and repainting:

When a GRP car body has a scruffy appearance due to scratches, chips and imperfect repairs, one has the choice of resurfacing with resin or painting. Make good all damage and fill scratches as previously described. Before resurfacing with resin, sand heavily to remove any

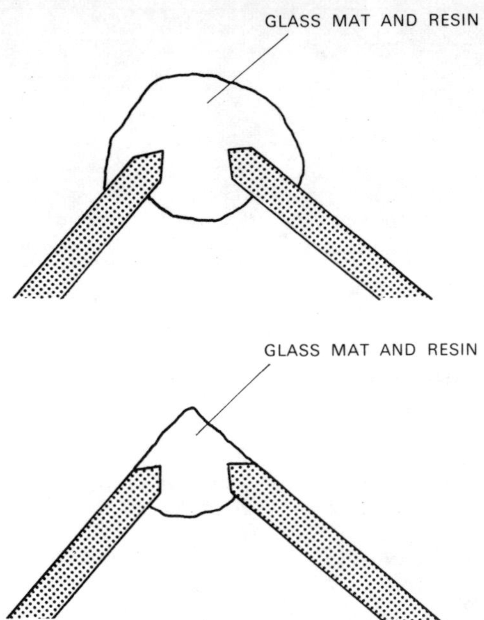

FIG 4:10   Repairing local damage to an angled section

traces of mould release agents and car polish, and to reduce the thickness of the gel coat. Remember that an over-thick gel coat will be brittle. Its purpose is to keep water away from the glass fibres and to carry solid colour, and apart from that the less of it the better. Do not use a laminating resin, but an isophthalic gel coating resin. Apply thinly by brush, and spread the resin out well, otherwise it will sag into 'curtains'. Probably two coats will be needed, because polyester resins do not mask as well as paint. Do not sand the first coat before applying the second. When the resin has set, burnish and polish the new surface. Re-surfacing with polyester resin should be more durable than painting, but an inexperienced person will probably do better with paint.

Painting GRP:

Preparation of GRP for painting is mainly a matter of getting it clean. New mouldings may bear traces of polyvinyl alcohol release agent and carnauba wax mould polish, and both of these repel paint. The first step is a wash down with white spirit which should be dried off with clean rag. Follow this with a thorough sanding with 320 wet-or-dry paper lubricated with plenty of water to which a domestic detergent has been added. Finish off with clean warm water and dry with a chamois leather.

Most primers take well on GRP. A styrenated alkyd primer is probably the best, but it must be sprayed. Another excellent primer for GRP is epoxy, which adheres well, but needs a warm workshop because it is sensitive to temperature variations. It also inhibits the cure of polyester resins, so it should not be used on very young mouldings. The test of a moulding is to tap it with a coin. If it rings, it is fully cured. If it sounds like cardboard it is under-cured and may need heat treatment. Good results on GRP can be obtained with two-part polyurethane or even a 'one-shot' polyurethane. Before painting a GRP panel, examine it for pinholes. This is a common defect, but the holes are easily filled with polyester putty.

Removing paint:

Never use a blow-lamp or chemical paint remover on GRP. Most car bodies are not made of fire-retardant resin, and will burn very well under a blow-lamp flame. Even if the laminate does not catch fire the surface will be pitted. Paint removers will attack the gel coat as well as the paint. Sanding is the only safe way to remove paint from GRP.

Speckled paint:

Speckled paint, which consists of globules of different paints which do not mix, is widely used on the insides of GRP boat hulls because it masks the rough side of the laminate. This material must be sprayed on and, because of the low pressure and large volume of air required, a large industrial air compressor is necessary. Consequently the private owner would be well advised to have this work done for him at a GRP factory or motor body paintshop.

Some striking effects, such as leopard skin or gold and silver lamé, can be obtained with speckled paint. As these paints have the remarkable ability to make rough surfaces look smooth, they can be used in place of conventional interior trim. In this case, of course, the insulating and sound-deadening effect of the trim is lost. . Another advantage of speckled paint is that it masks the smell of styrene which emanates from commercial GRP mouldings.

4:4 Working with GRP

Although GRP is more like reinforced concrete than sheet metal, it can be worked with metal-working tools such as hacksaws, files and twist drills. Always file, saw or drill away from the gel coat or face side towards the rough side to avoid chipping the gel coat. GRP is abrasive and if a great deal of sawing has to be done a diamond-edged circular saw blade may be used. Jig-saws attached to portable electric drills are effective, but shears and guillotines are useless because they crush the gel coat and wood saws chip it very badly.

Screws:

Self-tapping screws of the thread-cutting kind, such as GKN 'Z' blunt-end, may be used in GRP, but the size of the pilot hole must be kept down to the recommended size. The pilot holes must be drilled, never punched. Very small sizes do not grip well in GRP and the thread-forming kind intended for metal is not suitable. Never try to put a self-tapping screw or anything else into the edge of a laminate. It will merely prise the layers of glass mat apart, like screwing into end-grain wood.

All mountings and joints should be considered if possible at the design stage, when good provision can be made. While the moulding is being made it is easy to embed blocks of wood to take wood screws or tapped steel plates, preferably perforated to lock them in. Do not try to bond in large pieces of copper because this metal

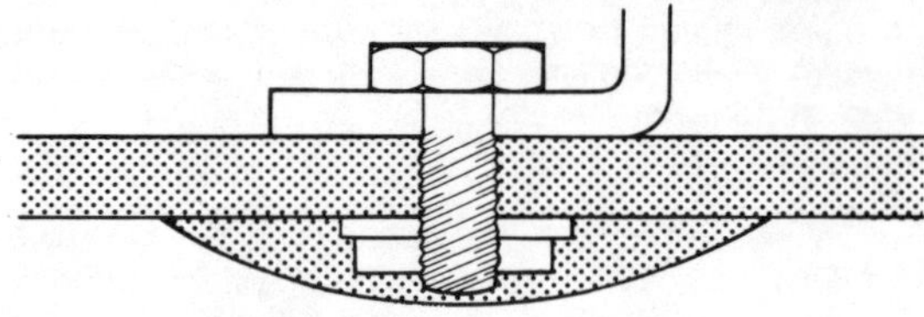

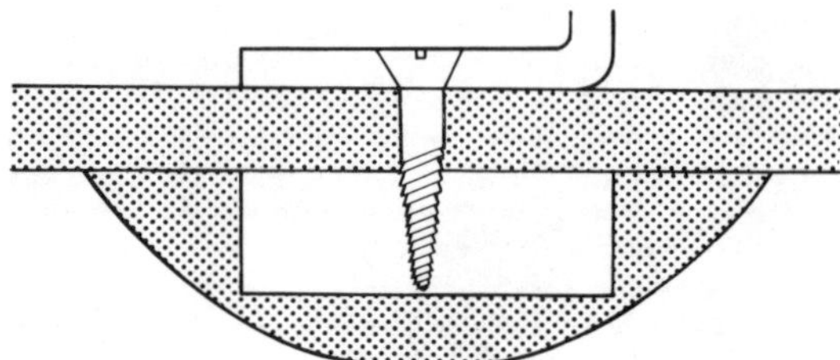

FIG 4:11   Moulded-in mounting points

inhibits the cure of the resin. Epoxy resin can be used safely with copper, so if copper must be used, it may be primed with epoxy resin before being embedded in polyester.

Rivets:

Hot rivets are unusable with GRP because the heat would damage the laminate. Even copper or aluminium rivets are to be avoided because the hammering will probably crack the gel coat, if not the base resin. If hammered rivets must be used, put a large washer under the head to spread the load over the gel coat.

A better type of rivet to use is the Pop rivet (see **Chapter 2**), which is spread into shape by the steady pull of a specially-shaped mandrel. The mandrel is pulled through the hollow rivet by means of a special hand tool. Even these can crush thin mouldings.

Tapped inserts:

GRP moulders use a number of makes of tapped insert, which are embedded in the laminate during lay-up. There is also a useful push-in tapped insert called the Blanc-lok which can be fitted at a later stage to a cured moulding. It is rather like a split thimble, knurled on the outside to grip the GRP and tapped inside to take a bolt. One type has a flange to take tensile loads. This type should not be loaded in compression because the serrations can push through the laminate. The plastics type of Rawlplug is effective in thick sections of GRP, and some of the toggle fittings intended for sheet metal and wallboards can also be used.

Bigheads:

Another proprietary fastener, intended for bonding into a laminate, is the Bighead bonding fastener which consists of a perforated 'penny washer' with a threaded rod welded to the centre. The perforations lock the washer into the GRP and leave the thread protruding. When using these with wet resin, protect the thread with release agent or a stack of nuts to prevent resin hardening in the threads. Some Bigheads are supplied with protective plastic sleeves.

Nails:

Any hammering is bad practice because it shatters the resin. Nails and upholstery tacks should not be used on GRP. If a tacking line is required, fasten a strip of wood or millboard to the laminate and tack into this.

Bonding GRP to other materials:

Bonding GRP to steel and aluminium is not easy and needs care. The metal must be entirely degreased, preferably with carbon tetrachloride, and not touched with the fingers afterwards. The metal is then primed with phosphoric acid primer, which must be thoroughly washed off after it has acted otherwise the process will continue inside the laminate. Rough metal surfaces bond better than smooth ones. The bond will not be as strong as the laminate and this method of attachment should be avoided in stressed structures.

Nuts are easily embedded in a laminate during lay-up and square nuts hold better than hexagonal. If the back of the moulding is accessible, it is possible to embed nuts on a finished laminate by glassing them over. It is easier to drill the laminate using the attachment as a jig, put in the bolts, screw down the nuts and glass over, rather than to try to position the nuts accurately first. Nuts will not hold in polyester if they are subject to continual racking; they will chafe a hole for themselves under the surface. Large plates to spread the load are the answer to this. The plates should be perforated to form a key.

Bonding to wood is not very satisfactory as a constructional method, and the most one can depend on is a wrap-round rather than adhesion. Polyesters are not glues and should not be used as such. A thin polyester primer should be used to soak into the grain of the wood, and this can be made by thinning general-purpose polyester with styrene. Styrene, although one of the constituents of polyester, is not often stocked by GRP retailers. If there is difficulty in getting it about 5 per cent of acetone could be used instead. Another way of thinning polyester so that it will soak into wood is to warm it by standing the tin in hot water. **It is dangerous to heat it over 50 deg. C (120 deg. F) because it catches fire easily.** Hot polyester needs far less catalyst, so cut the amount down to less than half the usual amount, otherwise the resin will go off before it can be spread. Do not try to bond to wood which has been treated with a preservative, because this will upset the cure.

Most porous materials such as hardboard, millboard, and canvas can be treated as wood. Rubber should be sponged with battery acid to make a key. Most of the plastic sheet materials will not bond to polyester or epoxy, but there is a grade of PVC used for lining GRP chemical tanks which can be bonded with a special type of polyester. But this type is not stocked by GRP retailers.

It is not possible to bond GRP to sheet glass. Phenolic laminates such as Formica can be bonded if the surface is roughened.

It is important to know that polystyrene foam is attacked by polyester resin. If they are to be used together the foam must be sealed with epoxy sealer or bitumen paint, or wrapped in polythene sheet. Foamed PVC is not so sensitive and may be laid up with the resin, though some softening does occur.

Both polystyrene and PVC foams are thermoplastics and may give trouble through softening if used as cores in sandwich-construction roofs in tropical countries. End-grain balsa wood is preferable as a core for tropical and sub-tropical service.

Bolted-through attachments are not suitable for plastic-cored sandwich mouldings, because the bolts compress the core. The correct construction incorporates metal spacing tubes between the inner and outer plates to take the load off the plastic core (see **FIG 4:12**).

Capping raw edges:

It is very difficult to mould a rounded edge by hand lay-up, so manufacturers usually carry the moulding beyond the line required and then either trim it with a knife while still soft, or saw it off when it has hardened. The raw edge is unsightly, easily chipped and allows water to work its way up between the resin and the glass fibres where it will eventually soften the moulding. In really high-class GRP work made for the aero-space industry and others, cut or drilled edges have to be sealed with resin but such refinements are not likely to be found on motor body panels. Various edge treatments are shown in **FIG 4:13**, but two of these can only be incorporated at the design stage. A metal, timber or rubber capping, fixed mechanically or with epoxy adhesive, is a practical way of overcoming the problem and of protecting this vulnerable part of a moulding. A suitable U-section rubber, which is usable for capping the raw edges of GRP wings and roofs, is obtainable from coach trimming suppliers.

4:5 Can I build a GRP body?

There is no quick and easy way of making a one-off GRP car body. The accepted method is to make a full-sized pattern of plaster over wire netting supported by wooden frames or 'stations' corresponding to cross-sections of

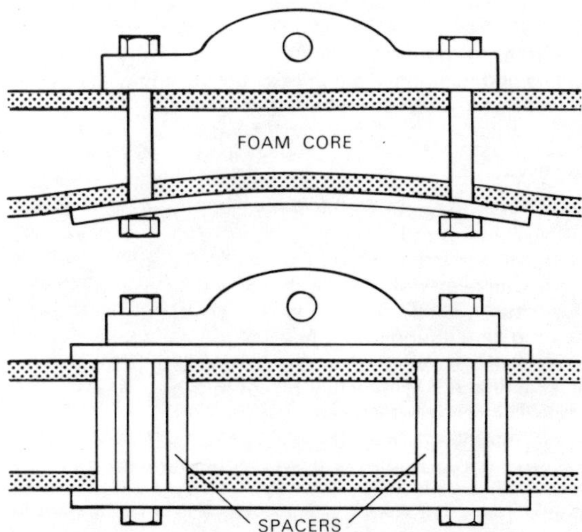

FIG 4:12   Attachments to a foam-cored sandwich

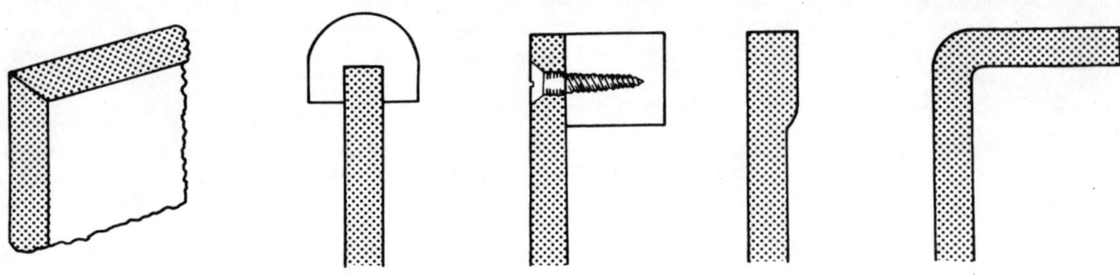

FIG 4:13   A selection of edging for mouldings

the bodyshell. The plaster is sanded down, sealed and painted with several coats of polyurethane paint. The mould is then laid up on the plaster, using several layers of glass mat or cloth with detachable part-moulds to accommodate any undercuts. The car bodyshell is then laid up in the female mould, which has been treated with mould release agent and wax polish. No moulding can be better than the mould from which it came and the surface of the mould depends largely on the time and care spent in making the male pattern or 'plug'.

The whole technique is not beyond the bounds of possibility for an amateur, but it is unlikely that a totally inexperienced person will produce a perfect moulding of size of a car body at the first attempt. It is far more economical to buy a professionally made bodyshell and mount it and trim it at home.

The alternative to making a pattern and a female mould is to lay-up a bodyshell on a male mould and rub down and fill the rough outer surface after it has cured. The labour involved in producing a good finish by this method is likely to be enormous.

If you must have a go, build a substantial timber frame on a plywood baseboard with plywood templates at 12 inch stations. Bridge the gaps between them with expanded metal or chicken wire about 1 inch below the finished surface. The assembly should be given two coats of varnish to prevent water from the plaster swelling the wood. Cover the wire with a $\frac{1}{4}$ inch layer of casting plaster mixed with shredded hemp to prevent it falling through the meshes. When this hard, apply a thick cream of plaster to within $\frac{1}{8}$ inch of the surface, covering the whole model in one operation to prevent warping. Follow with two finishing coats of thin, creamy mix, which is applied to two adjacent cells at a time and finished off with a metal spline, long enough to cover three adjacent templates. The second finishing coat can be smoothed with a smaller spline to fill in any low spots.

When you are satisfied with the shape and surface, fill the plaster surface with cellulose primer, stopper and filler as in paintshop practice. The primed and filled surface is then sprayed with a glossy coat of dark coloured cellulose, which will show up any irregularities. Low spots are filled with additional stopper and the high spots are sanded down and re-primed if necessary.

Laying-up on a male mould:

The first step is to apply a coat of unreinforced polyester resin, not forgetting the catalyst, and the accelerator if supplied separately. **Do not mix these two hardeners together, otherwise there will be an explosion which will blow your fingers off.**

It is impossible to maintain an even thickness, using chopped strand mat on a male mould, and the idea of smoothing it out by pulling down a layer of cotton or glass scrim over the mat does not work very well in reverse curves. The use of four or five layers of glass cloth, which costs much more than glass mat, is more satisfactory. But it still requires a great deal of heavy grinding, or hand rubbing, and the result is hardly worth painting, which only shows up the flats. On the other hand, the result may be no worse than the result of amateur panel-beating. Grinding will take all the resin off the cloth on the high places and the affected spots should be recovered with a coat of resin, which is extended over the whole body, and then sanded with a fine disc; further coats may be necessary to achieve a passable result.

The moulding is now ready for lifting from the male mould. It will have shrunk on hardening, but it can be separated from the male mould by hitting it with a rubber or hide-faced mallet, and inserting strips of hardboard into gaps between the moulding and the male mould.

It should be repeated that the novice is not likely to meet with success at the first attempt, so practise on small objects such as a model boat hull or a window-box until you know what you are doing. More details of GRP technique can be found in the information available from the firms who supply the materials.

4:6 Sources of supply

Satisfactory results are obtainable with the repair pastes, such as Cataloy, made by Holts Products Ltd. and obtainable at motor accessory shops. The same company provides a GRP repair kit, which includes some glass mat and surfacing tissue. The polyester resin is specially formulated for easy application and the amount of hardener is not critical. The bond obtainable with a polyester resin is not as good as that of an epoxy resin, hence the insistence on scoring the metal or drilling small holes in it to make a key. These kits are convenient for acquiring a very small quantity of material, but for more extensive repairs or alterations it is cheaper to purchase resin and glass separately from a GRP material supplier, such as Strand Glass who have shops in many towns (addresses can be found in a telephone directory). These specialist suppliers stock a wide range of requisites for GRP work and can also supply practical and technical information.

CHAPTER 5

Painting

5:1 Types of paint

The structure of paint:

All modern refinishing paints are mixtures of three main constituents; the vehicle (or binder), the pigment and the solvent (or thinner). The vehicle forms the film, binds the pigment particles together and adheres to the underlying metal or substrate. The pigment, so-called, does entirely different jobs in different kinds of paint. In primers it helps to resist corrosion; in fillers it builds up film thickness to fill irregularities and make flatting easy; in colour coats the pigment may consist of finely ground minerals or synthetic dyes, which give the paint its hiding power (opacity) and decorative finish. The solvent makes the mixture workable during manufacture and produces the correct consistency for application by brush, spray or knife. It evaporates when the paint has been applied, leaving the vehicle to form the paint film.

Traditional and modern paints:

The choice of paints is wider today than ever before, and confusing to the beginner because so many of them hide their identity behind trade names. But they can be divided into families according to their manner of drying.

1 Coach Paints. The earliest cars were painted by brush with coach colours made from linseed oil mixed with pigments or dyes. Linseed oil dries very slowly by absorption of oxygen from the air (oxidation), speeded up a little by the addition of 'driers' such as oxides of lead and manganese. The varnishes used to put a gloss on coach paints were also made with linseed oil, boiled with natural gums or resins.

2 Cellulose. Cellulose is made by dissolving cotton linters in nitric acid, acetic acid or ethyl chloride. The three types are indistinguishable to the user, but they are not all soluble in the same solvent, which explains why the paint manufacturer's solvent should always be used. Cellulose dries by evaporation of the solvent, but there are other volatile ingredients which take longer to evaporate. If the film is polished too soon the solvents will continue to evaporate under the polish and cause the whole coating to sink.

3 Acrylics. Acrylics are a blend of methyl methacrylate (better known in the UK as Perspex) and a synthetic plasticiser. Acrylics, like cellulose, dry by evaporation of a solvent.

4 Oil-based and synthetic resin paints. These harden in two stages; first the solvent evaporates, then the film hardens by oxidation. The drying time is slower than cellulose or acrylic but these paints can carry a higher content of solids.

5 Stoving enamels. These will not dry in air, but need baking in an oven to complete a chemical reaction between the two components of the vehicle. The repair trade uses 'low bake' enamels, while the motor manufacturers use 'high bake' enamels which show a characteristic shrivelled surface. They should not be confused with vitreous enamel which is opaque glass and far too brittle for use on car bodies.

6 Two-can paints. This last family does not dry by evaporation or oxidation, but by a chemical change (polymerisation) which is initiated by a hydrogen peroxide catalyst. They include two-can polyurethanes, two-can epoxy primers and finishes, and the polyester stoppers and polyester spraying fillers. They contain little or no solvent and once the catalyst has been added to the vehicle, the working life is very limited.

Most of the paints offered for car body refinishing are

blends of nitrocellulose and synthetic resins which need less hand finishing than 'straight' cellulose.

Identifying finishes:

Anyone who makes a hobby of restoring cars is likely to encounter all six kinds of paint, not to mention domestic enamels! As a rough guide, mass-produced cars made before 1949 had cellulose finishes and those built later had synthetic enamels or the modern baked finish. Specialist cars continued to be painted in cellulose or cellulose-synthetic blends. The test for cellulose is to rub it hard with a rag dipped in cellulose thinner. Cellulose will stain the rag, but other paints will not. Similarly, a rag dipped in turpentine will pick up colour from an oil-based paint.

Undercoats:

A primer is intended to make the whole paint system stick to the metal. It may have no great opacity, and is best when applied as a thin film. It is not intended to fill scratches or to be rubbed down. Etching primer is a special type of primer which improves adhesion to difficult metals and slows down the spread of corrosion if the paint has been accidently scored or chipped.

A primer-surfacer is intended to play a double role; to provide good adhesion and to fill scratches. It carries a much heavier load of pigment than a simple primer. It can be flatted to provide a smooth base for the following colour coats. Its disadvantage is that the pigment content reduces water resistance, so at least two full coats are required to give a thickness of .002 inch after flatting.

Fillers are heavily loaded with powdered slate or other pigments and they are intended to fill deeper scratches than a primer-surfacer. They can be applied in greater thicknesses, so more drying time is necessary. Fillers can be brushed or sprayed over an entire area.

Stoppers are undercoats very heavily loaded to form pastes, which are applied with a knife to fill dents and crevices. They are intended for local application.

Metallic paints:

The vehicle of a metallic paint may be a nitrocellulose/synthetic blend or an acrylic resin, as described in **Chapter 9**. The pigment is a transparent tint and the opacity, or partial opacity, is produced by flakes of aluminium which are tinted with one or more colours. The flakes act as mirrors, so there is a difference between a side view and a vertical view; the lesser the reflection the darker the shade. The difference will be greatest when all the flakes lie parallel with the surface and least when they lie at random attitudes. Thin, quick-drying coats tend to leave the flakes lying parallel with the surface, giving the most difference between face and side tones. Thick, slow-drying coats allow the flakes to settle at random angles, producing the least difference between face and side tones.

Matching metallic finishes is much more difficult than with solid colours, particularly if the original paint on the car varies in thickness. A wide range of effects can be obtained by varying the viscosity, the air pressure and the method. Full wet coats bring up the colour of the pigments, while dry coats bring up the tint of the

aluminium. The colour match may be tested by spraying a primed flexible strip of metal which is then held against the original paint. The problem is eased by spraying to a natural break or trim line so that minor colour differences pass unnoticed. Another method is to use 'blending clear' to dilute the metallic paint so that the original background colour will influence the appearance of the new. Metallics are not intended to be applied by brush.

Selecting a paint system:

When refinishing a car, whether by brush or spray, it is prudent to obtain all the materials from the same manufacturer, to make sure they are compatible. An example is the Belco system produced by the Paints Division of Imperial Chemical Industries Ltd., which is suitable for amateur use and available from retailers.

The components of the system, in order of use are:
1 Thinner, for cleaning bare metal, cleaning brushes and thinning viscous paint.
2 Anti-rust primer, for protection of the metal.
3 Primer undercoat; an important build-up coat and base for the colour coat.
4 Cellulose putty, for filling dents and imperfections.
5 Colour coat; a quick-drying cellulose gloss finish.
6 Finishing compound, to give the final smooth surface.

All these paints are designed to be applied by brush, which saves masking and the need to buy or hire plant. If the instructions are followed, brush strokes should disappear quickly to leave a smooth hard finish.

There are about 50 colours in the colour-coat range, matching most of the colours on popular cars. All the paints (anti-rust primer, undercoat and colour coat) are available in 250 ml tins, which is sufficient for 35 sq ft of car body. The cellulose putty and the finishing compound are sold in 250 mg tins and the thinner in 250 and 500 ml tins.

5:2 Preparation for repainting

The first step in repainting a car body is to decide how the surface should be prepared. In some cases the existing paint can be left in place and, with suitable rubbing down, will provide a base for the new coat. In other cases the old paint must be stripped off completely.

Loss of surface gloss is not in itself a reason for stripping off old paint. Old cellulose has a grey, powdery appearance called chalking. Rub part of it with abrasive paste. This may disclose sound paint which can be used as a basis for new colour. If the underlying paint is covered with a pattern of fine cracks (checking) it has perished and needs stripping. Other faults to look for are micro-blisters, which are small domes caused by prolonged absorption of water, cracking, peeling, flaking and chipping. Deterioration of old paint is not stopped by covering it with new. In fact, the strong solvents in the new paint may speed up the process.

If there is a possibility that silicone polish has been used on the body, special precautions must be taken. Refer to **Section 5:6**.

Abrasives:

Abrasive papers coated with silicone carbide (commonly called wet-or-dry papers because they can be used with or without water) have replaced natural materials like pumice stone. There is more than one system of grading but in all systems the higher the grade number the finer the abrasive. Wet-or-dry paper can be bought in discs or strips for sanding machines or in 11 inch by 8 inch sheets for hand rubbing. The proper way to use it is to cut the sheet into four pieces measuring $5\frac{1}{2}$ inch by 4 inch. These are folded lengthwise, making a strip to fit the hand, with abrasive on both sides so that it will not slip out of the hand during wet rubbing.

Use short parallel strokes, not a circular motion. Keep the wrist well down so that most of the work is done with the palm of the hand. Hold the fingers at an angle of about 30 deg. to the line of stroke, to avoid making finger furrows in the paint. Large, slightly curved areas can be rubbed by wrapping the paper round a special rubber block, or a thick piece of cork or felt.

Rubbing down old paint:

Wet-or-dry paper is used with cold water and detergent. A little hard kitchen soap is rubbed on the paper to ease the drag of the abrasive and help clean the paint. Start on the roof of the car and work downwards, changing the water in the bucket at least three times to prevent it becoming too soapy. Rub down a small area at a time then sponge it off and dry with a chamois leather. Do not leave the washing off until the whole body has been rubbed because the sludge is very tenacious when dry.

Among the contaminants to look for are tar spots, stains from petrol, battery acid, antifreeze, brake fluid and anti-squeak fluids, silicone and wax and minute particles of embedded grit, known as industrial fall-out.

Rubbing down levels the old paint and leaves a sound base. Fractured paint and rusty areas need rubbing down until there is no perceptible edge of paint against the metal. This is called feather-edging (see **FIG 5:1**).

An alternative method of rubbing down is dry flatting with stearate paper, which is self-lubricating, but a compressed air supply is needed to remove the dust and the body must afterwards be wiped down with white

spirit. Do not be tempted to save time by using coarse grinding discs. They leave deep scratches which have to be filled, plus burred edges which have to be covered.

Stripping to bare metal:

In the event of serious crash damage or perished paint making a complete strip down to bare metal a necessity, first clean off mud and grease, then remove any exterior fittings which can be taken off easily, marking them for identification on reassembly. Cover all rubber glazing strips with masking tape and protect the tyres. There is no need to mask metal fittings against paint remover, but they will need masking later if the car is to be sprayed. It is not difficult to clean paint remover from glass or chromium plate.

Do not use a blow-lamp on a metal car body. Paint removing liquids are very effective if given time to work before scraping, and they will not distort thin panels or damage interior trim. The difficult part is getting rid of all traces of paint remover after it has done its work. Traces of paint remover will cause the paint to remain wet in patches and this fault may not become apparent until the colour coats are put on, because some surfacers will dry over paint remover. Do not waste a good bristle brush on paint remover. Any old vegetable-fibre brush will do.

Close all windows and doors to prevent the upholstery being splashed and dab on the paint remover with an old brush, covering one small section at a time. In a few minutes the paint should lift, down to the filler coats, if not to bare metal. Scrape off the loose paint and dab on some more remover to soften the remaining paint. A broad-bladed flexible stopping knife is the tool to use for scraping loose paint.

A wire brush is very effective for removing traces of softened paint from crevices. Follow this with a good scrubbing with wire wool soaked in paint remover until the surface appears dry and shiny. This will remove stubborn patches of primer and filler. Finish with a solvent wash of white spirit or petrol, dried off with clean rags. An airline, if available, is useful for blowing out crevices.

Works primer:

Replacement wings and other panels may arrive with a coating of 'works primer'. It is not safe to assume that this paint will support a paint system, because some factory primers are intended only to prevent rusting in store. If this is the case it should be stripped off. Good primer should be thoroughly cleaned, sanded and painted with primer-filler. Consult the panel supplier about this.

5:3 Brush painting

The increase in car production during the last 50 years has led to the adoption of spraying to save time. This has given some people the idea that painting by brush is an inferior process and that it is not possible to get a good finish by this means. In fact a process thousands of years old is not inferior to the new one. A paintbrush in a skilled hand gives prolonged control of the paint, which is quite impossible with a spray gun. At one time a trained brush-hand would have been sacked for producing the 'kerbside finish' accepted by the public today.

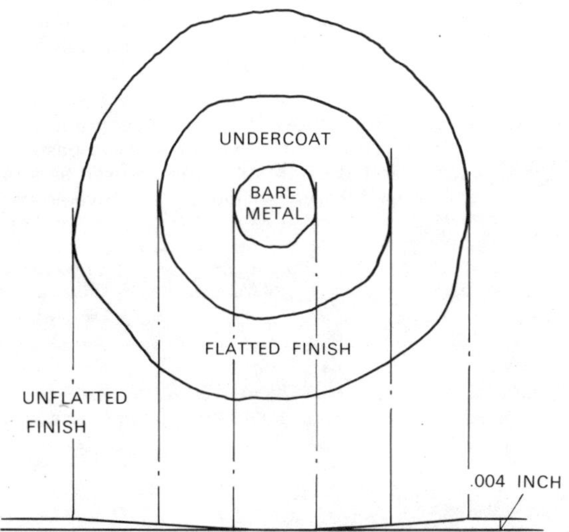

FIG 5:1 Feather-edging paint around a bare patch

The advocates of spraying forget that top-quality carriage work is still finished by brush, although the underlying filler coats may be sprayed. Whether brush or spray is used for undercoating, the rubbing down of these underlayers to produce a smooth surface is all-important. A lustrous finish will reproduce and even accentuate the defects of an uneven undercoat.

Brush marks are not an unavoidable feature of hand-painted colour coats. They usually indicate that the paint has not been correctly thinned or that it has not been fully brushed out and laid off. In other words, it shows that the painter does not know how to paint. Modern body finishes such as the Belco brushing system described in this chapter absorb their own brush marks to a great extent and are consequently easier to use than the older kinds of paint.

Choice of brushes:

The best craftsmens' brushes are made of semi-wild boar bristles, which wear down nicely to a tapered edge. In selecting a brush look for length of bristle and thickness. Take out a loose bristle and set light to it. If it burns away and leaves ash it is pure bristle, if it flares up and disappears it is probably vegetable fibre and suitable only for very rough work. Some modern brushes are made of nylon and other synthetic fibres, which are usable, but not as good as boar bristles because they are filaments, not tubes.

A new brush should be twirled in the hands to drive out loose bristles and dust and then broken-in on rough work, such as priming and filling. This will wear the brush down at the tip to give a correct taper and eliminate the splaying at the edges, which is found with a new brush. Even cheap brushes should be broken-in in this way.

Paintbrushes in use may be kept in water overnight, or even for several days provided the water is not allowed to evaporate. Rub the bulk of the surplus paint out of the bristles before putting them in the water. When the brushes are used again, the water is easily knocked out of them.

Varnish brushes:

Coach-painters' varnish brushes are oval and do not need breaking-in, but a new one should be suspended in raw linseed oil for several weeks before use, so that the dust will be floated out. Varnish brushes are kept under cover in linseed oil, so that they remain supple and free from dust. Some modern synthetic varnishes do not take kindly to linseed oil so it is advisable to clean off the linseed before using these materials.

How to clean a brush:

To clean a brush at the end of a job, or for a change of colour, rinse it out in turps substitute, petrol or paraffin and continue washing until the solvent is not stained by colour when the brush is put into it. Next remove the cleaning solvent by twirling the brush between the palms of the hands, making sure that the splashes do not fall on any newly-painted work. Bristles should never be wiped with fluffy rags, but a non-fluffy rag such as nylon can be used to wipe the stock. Never put a bristle brush into

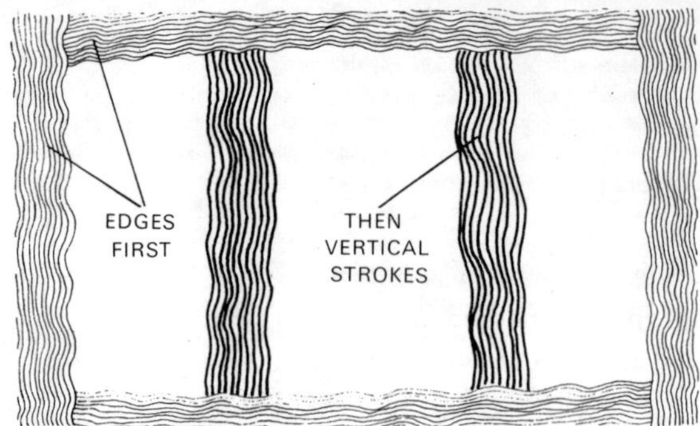

FIG 5:2   Sequence for brush painting a panel

water before it has been in paint. The bristles are open-ended tubes and water will run up and rot them from the inside unless they have been sealed with paint.

How to paint a panel:

Two sizes of brush will be required, a 1 inch or 1½ inch wide brush for edges and corners and a 2½ inch or 3 inch wide brush for the main surface. The correct sequence is shown in **FIG 5:2**, first using the small brush to do the edges and corners, followed by the large brush, well loaded with paint. Paint in two or three heavy vertical strokes so as to deposit sufficient paint. Then, using the same broad brush, spread the paint evenly across the whole surface. The final strokes of the brush, known as laying-off, are made first horizontally and then vertically. These last strokes should be made as lightly as possible to avoid brush marks.

It is important to keep the edge 'alive' which means running the broad strokes into the painted border before it begins to harden. It follows that no attempt should be made to paint a very large area, such as a complete side of a car, in one operation. Fortunately, car sides are broken up by the doors so it is feasible to paint each door separately, then the front and rear wings. The roof will probably be the largest unbroken area, and if it is necessary to make a join this should be on the longitudinal centre line where it is least conspicuous.

Varnishing:

Modern synthetic varnishes harden comparatively quickly, which means that a heavy flowing coat must be applied and brushed out before it sets up. Too thin a coat, applied timidly, will dry leaving bare patches, and too great a thickness will wrinkle in patches. Spread the varnish with a quick, stroking action of the wrist, keeping an eye on any heavy accumulations, and scrape the surplus varnish off the brush. Then cut across with the brush and scrape out the surplus again. Finish by laying-off downwards, using the tip of the brush gently but steadily. If any runs are forming in mouldings or around screw heads, stipple them out with a 1 inch brush. Work quickly and methodically, without slapping the brush about, which merely stirs air into the varnish.

Varnishing should not be done in very hot weather because the setting-up time is even shorter then. A dust-free atmosphere is obviously desirable: The painter should not wear fluffy clothing, and, if practicable, work should be surrounded by polythene curtains to exclude dust-bearing draughts. A pin in a cork is a useful little tool for picking out odd pieces of debris which may settle on wet varnish. The finished job should be left for at least 16 hours before any other work is done on it.

Brush painting step-by-step:

1 Preparing painted surfaces:

Wash with hot soapy water or detergent. Remove old polish with medium grade abrasive paper, using plenty of soapy water. Rinse off with clean water and leave to dry (which means dry as a bone, not still damp in patches). Scrape away loose paint and remove rust with a wire brush and abrasive paper. Feather-edge paint around bare metal areas with medium abrasive paper moistened with thinner. Wipe clean with a rag and thinner.

2 Preparing bare metal surfaces:

Clean thoroughly with thinner to remove grease and dirt. Remove rust with wire brush and abrasive paper. Metals other than steel should also be rubbed down with medium abrasive paper lubricated with thinner.

3 Rust-proofing:

Having removed visible rust, prevent its early reappearance by painting with anti-rust primer which contains red oxide and anti-corrosive pigments. This material has excellent adhesion qualities, but it must be given time to dry – preferably overnight, or for at least six hours in warm dry surroundings. This primer is the key to the whole paint system and if it comes adrift everything else will go with it.

When the anti-rust primer is dry, rub it smooth with medium wet-or-dry paper used with water. Sponge the surface with clean water and leave to dry. Take care not to rub through to bare metal. If this should happen, touch-in exposed areas with anti-rust primer and smooth again when dry.

4 Undercoat:

Undercoats are essential to build up the surface and to give adequate thickness to the system. Belco undercoat is designed specially for use over the anti-rust primer, but it will adhere to bare metal. Leave it to dry for at least two hours, then rub smooth with medium wet-or-dry paper.

5 Stopping:

Fill small dents, scores, lap joints and other imperfections with cellulose putty over the undercoat. Use a flexible knife such as a putty knife, and put the putty on in thin layers, leaving each half an hour to dry before applying the next, until the surface is level. Leave the final layer to dry for four hours then rub the surface down with wet medium abrasive paper until it is smooth and even. Sponge off with clean water and allow to dry thoroughly. Then apply another undercoat. After two hours' drying time there will be a smooth protective surface on which to apply the colour.

6 Finish:

Complete the job with the quick-drying cellulose finish which becomes 'touch dry' in a few minutes, lessening the risk of attracting dust. Apply the colour coat quickly and evenly with a full, broad brush. Brush marks should disappear as the paint sets up, but if it seems too viscous add a little thinner. Leave to dry for two hours. If the result is not satisfactory, rub down with fine wet-or-dry paper, used wet, and apply another coat.

7 Polishing:

Allow the final coat to harden for at least 48 hours, then apply the finishing compound thinned with clean water to a creamy consistency. Rub the surface evenly with a clean cloth using straight strokes, not a circular motion, taking care not to rub through the new paint on ridges or edges. Rinse with clean water, allow to dry, then rub clean with a dry cloth.

Notes:

Do not try to cut corners by skimping on materials or leaving out the primer, undercoat or putty. A glossy finish on an unprepared base only magnifies the defects which suggested that the car needed painting in the first place. Amateurs usually spoil the job because they are in too much of a hurry to get the colour on. A professional is not in a hurry, and he does not expect to do a week's work between one meal and the next.

All paints should be well stirred before use and strained through a paint filter or nylon stocking. Some modern stoved finishes remain active for a considerable time, and old cellulose can be softened by the solvents in the new. If you are in any doubt, paint a small unimportant patch to see whether the old finish will lift or bleed.

If lifting or bleeding does occur, apply a coat of primer undercoat over the whole surface, allow to dry for 45 minutes, then apply a second coat. Leave to dry for two hours, then rub down with medium wet-or-dry paper used wet. After rinsing down and drying, try again with the colour coat. If it still wrinkles, the car body needs stripping to bare metal.

Do not wax polish new paint for six weeks; this will allow the paint to harden completely.

5:4 Spray painting

The spray gun:

There are two basic types of industrial spray gun, the bleeder gun and the non-bleeder. The bleeder gun is simpler and less costly, but as the air flows constantly no pressure can be built up and its output is directly linked to the output of the compressor. The non-bleeder gun is more elaborate and the controls allow both paint and air flow to be adjusted independently. In both types air is fed in through separate passages and mixed inside the head. The three main components in the head are the paint nozzle, the air nozzle and the needle valve.

The paint nozzle lies behind the air nozzle and it meters the paint flow into the air stream. The air nozzle at the front of the spray head directs the air flow to produce correct atomisation. The needle valve runs through the centre of the paint nozzle and protrudes

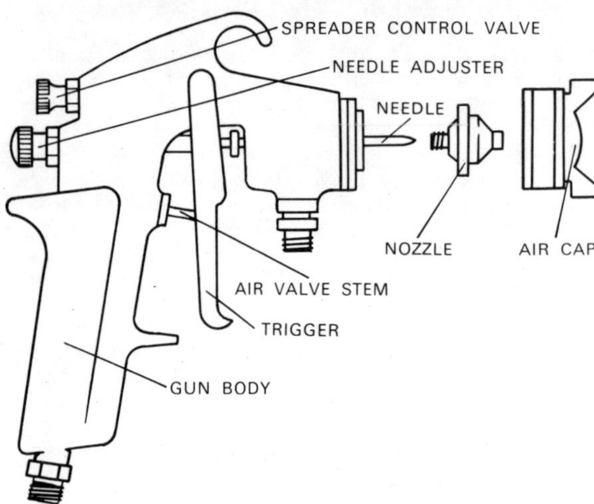

FIG 5:3 Components of a typical spray gun

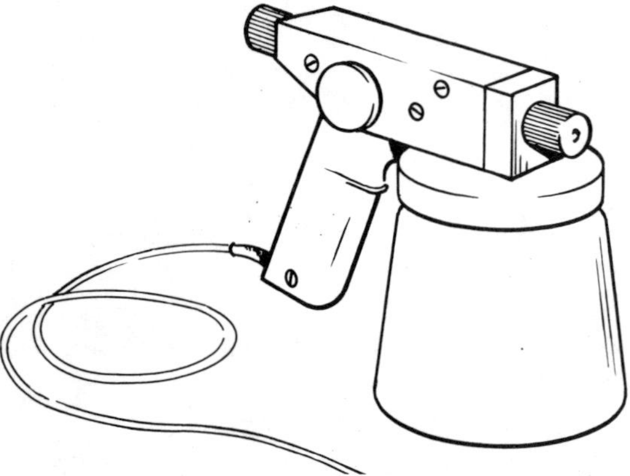

FIG 5:4 'Airless' spray guns require no compressor

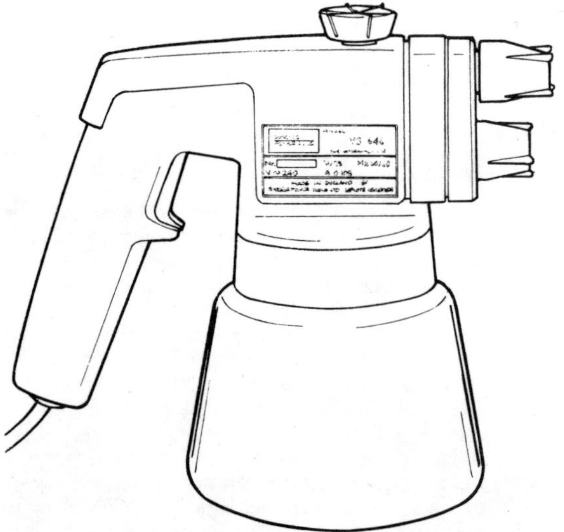

FIG 5:5 Another type of self-contained spray gun

into the air nozzle, and acts as a cut-off for the paint supply (see **FIG 5:3**).

The trigger first opens the air valve only. Pulling it further back lifts the needle valve off its seating and allows paint to be siphoned through the head. The amount of paint passing through the gun is dependent partly on the fluid orifice size and the needle valve adjustment, and partly on the viscosity of the paint and the air pressure in the container. The two external control knobs at the back of the gun are the fan-width control and the needle-valve retraction control.

There are also two container arrangements in common use; the gravity-feed gun with a plastic cup mounted on top of it, and the suction feed gun with underslung container. Most professional sprayers prefer the suction-fed type because its quart container holds enough paint to spray one coat all around a medium-sized car, whereas the gravity-fed type is usually too small. Another advantage of the underslung container is that the vent hole in the lid is at the back of the gun, so that paint does not spill out of it when the gun is tipped forward to spray horizontal surfaces. The top-feed gun also has a vent hole in the lid, and paint will spill out of it when a full gun is held at certain angles.

A spray-gun used for car painting uses from 7 to 15 cu ft of air per minute. Guns are usually sold with a general-purpose 'set-up' of needle valve, material nozzle and air cap which is suitable for most paints. A heavy-duty set-up, with a larger orifice in the material nozzle, is used for heavy-bodied fillers, flocks, speckled paint and so on. The air consumption is considerably higher when the heavy set-up is in use.

The commonest cause of a stoppage is paint blocking the vent hole in the container cover. A pin should be kept handy to prick this out. A second likely cause is clogging in the needle chamber or feed tube. To clean the needle, take off the screwed cap, unscrew the needle valve seating, and drop these two components into a tin of thinner. A blast of air should now dislodge anything in the mixing chamber. Clean the fittings with a small brush and replace. If the feed tube is blocked, take off the container, and note how the tube is positioned before dismantling and cleaning out with thinner.

Air compressors:

The important figure to ascertain before buying or hiring an air compressor is the volume of free air delivered per minute, which is about 75 per cent of the piston displacement. As a rough guide, an output of 4 cu ft/minute may be expected for each horsepower of an electric motor driving a piston-type compressor. To obtain the 10 cu ft/minute needed to keep a full-sized spray gun in continuous operation, the machine should have at least a 3 hp motor. The maximum air pressure need not be more than 100 lb/sq inch because most spraying is done between 45 and 70 lb/sq inch. To operate without pauses caused by pressure drop, the gun needs 10 cu/ft minute from the air receiver at any pressure. Pauses are maddening to the operator and lead to spoilt work. If the consumption of the air nozzle of the gun is known, it is easy to determine whether the compressor can keep the gun supplied.

The reader may be asking himself whether an industrial type of gun is necessary or whether good results are obtainable with less costly equipment. The smaller type

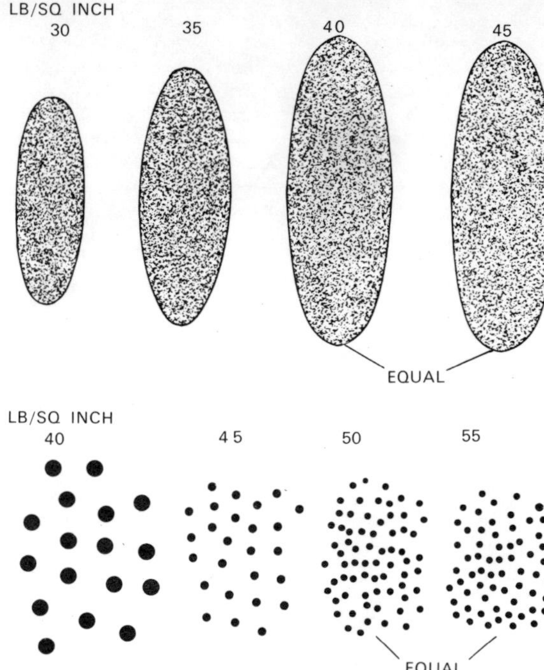

FIG 5:6 Setting up the gun for maximum spray size and finest atomisation

of equipment may be used, provided one realises the limitations of the machine and adjusts the working process accordingly. Spraying may have to be done with the paints at a lower viscosity, that is by adding more thinner, and this means spraying on more coats of paint. The speed of working will be slower and so greater care will be necessary to avoid runs and sags. It may also happen that the spraying quality will leave a lot to be desired. More intermediate flatting will be needed than is necessary with industrial equipment. Whatever the type of compressor, there must be an air filter fitted to prevent oil and water being mixed into the paint spray.

Spraying technique:

Spray-guns give an elongated oval spray, which emerges vertically or horizontally according to the position of the horns of the air cap. Most car spraying is done with a vertical spray, and the operator makes a series of passes across the panel, overlapping each by half to avoid leaving strips of paint-starved surface. The gun should be moving before the trigger is pulled and kept moving after the trigger has been released. This prevents too great a weight of paint building up at the edges. The gun should be held 6 to 8 inches from the work, and moved parallel with the surface, not swung in an arc from the wrist. This is easy enough on flat panels, but not so easy on curved surfaces which run into other curves.

The brush painter can control the paint manually for some time after it has been applied. If the viscosity is on the high side he can compensate by brushing it out, and he can distribute the paint evenly. The sprayer has no control over the paint after it leaves the gun; he has to rely on anticipation, acquired by experience.

Setting up the gun:

Stick a piece of paper to the wall, set the air pressure to 30 lb/sq inch and fully open the spreader and fluid needle controls. Hold the gun 6 inches from the paper, perpendicular to the surface, and spray for 2 seconds. Raise the pressure by 5 lb/sq inch and spray again; repeat the process by 5 lb/sq inch steps until the pressure giving the maximum spray size is established (**FIG 5:6**, top).

Take a second piece of paper, and with the gun 6 inches away from it and perpendicular, make a very fast pass, holding the trigger fully open. The gun must go fast enough to make the particles fall separately on the paper. Raise the pressure by 5 lb/sq inch, make another pass, and compare particle sizes. Repeat by 5 lb/sq inch stages until the pressure giving the finest atomisation has been ascertained (**FIG 5:6**, lower).

Spray pattern:

Before starting work at any time, fire a test burst on a piece of paper to check that the gun is operating properly.

SIDE PORT BLOCKED

DRIED PAINT IN NOZZLE OR NEEDLE BENT

AIR PRESSURE TOO HIGH OR PAINT TOO THIN

AIR PRESSURE TOO LOW

FIG 5:7 Faulty spray patterns and their causes

The spray pattern should be a long oval (or rectangle with rounded ends) about 8 inches high. A figure-of-eight pattern indicates too high air pressure, too wide a spray setting for the thinness of paint being used, or not enough paint coming through. An oval with 'lugs' at each end indicates that the air pressure is too high or that too much paint is feeding through (see **FIG 5 : 7**).

Cleaning the gun:

It is not necessary to dismantle a spray gun for cleaning every time it is used, but blowing a little thinner through it at the end of the day will save trouble. Do not leave a gun soaking in thinner or cleaning solvent overnight because this dries out the oil in the packing glands. Try not to drop a gun, and don't throw it about. It can be knocked out of alignment and ruined in this way.

Masking for single colour work:

In spray work, all glass, rubber, chromium and other parts must be protected from overspray by means of creped masking tape, the adhesive of which will withstand wet rubbing. One inch tape is quite wide enough. Half the width is used to stick the tape down on the car, and the other half is used to attach the masking paper. Masking paper is sold in rolls; it has good wet strength, no loose fibres and will not stain the work. Newspaper possesses none of these characteristics. Windows can be masked by winding them down a little, trapping the paper at the top, and sealing off with tape along the bottom and sides. Paper should be cut to fit the windscreen and back light, and taped to the rubber glazing strip. If the ends of the doors are to be sprayed, the trim panels must be masked and the seats and floor protected. It takes at least two hours to mask a modern car, but if it is not done properly much more time will be wasted in trying to scrape dried paint off rubber and chrome. Push-button door handles and other items difficult to remove should be covered with longitudinal strips of tape, not with tape bound around them.

Masking for two colours:

Allow the first colour to harden before masking to protect it from the second colour. Seal all joints in the masking paper to prevent any overspray from the second colour getting in. If the two colours are to meet at a moulding, then the masking needs to be effective as a protection only; but if the line is to run across a panel, masking tape with a good straight edge is necessary and a chalk guide line is useful for laying down the tape.

The thinner the tape the better, because paint tends to build up against the edge. Cellulose tape is thin and transparent, which is excellent when masking difficult places. It is not suitable if the second colour is to be flatted or wet rubbed because water disturbs the adhesive. If one is sure that the second colour will be left untouched until dry, then cellulose tape will serve.

An alternative is brown paper gumstrip used for sealing parcels. It has an accurate straight edge and is thinner than masking tape, but its disadvantage is that the adhesive is powerful and when removed it may peel away the colour coats underneath, which is a disaster. So the adhesive is modified with masking paste,

which plasticises the entire strip and makes it easier to peel away after use.

Masking paste is a material used to cover windscreens and windows in place of paper. The gumstrip used should be $2\frac{1}{2}$ or 3 inches wide. It is wetted along half its width with water and stuck down on whatever paper is being used for general coverage. The dry half of the gumstrip is then coated with masking paste and left to dry. When required for use, the dried, pasted half of the gumstrip is moistened with a sponge and applied to the panel. It will soften and cling to the panel and dry out in a clean straight line. Gumstrip so treated is very flexible when wet and can be made to curve in both planes, which is a very useful feature on some two-colour jobs. The masking should be removed as soon as the second colour has set to the point where it will not be damaged if the peeling tape touches it by accident.

Spray painting step-by-step:

For those who have suitable spray equipment and some previous experience of spraying, a recommended paint system is the ICI Belco PO30 line of car finishes available from suppliers like Brown Brothers or Thompson and Brown Brothers.

This system can be used over nearly all existing finishes without the use of special sealers and it can be applied to bare metal. It is available ready mixed to match most popular cars, and there is a range of basic colours and tinters which may be used to match unusual colours. Colour matching is beyond the scope of this book, but guidance will be found in the information sheet supplied with the tinters.

1 Cleaning:

Remove oil, grease, dirt and polish from existing paintwork with Body Kleen 901, diluted one part to four parts of water and applied with brush, sponge or rag. Stronger solutions will shift obstinate grease. After a few minutes, rinse by hosing down with clean water and, when the surface is dry, wipe over with cleaning petrol (petrol without additives) or a 1 : 1 mixture of methylated spirits and water. To remove silicone polishes, clean in the same way and then flat with 400 grade wet-or-dry paper used with a solution of one part Body Kleen to nine parts water.

2 Stripping:

If the old paint is to be stripped, wear protective clothing and apply Stripper 571 liberally with a brush. After removing all the old paint wash down with cleaning petrol or methylated spirits and water mixture.

3 Etching bare metal:

Mix one part Deoxidine 125 to two parts of water in a polythene bucket and flow it on to the surface with a long handled brush. As well as etching the metal, Deoxidine removes rust and grease, including the corrosive agents present in the fingertips. Brush it well into the surface and then rinse it off with a hose. If it dries and becomes sticky, apply more Deoxidine and rinse off at once. If it gets on to the skin, rinse it off at once. Deoxidine will attack zinc, so do not use it on zinc-coated steel.

There is a special etching primer, P565-5002, for this.

An alternative to Deoxidine is etching primer P565-5002 which is mixed 1:1 with an activator P273-5021 and allowed to stand for 10 minutes before use. This etching primer is particularly effective on aluminium, but cannot be used prior to the application of polyester materials, such as Cataloy or polyester spraying filler. Etching primer should be applied as soon as possible after cleaning, before the surface has become contaminated again.

For the private owner, refinishing one car, hand etching, using white spirit and abrasive paper not coarser than P360 grade, is cheaper and equally effective, although it takes longer.

4 GRP and wood:

Surfaces made of GRP (glass fibre) or wood require different initial treatment from painted steel bodies. Wash with warm water to remove traces of water-soluble parting agent and white spirit to remove wax. Wet flat with 400-grade paper to ensure good adhesion, then apply two or three coats of S/R Primer-Surfacer P540-line, applying the first coat by brush if surface imperfections are bad. Do not use any paint stripper on GRP or wood.

5 Sealing:

If the existing finish is maroon or red, which might bleed through into the new finish, apply a coat of Belco Sealer Black PO82-28, thinned 1:1 with Belco Fast Thinner 851-396 or 851-222, after preparation for painting. Allow this coat to air dry for 30 minutes and do not flat it. Apply at least two coats of undercoat before the finish, and when flatting these take care not to rub through to the sealer. If this should accidentally happen, spot in with BI Sealer and cellulose primer-filler before continuing the process.

6 Undercoats and stopper:

Complete coats of undercoat should be applied to stripped bodies and old, weathered finishes which are sound. If the existing finish is in very good condition, as in an accident repair, apply to damaged areas only.

There is a choice of cellulose or synthetic resin undercoats in the Belco system. The cellulose system is faster-drying and can be used for spot repairs as well as overall refinishing. The synthetic system has particularly good build to fill imperfections, is very easy to flat, but is not recommended for touch-up work. In short, use the synthetic system for rough bodies and cellulose for smooth bodies.

Cellulose undercoat: Apply three full coats of Hi-Build Filler Beige (PO84-678) or 505 Super Primer Filler White (PO84-505) thinned with an equal quantity of Belco Fast Thinner 851-396 or 851-222. Allow 10 to 15 minutes drying between coats and 30 minutes before wet flatting with P400 paper.

Synthetic undercoat: Apply two or three coats of S/R Primer Surfacer P540-87, thinned by adding one part thinner 850-33 to four parts surfacer. It is important to get the viscosity correct; this should be 25-28 seconds in a BSB4 cup. Dry each coat until the surface appears matt

(30 minutes in warm conditions) and wet flat the final coat after overnight drying. Be sure of complete flatting of the system by spraying a guide coat of one part colour to nine parts of thinner.

Polyester spraying filler: Where deep filling of irregular metal surfaces is required Polyester Spraying Filler P565-598 may be used. This is an off-white, heavy-bodied two-can product, which may be sprayed or brushed over well-sanded bare metal or over original stoved enamels.

Stoppers: Two types of stopper may be used with this system. The first is Polyester Stopper P551-1042, which is a two-can material suitable for application in thick layers. This must only be applied to well-scuffed bare metal or high-baked factory primers and finishes. It must not be sandwiched between coats of lacquer or used over etch primer. Activate the stopper with Activator P275-43, squeezing 3 to 4 inches from the tube for every 3 oz of stopper. Stir the two together thoroughly on a metal plate. The working life is only four minutes, so do not mix large quantities. If more than one layer is needed, allow 30 minutes for hardening, and remove any tackiness by wiping with petrol or cellulose thinner. This stopper can be flatted and feather-edged with paper not coarser than P280 grade.

The second kind of stopper for this system is Stopper PO83-line (grey PO83-44 and red PO83-49). Knife this in thin layers over the first coat of cellulose primer-filler or final coat of S/R primer-surfacer. Dry each layer for 15-20 minutes and the final layer for $1\frac{1}{2}$ hours before wet flatting with P320 paper. Spot-in any metal exposed during flatting with cellulose primer-filler.

7 Applying the colour coats:

Thin the Belco finish 1:1 with Thinner 851-804 and apply three single coats, allowing 15 to 30 minutes between coats and leave overnight for drying. This finish should dry with an excellent 'gloss from the gun' requiring no polishing. For the best possible results, apply two coats, dry overnight, then wet flat before applying the final coat.

8 Polishing:

If polishing is required, use 2B Rubbing Compound P562-32 by hand or machine, using a soft cloth or lambs-

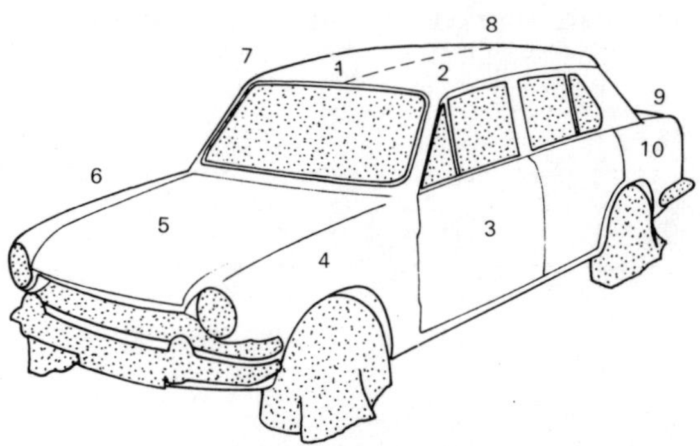

FIG 5:8   Sequence for spraying a complete car

wool mop, and finish with Car Polish No. 7. Do not apply any wax polish for six weeks, to allow the new paint to harden.

There is no doubt that a rotary lambs' wool polishing mop saves time, but it will 'burn' new paint if kept on one place too long. The household electric drill with a polishing attachment is rather fierce for this work, unless it has a variable-speed control in the trigger. Practice on a piece of scrap metal until you have learnt how to control the mop, which tends to run away with a beginner. Keep the mop flat to the panel, keep a steady pressure on it, and keep away from any projections. The lambs' wool mop itself must be clean and well secured. A rotary mop will not get into corners, which must be finished off by hand.

5:5 Refinishing special bodywork

Hand-made bodywork on special-bodied Bentleys, Aston Martins and other high-quality cars is usually panelled in aluminium, and needs much more filling than a pressed steel body. Some of these cars have ash framing under the panelling, so this should be checked for rot and renewed where necessary.

If the old body is to be stripped down to bare metal, take care to remove all traces of paint remover by washing with cleaning solvent and wire wool, followed by white spirit rubbed over with fine wet-or-dry paper, then more cleaning solvent wiped off with a clean cloth. Etch primers may be used for securing good adhesion to aluminium, but this precludes the use of a polyester spraying filler.

A heavy-bodied filler will be needed and this may be brushed, or sprayed if a filler set-up is available on the gun. On a hand-beaten aluminium body six filler coats may be necessary, each laid off at right angles to minimise ridges caused by brush marks. These can be applied two a day; one in the morning and the other in the evening. Stopping can be done on the primer or on the first coat of filler.

Surface irregularities will show through several filler coats because the filler tends to follow the contours of the surface as shown in **FIG 5:9**. The next step is to brush or spray a guide coat, which may consist of a little colour dissolved in white spirit. This evaporates quickly, leaving a stain. Its purpose is to show up the high and low spots and areas which have not been flatted. Rub down as directed by the filler manufacturer until the surface is level.

From this point onwards the procedure is the same as for refinishing pressed steel cars.

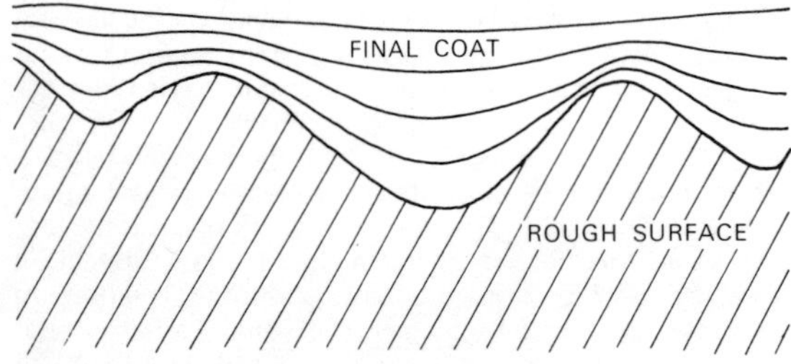

FIG 5:9   Filler tends to follow underlying contours

5:6 Silicone film removal

Polishes and waxes, both spray and wipe-on types, which contain silicone oils are extremely difficult to remove completely. They leave a residue in the cleaning rags which contaminates any surface on which these rags are used. Drastic measures are necessary to avoid 'fish eyes', 'craters' and other defects in new paint on a surface which has been polished with silicone-bearing material.

To find out whether a car has been polished with silicone, test-spray a small vertical area. If these polishes have been used fish eyes and craters will appear in the finish before it sets up. The test patch can then be wiped off with thinner.

The procedure for removing silicone polish recommended by the leading British distributor is as follows:
1 Wash the area to be repainted with a strong solution of detergent in hot water. Most of the commonly used household or car-washing detergents are equally effective.
2 Dry thoroughly and then wipe the surface with clean cloths wet with a solvent such as naptha or kerosene or one of the many wax-removing solvents and compounds.
3 Apply masking tape; bump out dents; sand broken paint to bare metal; lightly sand other surfaces to remove gloss; rinse with solvent and wipe with a prepared 'tack rag' to pick up dust and grit.
4 Spray primer coats on bare metal and allow coating to dry.
5 Spray colour coats.
6 If either the primer or finish coat does not adhere to the surface properly, the paint should be wiped off and the surface should be thoroughly cleaned again with solvent.

There are two departures from standard practice in this sequence. One is the use of disposable cloths soaked in a solvent to avoid picking up and transferring the residual silicone film. The other is a difference in the order of operations; the surface should be cleaned **before** panel beating and grinding to avoid the possibility of grinding the silicone film into the metal surface.

Cars should not be repainted near other cars which are being polished with silicones, and the paintshop should be kept clean and free from silicone on rags, clothing and spray equipment. Never use a gun to spray paint after it has been used to spray silicone polish.

5:7 Aerosols

If a spray gun is a crude instrument compared with a paint brush, what can be said of an aerosol – apart from the rude names flung at it by professionals and those who got bad results from their first attempt to use it?

In the first place it is a new technique, with different advantages and limitations and it needs a little practice to discover these. It is a rather expensive way of buying paint, but no other equipment is required and it is a very convenient means of obtaining small quantities of paint matching the standard colours of mass-produced cars. It is also a safe way for inexperienced people to buy metallic lacquers and other 'custom' paints. Some paint formulations need an industrial air compressor and a 'heavy set-up' on the gun, and it is easy to waste money in this way. Although you have no control over the viscosity of the paint in an aerosol, at least you know the gun is going to work.

The formulation adopted by Holts for their spray cans has two solvents. One half-dries very quickly to stop runs, then a slower-drying second-stage solvent takes over, allowing the surface to settle down and even out. As the speed of operation is low compared with an industrial gun it is advisable not to try to spray all round a car with one coat, because by the time you get back to the starting point, the paint there will have dried to such an extent that the join will show. With an industrial gun carrying a quart container it is possible to do this, but with aerosols the work should be broken down into sections using natural divisions of the bodywork as far as possible.

Hold the can at the recommended distance, usually 12 inches, and work methodically down the panel with a succession of horizontal passes, keeping an eye on the edges where paint tends to build up. Remember that any part which is painted twice will have twice as much wet paint on it as it should have. This weight of paint cannot hold up, anti-run solvent notwithstanding. If a run does occur, wipe the whole coat off with solvent and start again, or let it harden and then rub it down with fine wet-or-dry paper. Try to keep the spray always at right angles to the work, and always at the recommended distance from it. This is easier said than done on curved surfaces. Each pass should overlap the previous pass by one third of the spray pattern. If the paint 'loads up' on the surface this means you are spraying too close, overlapping too much, or moving too slowly. Even if it means wasting one aerosol, a practice run on a piece of scrap metal is advisable for a complete novice. He can then go on to less important parts of the car, such as the underside of the bonnet and boot lids and the inside of the boot and engine bay, before starting on the exterior pressings. As the roof is the largest and consequently most difficult unbroken area, it may be left until last, although normally it is done first.

If a spray can nozzle becomes blocked it can be pricked out with a pin. If the can is not empty and is to be used again on a later occasion the nozzle and feed tube should be cleared by holding the can upside-down and pressing the button. This will blow clear propellant through the system.

5:8 Faults in paintwork

Non-drying of primer:

This is usually due to traces of grease or paint stripper on the bare metal or rubbed paint underneath. Swab the affected area with white spirit; this usually does the trick and leaves the surface dry and normal when the solvent has evaporated. If this fails the part will have to be stripped, rubbed down level and re-coated with primer-surfacer.

Cracking and crazing:

Cracking is often observed when spraying the first coat of cellulose or car finish, after the surfacer has been flatted. It occurs when new paint is applied to perished paint which should have been stripped. The solvent in the new paint livens up the old and reveals fine hair-line cracks going in all directions. The remedy may be to spray on some more coats of surfacer, but if this does not work, the old paint will have to be stripped down to bare metal.

Lifting:

Sometimes the solvent in the new finish acts on the old finish as a paint remover, not producing mere hair cracks but lifting the old finish completely off the metal. This will happen if cellulose is sprayed on a car previously painted with air-drying synthetic enamels or domestic gloss paints, without an effective barrier coat.

Blushing:

This defect, sometimes called blooming, takes the form of a white cloud on newly-sprayed cellulose. It occurs in cold, humid weather, when the solvents have a re-frigerating effect on the air near the paint surface. This chilling causes the air to release its overburden of moisture on the wet cellulose, and this in turn brings about precipitation of the nitro-cotton content of the enamel, which shows white on the surface.

Blushing should be prevented by raising the temperature of the paint shop and by making sure that the car is not standing in a draught from outside, or one can wait until the damp weather has passed. If necessary, retarder thinners can be added to the cellulose in conditions where blushing may occur.

On 'straight' cellulose, which has to be burnished, blushing may not be a serious defect, because it may be possible to remove the white deposit without the necessity for re-spraying.

Peeling and flaking:

This defect, which occurs after a few weeks in service, is caused by poor preparation, which means that the new paint does not adhere to the old. The only remedy is to rub down the faulty parts and refinish, taking care to remove all traces of possible contaminants such as paint stripper, grease or polish.

Blistering:

Blisters are caused by distension of the paint film into a bubble by the pressure of trapped vapour. The vapour may be water vapour or solvent gas vapour from trapped solvents somewhere in the paint system.

In its simplest form, blistering is caused by spraying over a damp surface; for instance, spraying too soon over a flatted surface which has retained water from wet rubbing down. Local heating will vapourise the water and raise the paint film while it is still soft and flexible. Later, water introduced from behind the paint after it has hardened will crack the blister.

Water or a water-and-oil emulsion may be introduced by faulty air supplies. If the air filter on the compressor is not efficient, water and oil may be sprayed on the surface along with the paint, to be sealed down temporarily by subsequent coats. Then blistering occurs when the car body gets hot and the moisture vaporises.

Sometimes blistering is caused by osmosis, when water penetrates the top surface but cannot get out again. It travels along until it finds an area of poor adhesion, where it collects and forms a blister. This defect is usually caused by working in bad conditions. The remedy for blistering, however caused, is to strip to bare metal and start all over again, or at least rub right down until all traces of blistering have been eliminated.

Orange peel:

This defect, which is self-descriptive, is caused by poor spraying conditions, wrong air pressure, wrong paint viscosity, or an insufficiently heavy coat. The remedy is to flat down and respray, taking greater care in thinning the paint and keeping the air pressure correct.

Bridging:

This is an annoying fault on mouldings, where the paint film does not follow the contour but builds a bridge with a void under it.

The cure is to cut the unsupported film, rub down well and respray.

CHAPTER 6

Trimming

6:1 Coach trimming practice

The following notes are intended for those who have no previous experience of coach trimming. Neatness is the mark of good trimming – a cushion should look as if it grew like a fruit, untouched by human hand.

Tacking:

Of the four ways of holding trimming material in place, tacking is obsolescent and, in some modern cars, there there is no wood or millboard to tack into. The reader will come across tacking in the older cars still in service, and the system has its advantages for the beginner, because mistakes can be rectified, and temporary tacking enables materials to be strained into shape progressively.

Tacks vary from $\frac{1}{8}$ inch to $\frac{5}{8}$ inch in length, but $\frac{3}{8}$ inch and $\frac{1}{2}$ inch fine cut tacks are most frequently used. The $\frac{1}{4}$ inch and $\frac{1}{8}$ inch tacks are used on plywood, so that they do not project through the back face. Gimp pins ($\frac{3}{8}$ inch or $\frac{1}{2}$ inch) are used as finishing tacks, because their smaller heads look neater and they are easier to cover with braid. Gimp pins are usually painted black, but other colours are obtainable.

Professional coach trimmers used to hold 30 or 40 tacks in their mouths (not recommended for the beginner), and feed them on to the head of a magnetic tack hammer. They could drive in a tack with one blow, and work up an astonishing speed, which they had to maintain on piecework if they valued their job. For occasional private work a 'mag' hammer is not essential, but it has the advantage of leaving one hand free for straining the material while driving the tack. Tacks should always be knocked in at right angles to the work. If one goes in at an angle, take it out and try another. The base to which any material is tacked is termed 'the hold'.

Temporary tacking means knocking in tacks half way, so that they can be taken out again easily. By this means material can be pulled into position gradually, using two or three sets of temporary tacks.

Riveting:

Tacks can be used as rivets in plywood. The best way to do this is to place a metal plate behind the wood, so that the tack rivets itself. In the motor factories, staples have replaced riveted tacks in plywood and fibreboard.

Back tacking:

Back tacking is used to give a neat finish to a straight edge. The material is first tacked face down, then a strip of cardboard, plywood, rigid plastic or metal is tacked at the finishing line to give a straight edge, and the material is folded back over the strip to its correct face. Another braid-less finish is fold tacking, where the edge of the material is folded under and gimp pinned.

Finishing beads:

There are many designs of finishing beads which are used to cover a row of tacks or gimp pins and to give a neat finish. The commonest and cheapest is banding (see **FIG 6:1**). This is a strip of material with its edges turned in to meet in the middle. It is used in inconspicuous places where it will not be plainly visible. It can be made by hand, either with solution or on the sewing machine, or it can be bought ready made. It is fixed with evenly spaced gimp pins.

Another common bead is double-cord piping (see

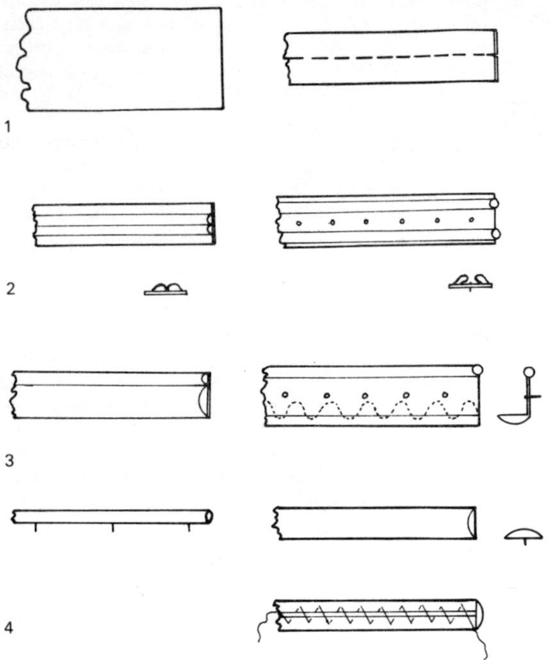

FIG 6:1   Some of the many forms of finishing beads

Key to Fig 6:1   1 Banding   2 Double-cord piping
3 Flexa bead opened and closed   4 Covered bead

FIG 6:1). As the name indicates, it has a double cord running through its length. It is usually bought ready-made in a colour to match the job. It is fixed by tacks or gimp pins, by opening the two cords and knocking home the tack between them. When the pin is home, the cords close up over its head.

'Flexa' bead is a fabric bead with a piping (see **FIG 6:1**). The tape of the piping is tacked to the job and the bead turned over to cover the tacks. A fine wire will be found interlaced along this bead to set it after it has been knocked into the correct position.

Covered bead is a metal or fabric bead covered with leathercloth. It can be bought in all colours, or it can be home made. To do this, the leathercloth is laid face down on the bench, with the bevelled side of the bead on top of it. The edges of the strip are then folded over the bead and sewn together. The bead has small nails (panel pins) at 2 inch intervals along its length (see **FIG 6:1**). These are knocked into the middle of the finishing line to give a neat matching finish. A bead block is used for the final fixing. This tool consists of a block of wood with a groove which fits the top of the bead. It will straighten out any bumps between the pin positions.

Fasteners:

Many types of fasteners are used in trimming. The following are most likely to be encountered:

Lift-the-Dot:

This fastener is undone by lifting the dot marked on one side of the female part. This releases the catch from the knob. These fasteners must always be arranged so that the dot is on the pulling side of the attachment point. The male part can be obtained to hold on fabric, wood or metal.

Veltex dot:

This is used on carpets. The fastening part lies on the underside of the carpet and only a pronged ring shows above, and this is almost invisible in a deep pile. The male part can be obtained to hold on wood or metal.

Durable dot:

The female part is similar to a press stud, and the male can be obtained to fit any hold. This fastener is also available in a baby size.

Turn button:

This has a fixed male part which fits any hold. The female part fits over it and the button is turned to secure.

Burco dot:

This fastener is similar in shape to the turn button, but fatter in shape. The male part fixes to any hold and has an eyelet fitted over it. To release this fastener, the button part is lifted slightly and then turned.

Trimount:

This fastener differs from the others in that it has only a male part which fits into a drilled hole. It is obtainable in various patterns and is used chiefly on doors and carpets.

There are special sets of punches available for fixing each type of fastener. If these are not available, a hollow punch can be used, using a knife to pierce any slots needed to accommodate the tags, which have to be turned over to secure the fastener to the hold.

Trimmer's stitches:

The heavier work is done with twine, preferably flax tufting twine, and No. 18 machine thread is used for lighter work. Yellow beeswax can be rubbed on twine or thread to make it run more easily.

There are two types of trimming needles, straight and circular. The circular needle is in fact half a circle and they are measured across the diameter from point to eye. They range from 1 inch to 6 inches and 4 inches is the most popular size. Straight needles run from 4 inches to 12 inches in length and some have a point at both ends to save having to turn the needle for the return stitch. Smaller sizes are used for thread work such as sewing piping and borders or basting loose covers.

Twine stitching is used to hold the cover material to a base where tacks or adhesive cannot be used, for example, when stitching a cover or hessian to a spring case, stitching felt, hair or fibre matting, or stringing on loose hair or fibre.

Hessian is sewn on a spring case by bringing it over the top and sides and stitching it to the bottom frame, using running stitches 1 inch apart. Invert the spring case so that the bottom frame is uppermost, with the

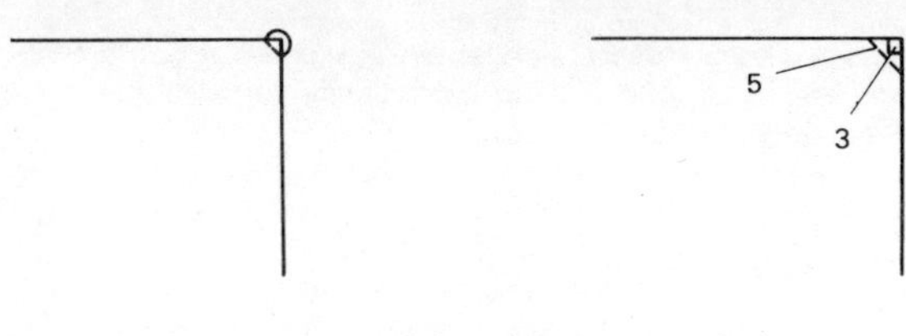

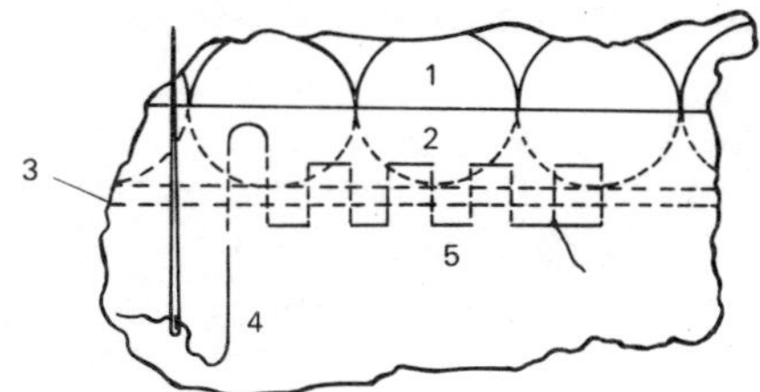

FIG 6:2 Running stitch used for stitching felt or hessian to a spring case

Key to Fig 6:2   1 Spring case   2 Hessian   3 Side frame   4 Twine   5 Stitches

FIG 6:3   Trimmer's slip knot

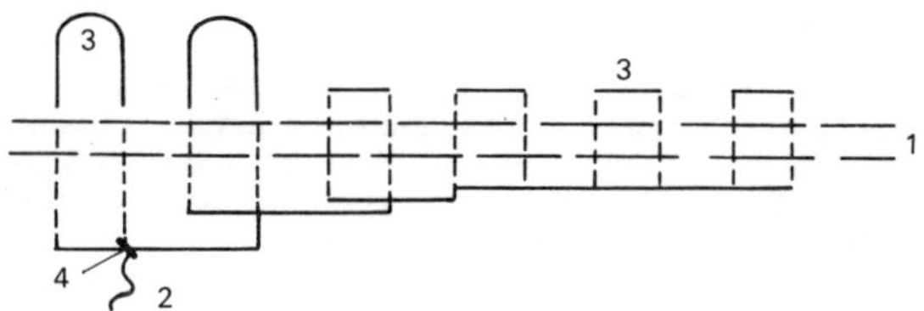

FIG 6:4   Quilting stitch

Key to Fig 6:4   1 Side frame   2 Twine   3 Stitches   4 Locking knot

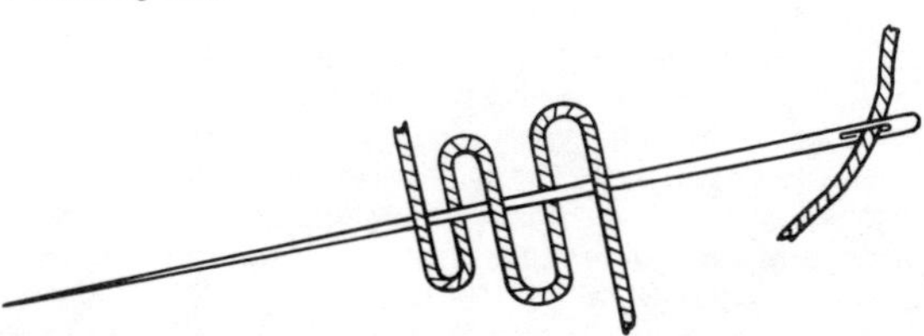

FIG 6:5   Stitch used for locking felts and rolls

hessian held in place by skewers. Insert the needle from the side, pointing diagonally upwards so that the bottom wire of the side frame is included in the stitch. Bring the needle back 1 inch to the left, returning to the line of stitching at the bottom of the side (see **FIG 6:2**). Pull the twine tight and fasten with a double slip knot (see **FIG 6:3**).

A modification of the running stitch is shown in **FIG 6:4**. This is used for sewing felt rolls and is called a quilting stitch. Travel 2 inches to the left and then back 1 inch to the right. As the needle comes through on its return, twist the length of twine twice round it and pull tight to lock the stitch (see **FIG 6:5**). Either a 4 inch circular or a 6 inch straight needle is used.

Another common stitch used when sewing the leathercloth border of a cushion to the bottom of a spring case, after the borders have been stuffed, is shown in **FIG 6:6**. In this instance, a raw edge of material is being stitched to the bottom of the spring case. Using a 4 inch circular needle, insert it about 2 inches in from the side-frame so as to include a bar or part of a spring. Pierce a hole in the leathercloth (which is held in position by skewers) about $\frac{3}{4}$ inch from the edge, bring the twine through, tie a double slip knot and draw it tight so that the leathercloth is fixed. Then, holding the length of twine in the left hand, make another stitch about 2 inches to the left with the other hand. Bring the needle over the twine held in the left hand and under the spring case hold (see **FIG 6:7**). Pierce the leathercloth and bring the needle through the loop formed by the left hand holding the twine, then pull it tight. This brings the cover into position and at the same time locks the stitch to the spring case. Continue round the spring case and tie off.

To secure the top machined part of the cover to the spring case, skewer the cover to the spring case, with the borders turned back so that the tape of the piping can be seen. With a 4 inch circular needle make a loop stitch through the felt which is held to the top frame of the

FIG 6:6   Stitch used for sewing border to spring case

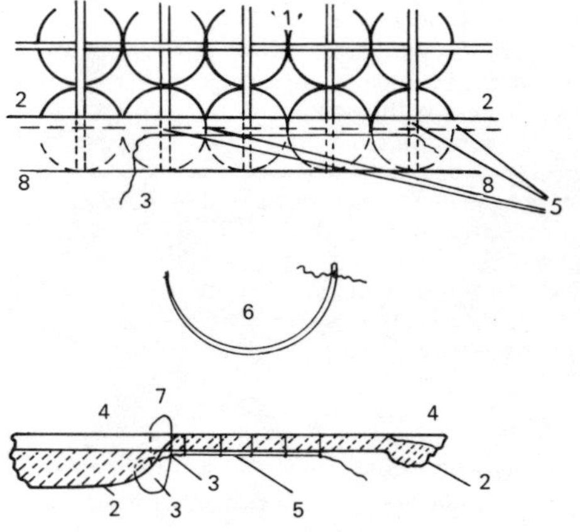

FIG 6:7   Stitching border to spring case

Key to Fig 6:7   1 Spring case   2 Edge of leathercloth   3 Twine   4 Case bar   5 Stitches   6 Circular needle   7 Knot   8 Bottom edge of spring case

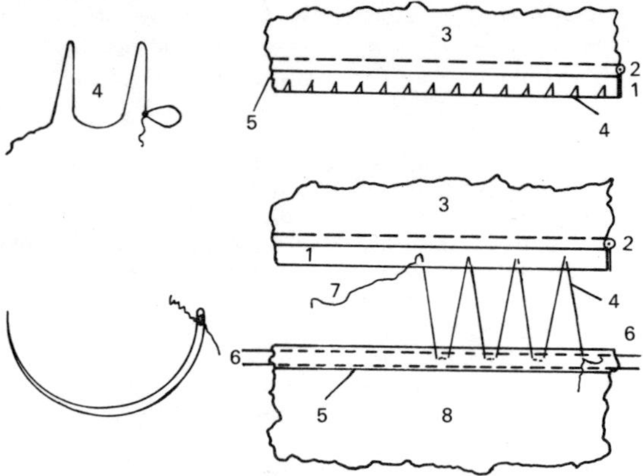

FIG 6:8   Stitching border to frame

Key to Fig 6:8   1 Tape of piping   2 Piping   3 Inverted border   4 Stitches   5 Felt roll   6 Frame   7 Twine   8 Side of spring case

spring case, tie a double slip knot and pull tight. This gives a start to the stitch. Then make a stitch right through the centre of the tape, piercing four thicknesses of material, the top, the border and the piping, which has two thicknesses.

The next stitch is made through the felt, forming a loop with its apex in the tape. After making another stitch through the leathercloth pull the stitch tight (see **FIG 6:8**). Never pull tight after the stitch through the felt, because this material will tear. The tape line of the piping has now been brought down to run along the outside contour of the top frame of the spring case and the cover is fixed to the top frame. The job is completed by turning down the border, stuffing it if necessary and stitching it to the bottom frame.

For sewing the bottom of the cushion and for fine work, such as hand sewing a piping line, a frenching stitch is

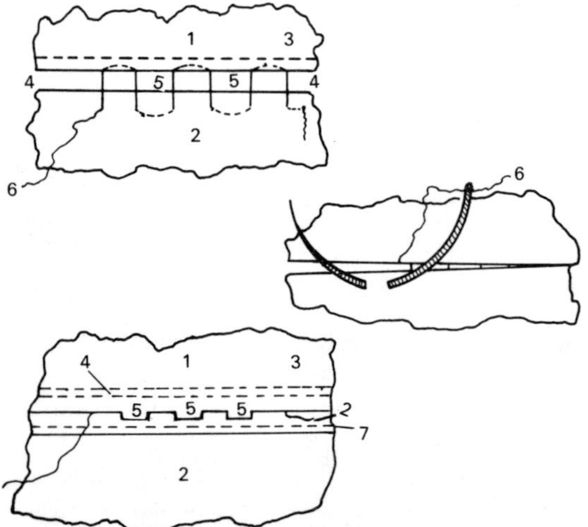

FIG 6:9   Frenching cushion base

Key to Fig 6:9   1 Black canvas   2 Leathercloth   3 Turned edge   4 Edge of leathercloth   5 Stitches   6 Twine   7 Frame

used (see **FIG 6:9**). This stitch is easier on fabric than on leathercloth, but if properly done it is difficult to distinguish from machining.

Black canvas is first laid on the cushion bottom, the edge of the canvas being folded in and skewered about 1 inch from the sides of the cushion. Knot the end of the twine to prevent its being pulled through and with a circular needle, make a 1 inch stitch in the leathercloth. The needle point is inserted in the flat of the leathercloth and pushed in, to reappear about 1 inch to the left, in line with the first insertion.

Pull the twine through and make the next stitch exactly opposite in the folded edge of the canvas; repeat the stitch, first in the leathercloth and then in the canvas and draw the twine tight. This stitch draws the two edges together so that the twine does not show. For finer work, use a $1\frac{1}{2}$ inch circular needle, making $\frac{1}{4}$ inch stitches.

The running stitch, previously described, is used for sewing a border to the body of a cover, when a sewing machine is not available. Use a crewel needle and No. 18 thread. Make $\frac{1}{4}$ inch stitches close to the cord of the piping and pull each stitch tight. For a stronger job, repeat the stitch in the opposite direction, so that two threads go through each hole. This stitch is also used for basting piping, using 1 inch stitches in the centre of the piping tape. Always use twine long enough for the job.

When fixing cushion covers to a spring case, it is not essential to stitch them to the top frame of the spring case. They can be pulled over and stitched to the bottom frame, but stitching to the top frame is more satisfactory because it does not compress the spring case.

Machine stitching:

A power-driven machine is not necessary, but it is quicker than treadle or hand operation. Some jobs can be done on a housewife's machine using a leather needle, but trouble may be experienced with the heavier threads because the shuttle is designed to take a small quantity of the finer threads. Some heavy work can be done on a domestic machine with two helpers; one to turn the handle and another to draw the work through.

The types of machine used in motor body trimming range from the heavy Singer 132K, 45K and 31K to lighter machines such as the 96K. Some have an oil bath for the thread, but if this is not fitted, the thread can be soaked in oil by immersing the whole reel. Lubrication is particularly helpful when machining leathercloth and other plastics.

Whilst machining, watch the needle and use the edge of the foot as a guide to keep straight. Edges up to $\frac{1}{2}$ inch wide can be gauged by eye (see **FIG 6:10**). The distance from the needle to the centre of the foot is about $\frac{1}{8}$ inch, from the needle to the outside of the foot is $\frac{1}{4}$ inch. Keep an eye on the width of material outside the foot, making it equal to the distance from the stitches to the outside of the foot and this will give $\frac{1}{2}$ inch edge. See that the tension is correct (see **FIG 6:11**) and not making more than 10 stitches to the inch, or the material may split.

Fluted leathercloth is machined to the calico line as follows: Lay the creased line of the leathercloth on top of the calico and enter the needle through the folded underside, passing through two thicknesses, $\frac{1}{8}$ inch from

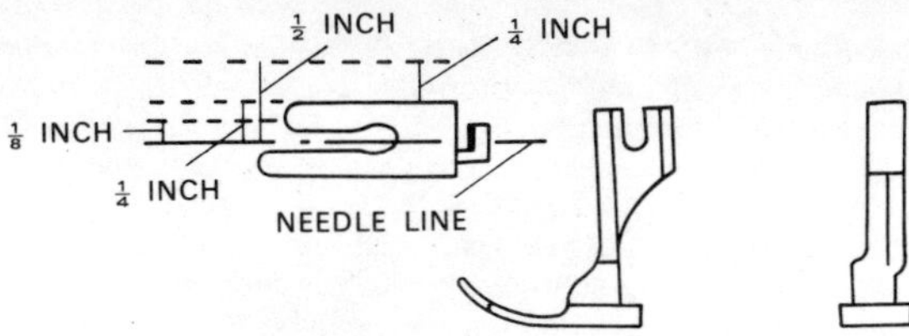

FIG 6:10   Flat foot for sewing machine

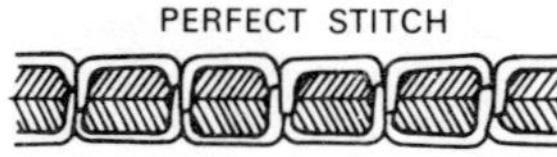

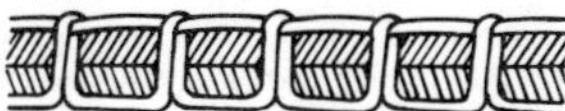

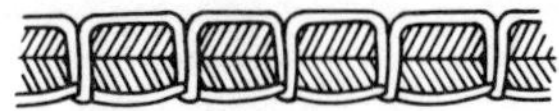

FIG 6:11   Effect of incorrect thread tensions on the stitches made by a sewing machine

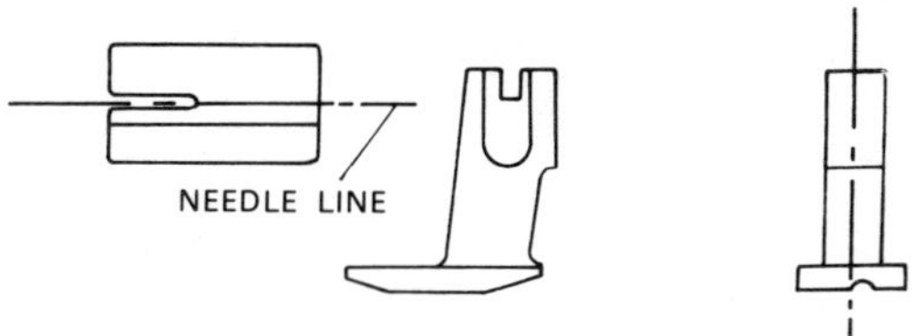

FIG 6:12   Piping foot for sewing machine

the fold. The object of this is to ensure that the stitches do not show on the finished job. Make sure that machining starts on the correct line on the calico and be careful to keep straight, otherwise the whole cushion will not be symmetrical.

A piping foot (see **FIG 6:12**) is necessary for all piping and any work which includes piping, such as borders. When making piping, run the machining a little way back from the cord, so as to allow the next line of sewing to come right up against the cord. Then the first line of stitching will not be visible on the completed work.

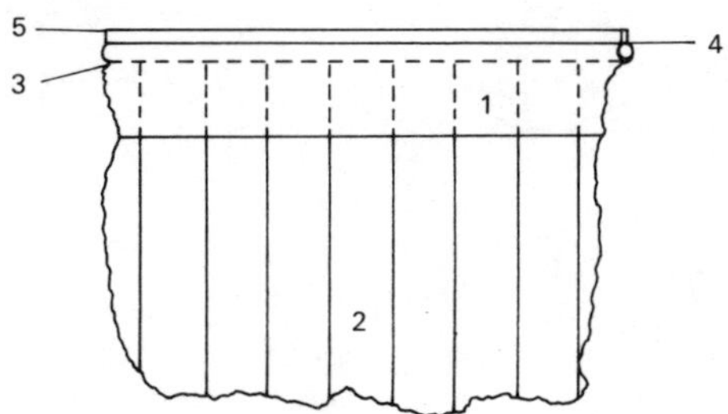

FIG 6:13   Machined border

Key to Fig 6:13   1 Border underside   2 Fluted body
3 Piping   4 Machined line   5 Edges

In bordering a cushion, the body of the job is laid face uppermost. The piping (which can be machined on to the body) is laid at the edge and the border laid on top, face downwards, so that all the edges are together pointing outwards from the body of the job (see **FIG 6:13**).

The needle enters the fabric close to the cord, but not close enough to damage the piping. Make sure that all salient points meet correctly. It is best to work outwards from the centre, as borders are liable to creep. Check this while sewing is in progress. When finished, turn the job the right way round and beat the border with a hammer along the outside piping line.

Joins on borders are machined with the face surface inwards ($\frac{1}{2}$ inch back), then turned and machined $\frac{3}{16}$ inch back from the joined edge. The sewing line will pierce three thicknesses. This is called face machining (see **FIG 6:14**).

FIG 6:14   Face machining

Corners should be silk machined. This is stronger and is necessary on a face mitre join. Silk machining is done by joining the two edges face inwards, machining $\frac{1}{2}$ inch back, turning the material and pressing or beating both of the $\frac{1}{2}$ inch edges back and outwards. Another piece of material is then laid face uppermost under this turned join to reinforce it. Both edges of the join are face-machined $\frac{1}{8}$ inch back. This stitch gives a neat appearance with two lines of machining showing on the face (see **FIG 6:15**).

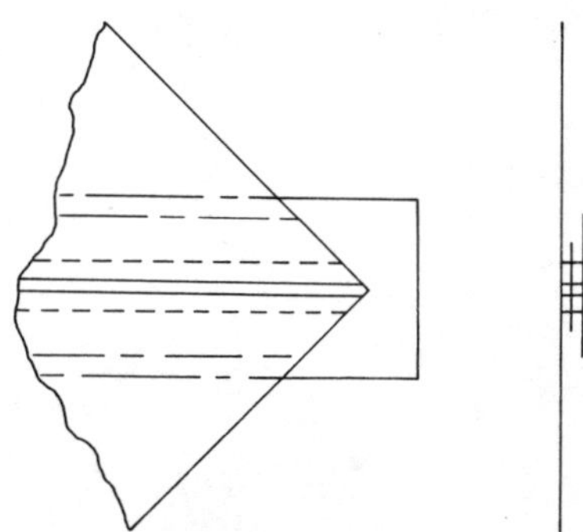

FIG 6:15   Silk machining

Straining:

Straining is an important part of the trimmer's art. A good deal of fullness can be dispersed by straining, which saves making pleats and cuts. **FIG 6:16** shows how to strain large and small areas. Strain first at the centre and 45 deg. on each side, followed by a temporary tack in between those tacks already in position.

On a large bend or dome it may be necessary to strain many times before the fullness is dispersed. **FIG 6:17**

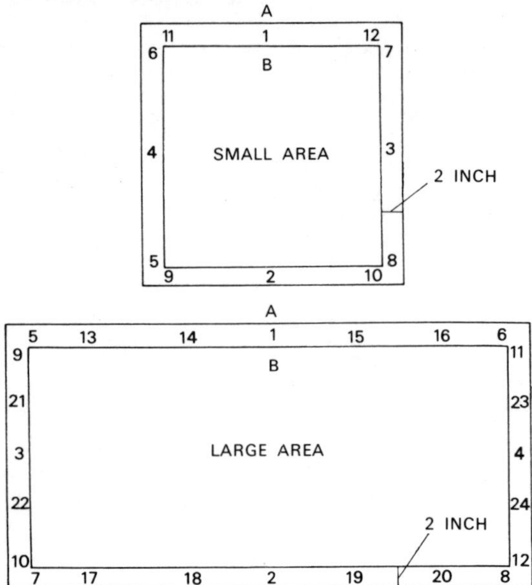

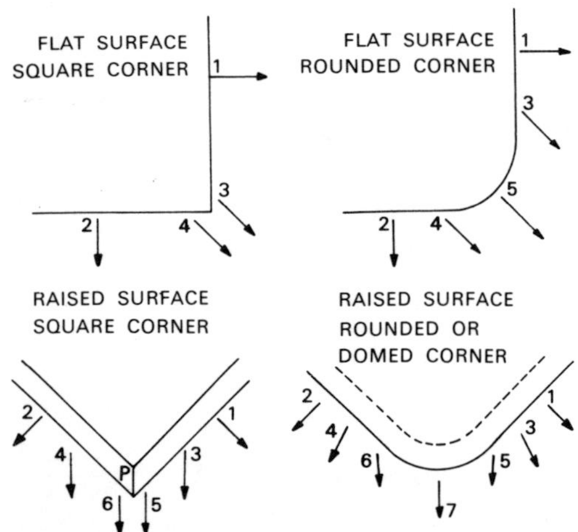

FIG 6:16   Straining

Key to Fig 6:16   (A) Edge of material;   (B) Cutting line. Figures 1 to 24 show order of temporary tacking. 1 to 4 are slightly strained, 5 to 12 strained tight diagonally outwards, and 13 to 24 provide final tight strain

FIG 6:17   Dissolving fulness at corners by straining. Numbers 1 to 7 indicate order of placing temporary tacks. ➔ shows direction of strain, and P indicates temporary pleat

shows the straining sequence for dissolving fullness at corners.

When straining on a hard surface, such as a metal or wooden roof with only wadding between the fabric and the panel, there is plenty of scope, but if straining is done on a sprung and padded surface, such as a seat cushion, it must not be carried so far as to depress the springs. In this case the surplus must be disposed of by pleats.

Straining can be done with the hands or with special pliers known as strainers. These have a ribbed jaw to grip the fabric, but they need some firm surface, such as a piece of board, to serve as a fulcrum. Hand straining is done by using all the weight of the body, taking advantage of any available leverage and the work is easier if there is a second person standing by to knock in the temporary tacks while the material is under strain.

Leathercloth strains more easily when it is warm. Hessian and other undercoverings can be strained with an awl, which is pierced through the material and anchored in the base at an angle. It is then used as a lever, pulling the material with it as it rises to the vertical position.

Pleats and cuts:

The object of a pleat is to take in any unwanted fullness at corners and curves and so present a neat appearance. Pleats fold either outwards or downwards according to their location. On an outside curve the pleats would fold outward from the starting point and on a side they would fold downward with each pleat lying the same way. Where several pleats are required, they should be evenly spaced and match up on both sides.

The commonest type of pleat is that used over a curve. The fullness is laid to one side, then folded back so that it lies neatly on top, forming a straight pleat, square to its base line. This pleat is made when even a small fullness has to be taken in. It may be a single pleat, or one of several going round a curve (see **FIG 6:18**).

Another common pleat is that used at right angle corners (see **FIG 6:19**). To make this pleat, the spare

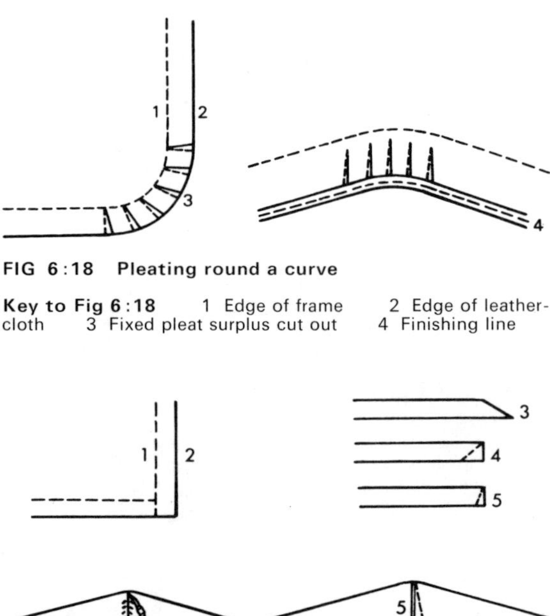

FIG 6:18   Pleating round a curve

Key to Fig 6:18   1 Edge of frame   2 Edge of leathercloth   3 Fixed pleat surplus cut out   4 Finishing line

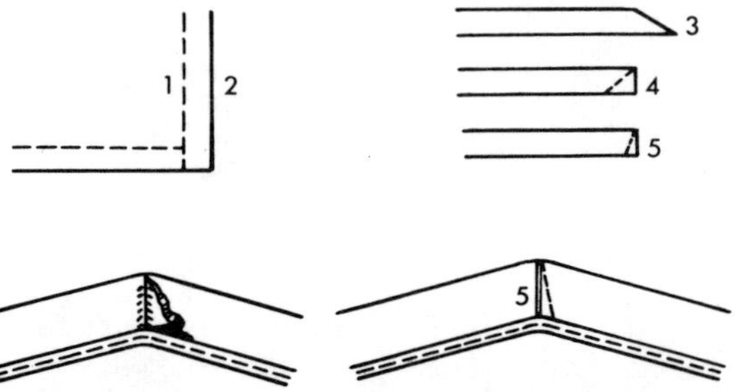

FIG 6:19   Pleating a right-angled corner

Key to Fig 6:19   1 Edge of frame   2 Edge of leathercloth
3 Folded diagonally   4 Fixed pleat surplus cut out
5 Finishing line

material is turned to one side and secured with one tack or gimp pin. The surplus fullness is generally cut out to avoid bulkiness. This must be done carefully, because if too much material is cut out, the pleat may show a raw edge. The cut should therefore be made well back from the fold. When pleating cloth into small pleats, it is best not to cut out any material, as it might fray.

A pleat once used in leatherwork, but uncommon now, runs around a semi-circle, such as the end of a centre armrest. The whole semi-circle is divided into small fullnesses by means of temporary tacks. Each pleat is made by raising the material with a regulator and lifting the fullness. (A regulator is a small pointed tool like a bradawl.) These pleats remain standing at even distances all round the semi-circle. The finishing line is usually in a groove, studded or braided.

Pleats are used to take in fullness on visible parts; cuts are used to facilitate the folding of material where it will be hidden, for example when covering a door casing. When turning over material on an outside curve, straight cuts are made about $\frac{1}{4}$ inch beyond the edge of the plywood. When folded over and stuck down these open into V-shapes. For an outside curve, V-shapes are cut out and when these are turned on to the back and stuck down they close up to give an even surface (see **FIGS 6:20** and **6:21**).

Modern trim:

By contrast, there is little or no craftsmanship in the upholstery and trim of modern production cars. Gone are the diamond, half-diamond, organ-pipe and square button pleated styles, together with silks, lace, tacks and mag hammers. The cushion of today is likely to consist of a polyester foam moulding sitting directly on corrugated springs and covered with PVC clipped to the seat frame. The vestigial flute lines are hot-press marks on the surface. It will still be a sewn cover, with piping in the seams, and, ironically, it will probably outlast the steel body. All it needs is an occasional clean to take the grime out of the depressions of the imitation leather grain.

6:2 Types of material

Trimming materials:

Cowhide is still the best material for car seats, except in tropical countries where it becomes too hot to sit on if a car is left in the sun. Leather is expensive because the preparation is very complicated and there is always some wastage caused by the irregular shape of the hide. More-over, it is difficult to find an unblemished hide; those of hill-bred cattle have the least barbed-wire scratches on them. The original purpose of fluting was to enable a defective part of a hide to be cut out and replaced with a strip taken from the edge. Hide is difficult to cut and sew, quite apart from being expensive, and is best avoided by an inexperienced trimmer.

The first leathercloths were fabrics treated with linseed oil. These were followed by fabrics coated with nitro-cellulose, of which Rexine is the best known make. The coating tended to crack with age, but it is still useful for applications not requiring flexibility. Modern leather-cloths are fabrics coated with polyvinyl chloride, poly-thene or nylon. Unsupported PVC sheet is available for

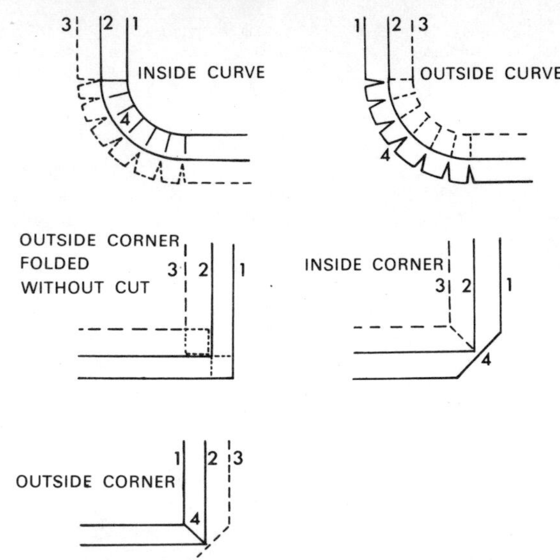

FIG 6:20 Cuts for inside and outside curves and corners

Key to Fig 6:20 1 Edge of leathercloth 2 Edge of casing
3 Edge of leathercloth when folded 4 Cuts

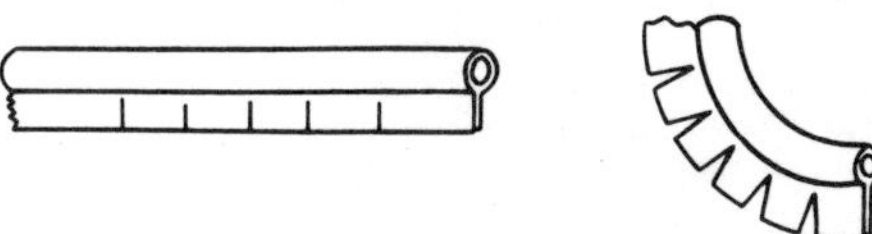

FIG 6:21 Nicks in door piping around curve

deep compound curvature, but its tensile strength is low compared with the fabric-backed variety. For instance, a .015 inch coat with a .005 inch backing is 200 per cent stronger than a .020 inch unsupported sheet. The leather-grain pattern is rolled or stamped into the PVC surface while it is in a plastic state and a two-colour effect can be obtained by running a finishing solution into the hollows of the grain. Various finishes can be achieved in the final varnishing of the material – bright, semi-dull or dull. Early types suffered from migration of the plasticiser in the PVC, which made the surface sticky, but this has been overcome by the use of a sealing lacquer.

In recent years a number of hard-wearing and easily cleaned cloths have been developed from man-made fibres, which are more suitable for car seats than any traditional fabric. Some of these are nearly as expensive as leather.

Repp, moquette (cut and uncut) West of England Cloth, whipcord, tapestry and many other fabrics have been used for car upholstery. A combination of leather wearing surfaces and moquette panels has long been popular for public transport seating, where heavy wear makes it the cheapest material in the long run.

A woollen fabric known as coach cloth was used for the roof lining of older cars, but this has been replaced in modern mass-produced cars by lightweight plastic sheet with a backing of polyester foam for heat and sound insulation. A suitable adhesive for this material is marketed under the trade name 'Clan'. Unsuitable adhesives can cause corrosion troubles due to chemical reactions, so the leathercloth manufacturers' recommended adhesive should always be used.

Undercovering materials:

Hessian is the conventional material for covering spring cases. This is a coarse jute canvas, obtainable in various widths and grades. Black canvas, used on the underside of cushions, is also available in various widths. Calico is used as a base for flutes or as an undercovering for plain work. It is also used to secure rubber latex to a base by means of solution. Grey and black felt, used respectively at the bottom of cushions and as a sewing base, can be obtained in several widths.

Stuffing:

Various materials used for filling and padding pieces of work come under the category of stuffing. The usual form of stuffing consists of hair or fibre, with perhaps a layer of wadding on top. Wadding is not essential under a leather or leathercloth cover, but must be included when the cover is of cloth, otherwise the bristles of the hair or fibre will work through the cover. If the top cover has been fluted, wadding or latex foam will have been placed in the flutes, and need not be duplicated on top of the fibre.

Wadding is obtained in various widths, usually 18 inches, and sold in 12 yard rolls. It can also be obtained in strips, ready for fluting. Cotton linters is a soft mixture, like thick wadding and made in various lengths and widths. It is usually rolled, with tissue paper between the layers. It provides a soft finish.

Rubberised hair is a mixture of hair and rubber made in sheets 3 ft by 6 ft and 2 inches thick. A similar material is made using coir or coconut fibre instead of hair. This is ideal for stuffing cushions, either on its own or in conjunction with a spring case. Wadding or cotton linters must be laid over it, to prevent its rough surface being felt through the cover. Hair or fibre is sold loose in bags, or in the form of a mat. The mat has a hessian base on to which the hair or fibre has been woven.

If loose stuffing is put on the top of a spring case, the case is first covered with hessian, which is brought down the sides and sewn to the bottom frame, or tacked to a wooden base. Two or three strings of twine are placed down the length of the job on the upper side and tied at each end to the spring case. The twine is also attached to the spring case at the centre to prevent ballooning. The fibre or hair is picked up and teased out with the hands to break up any lumps. A large handful is placed under the twine and teased out further from the top. This is repeated until the whole surface of the spring case has been evenly covered and the twine is invisible.

If the mat type of stuffing is used, the mat is cut 2 inches larger than the spring case so that it will fold over the side frame. It is then fixed to the case with twine, using a running stitch or quilting stitch.

After a finished cover has been fixed in position, the borders are filled with stuffing if necessary. Sometimes only the front border is stuffed. Loose hair, fibre or cotton linters are used for filling borders. The material is placed by hand, but a stuffing iron may be needed to reach awkward places. A finished cover may be fixed to the top frame of a spring case before turning the borders over to be fixed at the bottom. Alternatively, the cover is pulled right over and temporarily fixed at the bottom before the borders are stuffed. The cushion is then inverted and grey felt placed on the bottom to give a cushioning effect between the spring case and the car base. The felt is covered with black canvas sewn to the cover with a frenching stitch.

Years ago, moss, seaweed, whalebone shavings and other industrial wastes were used in cheap furniture, but not generally in cars. The best stuffing was long white horsehair, which is unobtainable now. Any horsehair is valuable and can be sold to furniture restorers if it is to be replaced by modern motor trimming materials.

Adhesives:

The modern adhesives which have replaced rye paste in trimming, can be classified as solutions and cements. Solution is used extensively, because it is quick in action and does not soil the leathercloth should it get on to the face side by accident. The bond is not very strong but adequate for requirements. Dunlop S.758 is recommended, because this compound is soluble in T559 solvent so mistakes can be corrected.

Solution should be applied to both surfaces, using a brush for wood and a scraper for fabric. It should be spread quickly and not worked over. Leave to dry for five minutes. When both surfaces are dry, bring them together and if the fabric is in the correct position, sweep the hand over it to make it adhere. If the position is incorrect and the fabric has to be lifted, it will take the base film with it and both surfaces will need fresh solution. Try to avoid this, because the remains of the old solution will show as lumps under the material.

Cement, such as Bostik 321, is more viscous than solution and gives a stronger bond. It can be used to stick fabric to metal. It is not so easy to clean off hands or material, but paraffin is the solvent to use. Cement is applied to both surfaces, using a brush and scraper and left for about 10 minutes to become tacky. It is then pressed or rubbed down. It may require weighting down for 24 hours while drying on bends and folds. If wrongly placed, cemented material can be lifted and corrected without trouble, but it is not easily removed when the cement is hard.

6:3 Retrimming a car

The internal trim of modern mass-produced cars has been simplified by the use of moulded stuffing and adhesives to enable semi-skilled labour to be used on the production line. But it is the older car which probably needs re-trimming, so we shall go through the process of stripping out and renewing the conventional leathercloth fluted trim of a popular car of the late 1950s or early 1960s, and deal with more modern developments later.

It would be impossible to describe all the numerous designs of trimming in this book, so unless he is experienced the reader should use the old covers as patterns for the re-trim. Thoroughly examine each piece as it comes out. By doing this a lot will be learnt which will help in the new work. The work divides into two categories; bench trimming, which is the covering of seats and squabs, and trimming the bodyshell. In bench trimming it is best to strip and trim each piece completely to avoid confusion. Keep a notebook handy for jotting down dimensions and making sketches. Put all screws into one tin and all the fittings into another. Remember that a lost fitting may be irreplaceable.

The quantities of materials required will vary with the size of the car, but 10 to 12 yards of leathercloth, 50 inches wide, is needed for the seat covers and $2\frac{1}{2}$ to 3 yards of coach cloth, also 50 inches wide, for the head linings and fillets. Head linings are sometimes trimmed in leathercloth, but it is easier to get good results with coach cloth. A lighter weight of cloth could be used for linings and cloths such as moquette or repp could be used in place of leathercloth for the covers.

Other materials needed are 3 to 4 yards of 50 inch calico for backing the flutes, hessian (for covering spring cases) and wadding. It may be possible to use the wadding which is already in the flutes and if the original hessian is in good condition there will be no need to replace it. Such items as piping cord, rubber tubing, hair of fibre may be used again if in good condition. Sundries required consist of 1 dozen 4 inch skewers, 1 circular needle (4 inch), 1 lb each of $\frac{3}{8}$ inch and $\frac{1}{2}$ inch tacks, $\frac{1}{4}$ lb of $\frac{1}{4}$ inch tacks, $\frac{1}{2}$ lb of $\frac{1}{2}$ inch gimp pins, $\frac{1}{2}$ lb of $\frac{3}{4}$ inch panel pins, a pint tin of adhesive solution, a small ball of thin, strong twine, the usual hand tools and the use of a sewing machine, preferably a Singer 31 or 45K industrial model, but much can be done with a domestic machine fitted with a leather needle and operated slowly.

Dismantling:

The first thing to do is to take out the front bucket seats or bench seat. If these are on runners, press the lever and slide the seat off. Some seats have a stop on the runner; this must of course be removed before the seat will come out. The rear cushion is lifted out next. This usually has no fixed hold and comes away easily. The rear squab, which comes next, may be fixed or not. Some lift straight out; others fit into holes or slots and need to be pulled forward and then lifted. Fixed squabs are either bolted or screwed. Locate these screws or bolts and remove them, not forgetting that the heads may be in the boot. Remove the carpets and all fittings such as sun visor and interior lights.

Next take off the leathercloth from the wheelarches. This may be stuck on, or may be in the form of casings (boards covered with leathercloth). Then strip off the heelboard, which is the vertical panel under the rear seat. Take off the centre pillar finishers, dash casings and all other small casings and fillets. These may be found in the recess of the roof above the rear seat, round the sliding roof aperture, rear window and squab shelf. They may be fastened with screws, clips or panel pins.

To remove the door casings, first take off the handle lever and the window winder. This is easy if the screws are visible, but some types may be puzzling. In these the handle is usually held by a peg and spring. Insert the blade of a screwdriver just behind the lever and turn the screwdriver 90 deg. This depresses a spring, making the spindle just visible. Now one can see the peg, which is tapered. Tap it out, being sure to tap the small end. As this is a tricky operation, one person should hold the

screwdriver while another taps out the peg. Be careful not to lose this peg, because a replacement will not be easy to obtain. In another type, there is a circlip which engages through two slots with a 'flat' on the spindle. It is dismantled by means of a screwdriver as described above and eased out of its position. Take care that it does not fly off and get lost.

Some cars have covered fillets round the upper part of the doors. These should next be removed. They may be fixed with screws, nails or clips. Try a little gentle levering here and there with a screwdriver to discover the method of fastening. There may also be a metal pressing or polished wood fillet to be removed. Some screws have a Phillips recessed head, which needs a special screwdriver. There is more than one size of recess, so more than one Phillips screwdriver may be required.

The door casing may be secured in any of the ways mentioned in the previous paragraph and should be removed when the method of fixing has been detected. Many of them are tucked under a flange along the top and fixed with screws or clips at the bottom. The method of fixing is usually mentioned in the Workshop Manual for the model in question, because mechanics have to remove these panels to adjust door gear.

The inner part of the door is now revealed and this is as far as one need go, unless the glass channels or winders need repair, or the bottom of the door is badly corroded.

Take off all the door and quarter casings in the same way. All the fillets should be tied together in sets labelled 'N/S Front Door' and so on, to avoid getting them mixed up, as they may not fit nicely on any other door.

Take care not to damage the old material more than is unavoidable, as it will be needed for reference when retrimming. If nails should slip through a fillet or casing when it is being taken out, extract them afterwards. Never use force in removing fillets and casings. They will come out, so discover what is holding them.

Removing sliding roof:

Removing the sliding roof is another journey of exploration, as there are many variations of design. The commonest type is taken off as follows. Turn the handle and slide the roof back until it is one-third open. Take out the screw stud in the centre of the handle, thus releasing handle, spring etc. If there is a covered bar on the front, this should be unscrewed and removed. There may be two screw studs on each side at the front end. When these have been removed, the bar holding the roof to the slides should be free. Lift the front end of the sliding roof and slide it forward off the car. Some cars have a sliding roof which slides back on the outside of the roof. In this case, there is usually a rubber buffer; this should be removed and the roof slipped backwards off the car.

The car is now stripped of all trimming except the cloth interior roof and back-end, while on the exterior roof a fabric half-roof remains in the case of sliding-head models. Fixed-head models may have a fabric whole roof or a sheet metal roof.

Although we have assumed that the whole of the old trim is to be stripped out, it should be noted that leathercloth may be re-surfaced by brushing or spraying one or two coats of Leathercoat, or similar paint containing leather dust. These paints contain a surplus of plasticiser, which is absorbed by the original coating of the leather-cloth. The two layers are thus combined.

Stripping headlinings and roofs:

Stripping is done with a medium-sized screwdriver or a long half-inch cold chisel, using a mallet, not a hammer. Place the end of the chisel at the side of the head of each tack and strike it at an angle; this will lift out the tack. When stripping tacked material, it is best to place the chisel under the material to knock out the tack. Looking at the headlining, one can see the rows of tacks to be removed from the back, front and sides, unless the finishing line is still covered by double-cord piping or beading. In the latter case, these strips will have to be taken off before knocking out the tacks. Starting at the nearside door, remove all the tacks round the roof.

The lining is now hanging down on all sides, but is still held to the roof by strips of cloth across the middle. These strips are called lists. Starting from the front, knock out the tacks along the first list rail, leaving the lists still sewed to the lining and work back from rail to rail until the lining is free. In some models, metal bars, fitted across the roof, take the place of wooden list rails; these are pushed through the lists and screwed to the body at each end. Release the screws and roll up the bars with the cloth, to be removed at a later stage. Other models have bars which clip to the roof; these should be released from the clips. The wooden roof battens of older cars are used as list rails.

Next remove the back cloth, or back curtain as it is called. The tacks should be lifted out in the following order; round the back window, round the side windows along the bottom finishing line and along the top finishing line. Having freed the lining, fold it up and store for future reference.

It may be necessary to reverse the process and take the back curtain out first and then the headlining, if the original trimming was done in that fashion. Some roofs have a recess at the back over the rear seat. These should be dealt with in the same way, but the cloth may be in two pieces. Others have cloth solutioned to the metal roof. This cloth can be stripped off by pulling at a loosened corner.

In the case of a sliding roof, first remove the tacks round the edge of the opening. Strip off all remaining trimming such as draught piping round the doors.

Exterior roof covering:

Some sliding roof models have a fabric top on the back half of the exterior roof. Using the same methods as for stripping the interior, strip this fabric top, after removing any bead or metal strips from the sides and any remaining rubber strips. Lift off the fabric and store with the rest of the old materials. Other models have slide runner channels covering the tacks at each side. In such cases, remove these channels, knock out tacks at front and sides, lift the fabric back and unscrew the metal plate which holds down the back end. The wadding is now revealed. If it is in good condition, it should not be disturbed. If it is not fit to use again, lift it out; it may be held by a few tacks. The hessian underneath should now be taken off, knocking out the tacks which are holding it, and any other left in the wood.

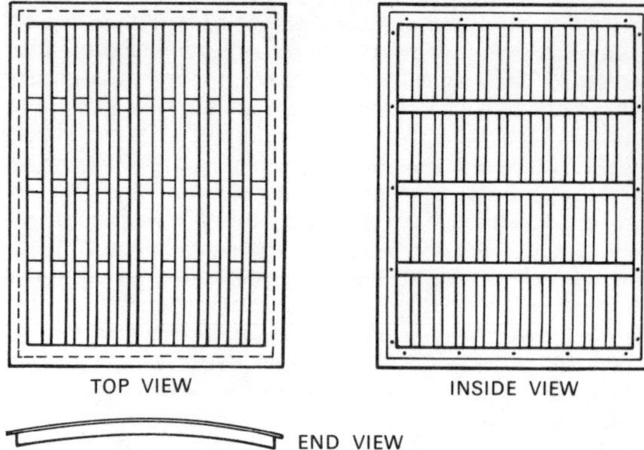

FIG 6:22   Wooden frame of fixed roof

Some old fixed-head cars have a fabric roof on a wooden frame which can be detached for stripping and recovering on the bench. This frame rests on a body flange and is secured by screws from the inside of the car. Undo these screws and give the roof a sharp tap at each corner to break the seal, so that the frame can be lifted right off. Other fixed head models have a fabric roof with beading showing right round the edge. To strip this type, unfasten the beading and treat the fabric as described for the half-roof sliding head type. The car is now completely stripped of trimming and now is the time to look round carefully for corrosion and other damage. Check the sliding head runners for corrosion and ascertain whether the drain tubes are in good condition.

The next stage is to replace the exterior roof covering.

Back half of sliding roof:

Black leathercloth of heavy gauge is generally used for exterior roofs. Using the old cover as a pattern, cut this fabric with about 2 inches to spare all round. Then cut some hessian to the same size and tack it to the roof, straining it tight. Tack this about $\frac{3}{4}$ inch inside the finishing line. Turn the surplus over and fold it inwards, putting a few tacks to hold it down. This prevents the hessian from fraying and is standard practice. Next place the wadding on top of the hessian and then tack the fabric on to the roof, equalising each side.

To do this, lay the fabric on the roof, equalising each side. Place a tack at one corner about 2 inches in, using the temporary tacking method. Temporary tacks are those knocked only half way in, so that they can easily be removed in case of error. Lightly stretch the fabric to the second corner and tack; repeat until there is a temporary tack at each of the four corners. Then strain the fabric gently to each side, putting a temporary tack in the middle of the side. The roof is now stretched out without creases and is held by eight of these tacks, which should be on the finishing line. Working out from the middle of each side, tack off at 1 inch intervals. Do not strain the first side too much, because the other side is still held by temporary tacks. After finally tacking to one side, repeat the operation on the opposite side. This time the fabric may be strained very tight. Always work from the middle of a side, allowing the fullness to

64

dissolve itself at the corners. When finished it should be as tight as a drum. The straining is done by hand without the aid of strainers. Cut off the surplus material with a sharp knife so that the edge of the fabric is flush with the finishing line. The metal or rubber strips which were taken off the roof should now be replaced over the rows of tacks. Gimp pins can be used instead of tacks for the final finish. In the case of a roof which has been back-tacked at the back end, follow the same method up to the point of tacking the hessian; then tack the back end with the face of the fabric downward and the rest of it hanging over the rear. Place the tacks about $\frac{1}{2}$ inch in all along the back end. Replace the metal strip, fold the fabric, stretch to the front and sides and continue as previously described. Replace the slide runner channels.

Fixed exterior roof:

Proceed as in the case of back half of sliding roof, but as the sides are longer the temporary tacking should be at 6 inch intervals. This type of roof requires more straining. When finally tacking, the temporary tacks may be knocked right in, provided they come in line with the finished row of tacks. A little Dum Dum black putty or similar water seal should be smeared around the edge and the beading replaced. Clean off any surplus sealant which may have oozed out.

Fixed frame roof:

Following the instructions given for stripping the frame type of roof, place the frame face down on the bench and knock out the tacks around the sides; then lift the frame off the bench and take off the fabric. Turn the frame over and strip off the wadding and hessian if it needs renewing. Clean the metal flange and repaint the whole frame if necessary. When dry, tack on hessian, lay on the wadding and place the fabric over it. Then, holding frame and fabric, turn them over so that the inside is uppermost. Wrap the fabric over the flange and temporarily tack the middle of each side; strain to each corner, working outwards. Whilst tacking each side, a better hold for straining will be found if the frame is placed on end. Tack off at 1 inch intervals into the wooden batten close to the metal flange; fold in the corners and tack. Be careful that the edge of the flange does not cut through the fabric while working. Cut out any surplus material at the corners and trim level with the wooden batten on all sides. Smear sealant on the edge of the roof and fix it into position on the car. Screw from inside the car and tighten, starting at each corner and working round until the roof is properly pulled down. Clean off any surplus sealant.

Sliding roof:

In retrimming this roof, cover the exterior first, using the same general methods described above. Tack to the previous tacking lines, using the temporary tacking method until satisfied with the exterior. The fabric should be tight and clean. Use gimp pins for the final finish and cut off any surplus fabric. Then attend to the interior cloth side.

Solution can be used instead of tacks. This is painted on to the wood by means of a 1 inch brush; a scraper of wood or metal 2 inches by 3 inches is used to apply solution to cloth. Allow it two minutes to dry, then stick along one side, strain to the other side and stick. Be sure that the fabric is cut clear of the slides. Each end may now be tacked. In some cases these ends are folded in and gimp-pinned, following the previous trim. All important parts should be held by gimp pins. Locate any holes which have been covered with cloth and are required for the screws; mark them with an awl. If there is a wooden bar, this should be covered with cloth. Some sliding roofs have a metal finish and so need new interior cloth only. In this case the cloth is first back-tacked at the front edge. The roof is now finished and should be stored until the body has been trimmed.

Cutting new material:

This section describes the cutting out of all the parts. In practice, it is wise to cut out one item (for example, the rear cushion), machine and trim it, before going on to the next. Compare each finished article with the corresponding piece of the old material, to make sure it is a replica.

When cutting out, use sharp scissors (10 inch is a suitable size), and allow an extra 2 inches all round for working, except where a side of leathercloth has to be machined, in which case cut it the same size as the old cover. Take great care in cutting, because the material is easily spoiled. Where pieces are in pairs, remember that the pattern must be reversed for the second piece. Make sure that the material and the pattern are both laid down the same way (that is, both face downward). It is a common error to lay the pattern upside down. Keep referring back to the old covers.

Planning and marking out:

It is worth making a one-fifth scale plan on a piece of paper 10 inches wide to see how all the pieces of

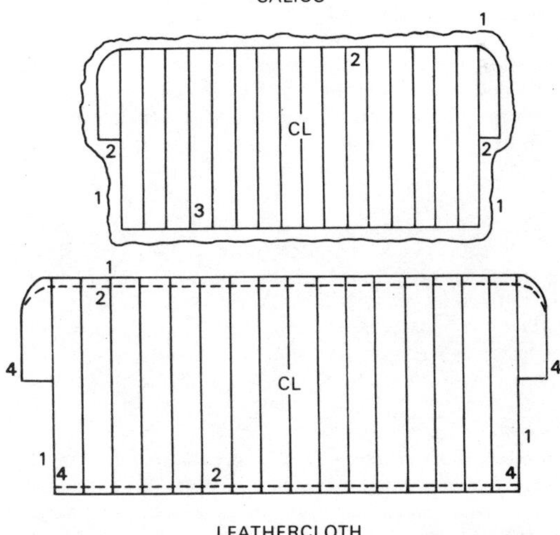

FIG 6:23   Marking-out calico and leathercloth for rear squab

Key to Fig 6:23   1 Cutting line   2 Finishing line
3 Flute line   4 Machine line   CL Centre line

leathercloth or other material can best be cut out of a
50 inch wide roll. This will show exactly how much
material is required for the job and will avoid waste.
Generally it is best to attend to the outside of the roof
first, then the headlining, rear cushion and squab,
leaving the front seats until last.

Each piece needs marking with: **1** finishing lines;
2 fluting lines – where required and **3** cutting lines.
Fluting lines may be marked out with a piece of wood of
correct width, for example 3 inches wide for fluting
lines on the calico and $3\frac{1}{2}$ inches wide for the fluting
lines on the leathercloth. Alternatively, points may be
marked on the finishing lines with an awl or pencil dot
and joined up with chalk, crayon or indelible pencil lines.
The fluting lines of leather or leathercloth are creased.
The cutting lines are marked $\frac{3}{8}$ inch outside the finishing
lines where the line is to be machined, but 2 inches
outside where the line has to be tacked or hand sewn.
Lay the material flat and smooth before marking out.
Letter the centre points, back, front etc. to avoid confusion. The fullness allowance for wide flutes may be
extended to $\frac{3}{4}$ inch. The allowance will never be greater
than this, or less than $\frac{3}{8}$ inch.

Cutting cloth:

This is a fairly simple operation. Lay the pattern on top of
the material and mark round the edges with tailors' chalk.
Do not cut out any holes which may be on the pattern
(such as the rear window) as this is done at a later stage.
See that the cloth is correctly laid, with the nap brushing
to the front in the case of the headlining and downwards
in the case of the back curtain. Two inches of cloth must
be allowed for each list, when the method of listing
described in this book is used. For example, if the old
headlining is 60 inches long with four lists, the new
lining will be cut 68 inches long. The pieces of cloth at
the sides of a sliding roof headlining are cut separately
and sewn on to form two 'legs' running to the front.
Recessed linings are cut to pattern, allowing extra for
working.

Cut the calico in the same way, allowing 2 inches
extra all round. There will be six pieces in all; rear squab,
rear cushion, two bucket squabs and two bucket cushions.
The bucket pieces may be in pairs. Mark the calico for the
finishing lines and fluting lines (the former usually
follows the contour of the piece). Flutes vary in width, so
the best plan is to measure the flutes on the old material
and copy them. Taking 3 inches as the average width of
flute, mark the calico in 3 inch parallel lines, square to the
base line, running from top to bottom or front to rear.
Count the flutes from the centre (which may be in the
middle of a flute or at the edge of one). The end flutes
may be from 2 inches to 4 inches wide.

Cutting leathercloth:

Fullness has to be allowed on the fluted part so that the
wadding can be inserted. Half an inch fullness is generally
allowed, so if the calico has been marked in 3 inch flutes
the leathercloth will be marked in $3\frac{1}{2}$ inches. Always
count the flutes on calico and leathercloth so that they
line up correctly, working from the centre. For example,
16 flutes at 3 inches on calico = 48 inches, 16 flutes at
$3\frac{1}{2}$ inches on leathercloth = 56 inches. If you were to undo

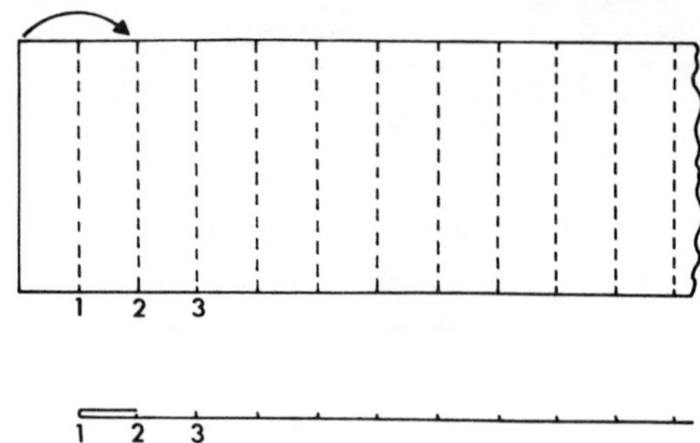

FIG 6:24   Creasing leathercloth

Key to Fig 6:24   1 First crease line   2 Second crease
3 Third crease, and so on

the machining of an old cover and stretch the flutes out,
it would illustrate this point. The end flutes are also cut
with $\frac{1}{2}$ inch extra for fullness. It is a good idea to mark the
fluting lines and the finishing lines on the leathercloth
before it is cut off the roll. These fluted pieces should now
be creased ready for machining. Starting at one end, fold
the material to the first flute line, so that the line is still
visible and crease. Creasing may be done with a sleeker,
the handle of scissors, or by beating with a hammer.
Rub the fold with pressure so that the crease shows on
the face side; fold to the next line and repeat until the
piece is finished (see **FIG 6:24**). The object of this is
straighter and easier machining. It is not necessary to
crease when cloth is used, as this lies easily and can be
machined to the folded line.

Cutting borders:

Cut borders to pattern, marking 'top', 'centre' and so on,
to save errors in machining. It is wisest to make a brown
paper pattern from the old border, because sizes and
shapes vary considerably. Or the old cover could be
unpicked and the border itself used as a pattern. If a
brown paper pattern is used, label it correctly and again
double-check that it is laid the right way on the leathercloth. Study the old covers to see where each piece goes
and how it is machined.

Cutting piping:

Piping may be cut from scrap or across the roll of leathercloth. It is 1 inch to $1\frac{1}{4}$ inches wide and is usually machined
in long lengths to be cut as required. The pieces are
joined by overlapping $\frac{1}{2}$ inch. Draught piping for the
doors is cut in 3 inch to 4 inch widths.

Cutting casing covers:

Cut casings to pattern so that they pair up correctly; also
wheelarches, centre pillars, bucket seat backs, heelboard
and all other pieces. Door pockets should be measured
for flutes. The plywood or hardboard casing could be
used as a pattern, allowing extra for turning over at the
sides, but do not cut any apertures such as pocket holes
at this stage.

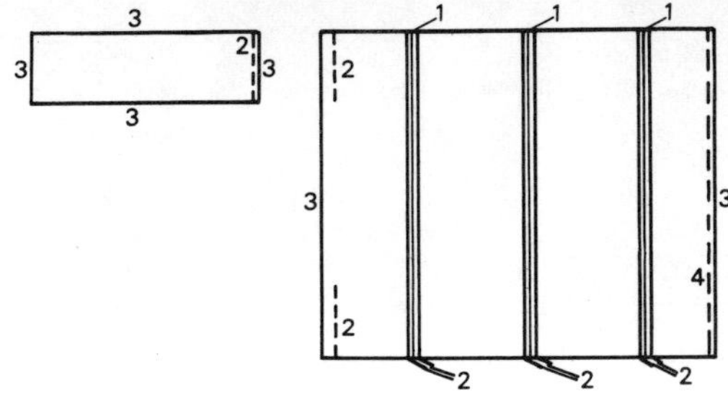

FIG 6:25   Machining head lining

Key to Fig 6:25   1 List line   2 Machine line   3 Cutting line   4 Finishing line

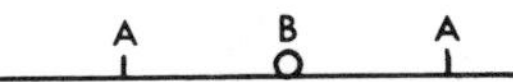

FIG 6:26 Section through lists. (A) Machined list for tacking; (B) list open for list bar

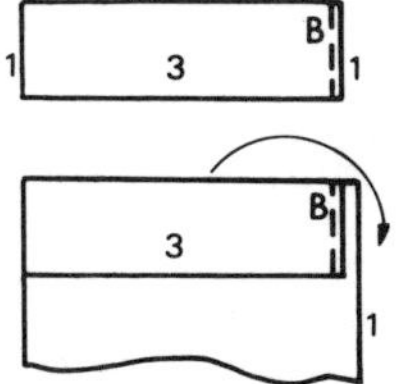

FIG 6:27   Scrap view of sides machined to head lining

Key to Fig 6:27   1 Cutting line   B Machine line   3 Sliding roof sides (i.e., 'legs')

Machining:

A Singer 31K or 45K industrial sewing machine should be used for this type of work, but if neither is available, some of it can be done on a housewife's machine and the heavier pieces hand sewn, or the work could be given out to an upholsterer. For the sewing machine, two feet will be required, a plain foot and a piping foot, as shown in **FIGS 6:10** and **6:12**.

The small amount of machining on cloth headlinings can be done on an ordinary household sewing machine. On the headlining there are the lists and the joins to be machined. To mark out the lists, carefully measure the distance between each batten, or take the measurements from the old headlining. Starting from the end finishing line at the rear window, allow 2 inches extra and mark each batten line in chalk across the width of the cloth. Then 1 inch to each side of these lines, mark another line, thus making three parallel lines; these sets of three lines each represent a list (see **FIG 6:26**). Fold the cloth so that the outside lines meet and the middle line forms an edge. Set the machine at 10 stitches to the inch and machine down the outside line. This makes a 1 inch tuck, which may be tacked to the roof, or through which a bar may be inserted. Machine each list in this fashion. Joining is done by placing the cloth edge to edge and machining it $\frac{1}{2}$ inch back (see **FIG 6:27**). All machining is done on the inside of the roof lining.

The machining of flutes for seat covers and squabs is generally done on a 31K machine, but could be done on a housewife's machine if taken slowly. For this work, the machine is set at 8 stitches per inch. Lay the calico so that the first flute line on the left is under the foot of the machine and the rest of this material lies to the right. Place the first creased flute line of the leathercloth on top of the calico and machine about $\frac{1}{8}$ inch inside that line, making sure that everything is in line (see **FIG 6:28**). Fold to the next line and machine along it; continue until the work is finished. At the beginning of this operation the calico lies on the right and the leathercloth on the left. On completion, there is a calico base with a leathercloth top, forming a series of tunnels which are the flutes.

Piping is machined by placing both edges of the leathercloth together with a piping cord inside the fold so formed. A piping foot is needed for this operation, which must be carried out on an industrial sewing machine. If such a machine is not available, the piping may be solutioned instead. In this case, solution the leathercloth and allow to dry. Lay the cord down the centre, fold the leathercloth over it edge to edge and stick. Then slightly stretch it on the bench and temporarily tack each end. Run a garnish awl down one side close to the cord to give a good finish. Alternatively, ready-made plastics piping may be bought, in matching or contrasting colours.

Machine the piping to the cushion sides and so on, using the piping foot on a 31K or stitch it by hand using 1 inch running stitches. For machining borders to the fixed piping and the body of the piece, adjust the machine to 6 stitches per inch. Keep all edges together and machine on the inside. When finished, turn it the right way round. It is always best to work outwards from the centre, because the border is liable to creep.

See that the proper sides are machined and that any marked points meet at the correct places. Choose the thread according to the machine used and the job to be done; No. 40 thread for light work, down to No. 25 for the heavier work. If the sewing is to be done by hand, place all the edges together and secure the job to the

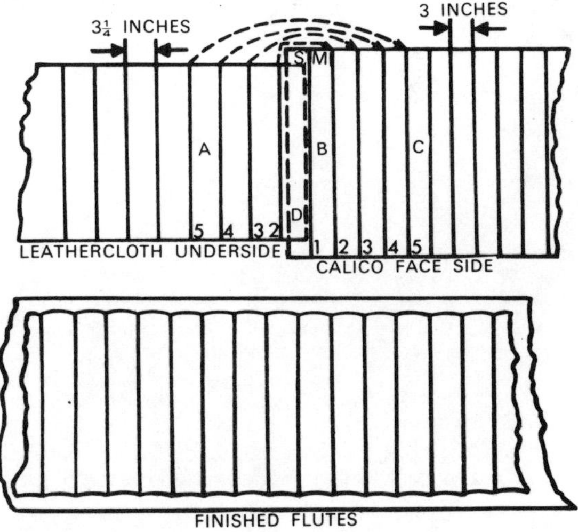

FIG 6:28   Machining flutes

Key to Fig 6:28   (A) Creased lines in leathercloth; (B) Folded crease line;   (C) Marked flute lines on calico; (D) Machined line;   (SM) Sewing machine

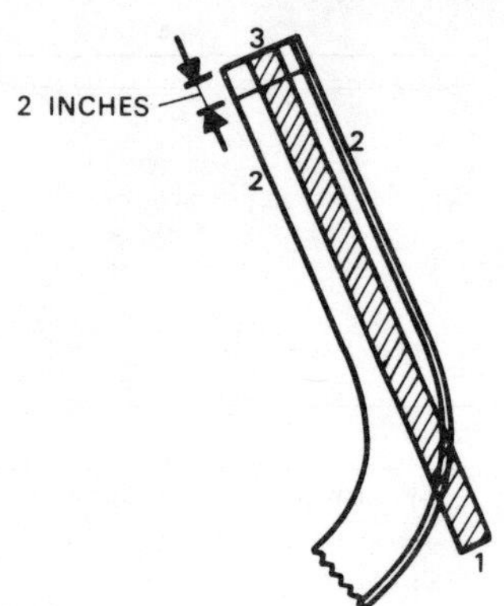

FIG 6:29   Stick method of inserting wadding

Key to Fig 6:29   1 Fluting stick   2 Wadding strip
3 Folded end of wadding

bench by sticking a skewer through the edge at the starting point. In this case use No. 18 thread and sew with running stitches $\frac{1}{4}$ inch apart keeping close to the cord. A sewing awl could be used for piercing the holes. Keep the work slightly strained and the thread tight. It is a good idea to wax the thread.

Where a border or piping is to be machined on to a fluted piece, the wadding must be inserted in the flutes first. This is done as follows. Split the wadding, which is 18 inches wide, down the middle to form 9 inch strips. Fold the strips into three thicknesses of the desired 3 inch width. This is for 3 inch flutes; modify these folding instructions for larger flutes or inferior wadding. For inserting the wadding, a thin flat stick or metal plate about 36 inches by $1\frac{1}{2}$ inches is required. Lay the stick on the folded strip of wadding and turn about 2 inches of wadding up over the end of the stick to give a hold for pushing (see **FIG 6:29**). Insert this end into the near opening of the flute and push it in gently until it protrudes at the other end. Draw out the stick leaving the wadding inside the flute and pull the wadding back gently until it is flush with the far end. Cut off the near end with a pair of scissors and proceed with the next flute. Wadding can be obtained in the correct width for standard flutes, with a strip of paper down the middle.

Refitting the body trim:

The headlinings can be installed first, or the draught pipings and other edgings according to which was done first on the original job. The tacking line on the body may be of wood or compressed fibre, or there may be holes at intervals in the metal lining backed with wood or fibre. Follow the previous tacking line.

Headlining:

First mark the centre point on the list rails and on the lists. Tack the list nearest to the back window to the first list rail with one centre tack. Make sure that the machine line lies about $\frac{1}{4}$ inch below the edge of the list rail. Stretch the list as far to each side as the rail will allow and tack. Then tack off at 2 inch intervals, keeping the machine line straight. Work back towards the front of the car to the next list, tack at the centre and repeat as before until all

the lists have been tacked. The cloth is now held by the lists, but is sagging.

If the model has metal bars holding the lists, push the bar through the machined loop of the list, taking care to choose the correct bar for each list, as these may differ in length (see **FIG 6:31**). This job is best done outside the car. See that the centre of the cloth is in the centre of the bar. Some assistance will be needed to fix the bars. One person should hold the bar of the list nearest the rear window in the centre, while a second person screws each end. Continue until all the bars have been screwed in position.

The sides and ends are now tacked. Stretch the cloth tight and tack the back end, then stretch and tack the front end. The cloth is now tight from front to rear. If there is a sliding roof, first tack the centre rear of the opening, then stretch the side legs forward and tack; finally tack off each side of the opening. The narrow opening in front of the sliding roof, above the windscreen, can be covered with a separate piece of cloth or a screwed-on covered casing (sometimes called the front header).

Stretch at each line list, on each side and tack off at 1 inch intervals (see **FIG 6:30**). Cut off any surplus

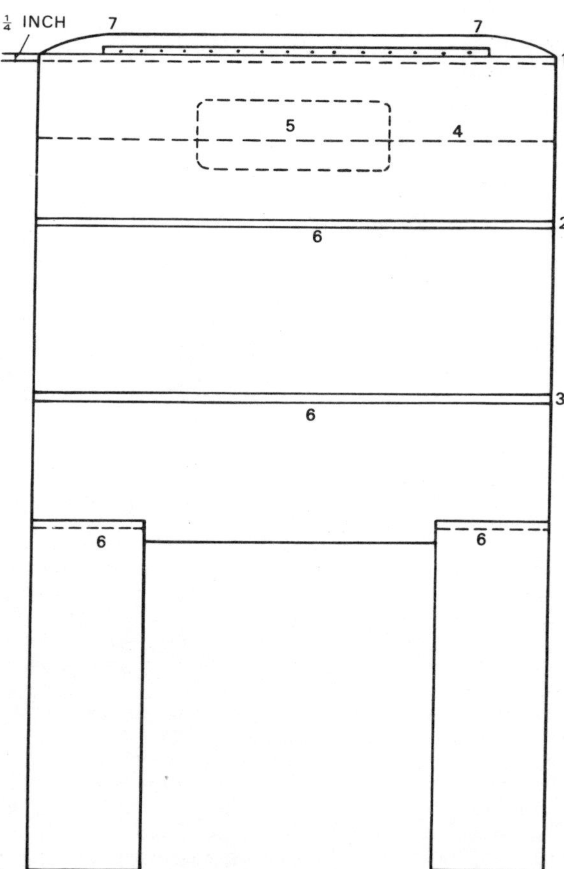

FIG 6:30   Hanging head lining

Key to Fig 6:30   1 First list tacked   2 Second list tacked
3 Third list tacked   4 Rear cutting line   5 Rear window
6 Machined line   7 List rail or batten

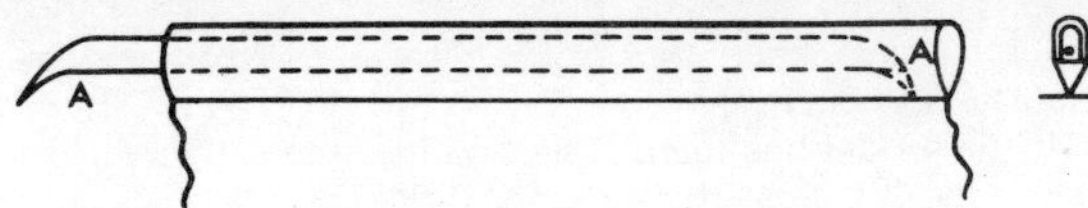

FIG 6:31   List bar inserted in list. (A) screw hole in curved end of bar (note that bars differ in length)

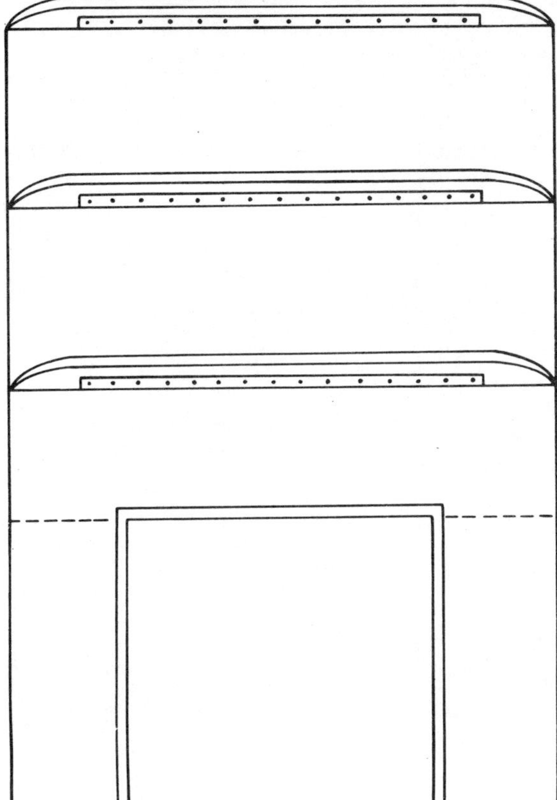

FIG 6:32   View of fixed head lining as it would appear if roof were removed

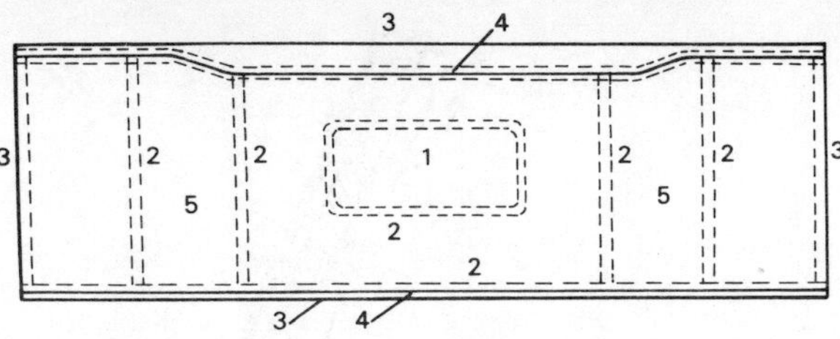

FIG 6:33   View of back curtain laid flat

Key to Fig 6:34   1 Rear window   2 Wooden batten
3 Cutting line   4 Finishing line   5 Corner curve

cloth and keep it for use in covering small fillets. Some roofs have both list bars and tacked lists, other have the back curtain and headlining in one piece.

Back curtain:

Place the first tack in the centre at the top. The centre is most simply gauged by measuring the centre of the back window. The tacking line will be the same as for the headlining, the tacks going in between those holding the headlining. See that the material is high enough in the centre to allow for any rise in the tacking line at the corners. The cloth could be folded inwards along this line to save cutting off later. A very sharp knife might accidentally cut into the head lining as well.

Stretch each side at the top to the beginning of the curve and put in another tack; tack off between these. Stretch down and tack bottom centre; stretch outwards and tack the bottom corner parallel with the top line. Tack off as before.

Follow the old top line around each corner, but do not stretch; rather let the cloth lie easy and tack off. Stretch down and tack round the bottom corners. Then tack off round the quarter window on the finishing line. The back curtain is now stretched in position and tacked off all round except for the rear window (see **FIG 6:33**) which should not be cut out until it is finally tacked or solutioned.

To tack the rear window, push the cloth against the window ledge with the fingers and tack all round half way in the ledge. Then cut the cloth by running a sharp knife round the ledge next to the glass and lift out the cut piece. If the car has a casing round the rear window, follow the previous finishing line.

Solution can be used in place of tacks for fixing round the rear window. In this case, before hanging the back curtain, solution a 2 inch wide outline of the window on the back of the cloth where the window will come (the 2 inch width will allow for some error in calculation). This should be done on the bench. Brush the window ledge with solution. When the curtain has been fixed, rub a finger round the ledge to stick the cloth; then cut out the aperture.

Cut off all surplus cloth and cover all tack lines with double cord piping, beading or similar material. If none is available, the tack line can be concealed with long strips of millboard or thick cardboard, $\frac{1}{2}$ inch to $\frac{3}{4}$ inch wide, covered with cloth and fixed with $\frac{3}{4}$ inch panel pins about 6 inches apart. Any interior light or other roof fitting should be installed next. Cut no more holes than are absolutely necessary. For the roof light, feel for the wires under the cloth, pierce the cloth with a knife and draw the wire through the cloth ready for reconnection.

Wide rubber draught piping is tacked or solutioned round the doors. The piping (which has been made up on the bench as previously described) is stretched tightly in position. Nick the tape so that it fits at the bends and corners (see **FIG 6:21**). Use larger tacks for this job, or metal cutting screws with cup washers for a better hold.

Next attend to the heelboard, bottom sides, wheel-arches, valances and squab shelf. These will be either stuck on or gimp pinned. Glove boxes can be relined with cloth cut to the pattern of the old lining. Use a brush to solution the box and a scraper for solutioning the lining. Fix when dry.

It is sound practice to use the smallest tack that will hold each job. When the tacks must show on the finished job, use either gimp pins or panel pins to give a neat appearance. Complete body trim by tidying up any raw edges.

Bench trim:

The seats and other parts which have been taken out of the car are stripped and retrimmed on the bench. It is best to strip, cut, machine and retrim each piece completely before going on to the next. This enables one to concentrate on one particular piece and to refer back to similar pieces not yet stripped, which will probably be frequently necessary for anyone who has not done the job before. Before re-covering, attend to any repairs to the spring cases or stuffing. If the stuffing is in good condition, do not disturb it.

Stripping bench trim:

Turn the rear squab face down on the bench and knock out all the tacks holding the cover to the board. The cover may have been tacked to a compressed fibre strip enclosed in a metal cage attached to the spring case, or it may have been sewn on to the spring case itself. In the latter case, the twine will need to be cut to release the cover. If the squab has a centre armrest, this should be removed and stripped separately.

Strip the rear cushion in the same way. If there is no board, the cushion will be sewn with twine. Cut the twine holding the black canvas and then that holding the cover to the spring case. Save the canvas and felt to be used again. Some covers are fastened to the spring case with clips, which need to be released.

There are various types of bucket seats. Some have a fixed cushion, and others a lift-out type. The fastening can be found by looking at the underside. The bucket squab may pull off over the top, or there may be a bead line around the edge. In this second case, remove the beading and knock out the tacks round the line, thus separating the front from the back, to give two pieces. Save any loose millboard or felt for re-use. Do not disturb the runner plates unless this is unavoidable. The runner plates on the floor of the car should be left alone, too, unless the floor carpet is trapped under them.

Strip fillets by carefully pulling off the cloth so that none of the plywood gets broken. If any should break, thick cardboard or millboard can be cut to the shape of the old fillets. To strip door casings, first release the pockets, if any. Any broken door casings should be replaced with plywood. Next strip the centre pillar casings and all other casings. The wheelarch casing may be in two parts if an armrest is incorporated. Again, save all the old covers and pieces for patterns and later reference.

Retrimming seats:

Assemble the rear squab by placing the new cover over the spring case; see that it is put on the right way up. Temporarily tack at bottom centre, strain outwards and temporarily tack bottom corners. Strain up and repeat temporary tacking at top. Then temporarily tack the top and bottom, straining the work tight. Make sure the cover is straight and square with the sides fitting properly over the spring case. If the sides are shaped for the side armrest, fasten them over the spring case by skewers under the

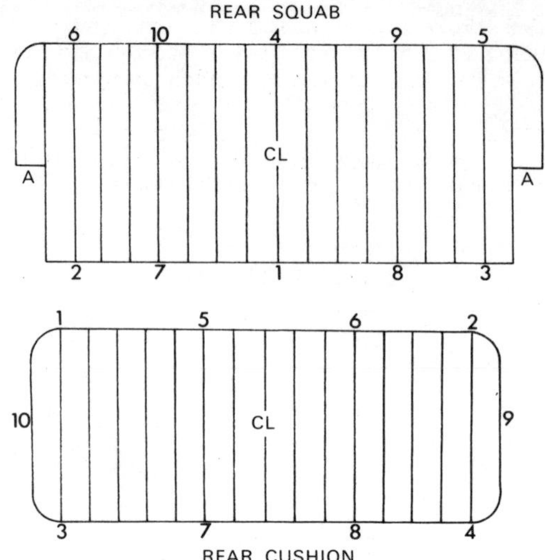

FIG 6:34   Order of placing temporary tacks and skewers when recovering rear squab and cushion

Key to Fig 6:34   (A) Skewers   CL Centre line

piping line so that they fit neatly (see **FIG 6:34**). When the fit is satisfactory, tack off all round, making sure the flutes are straight. Cut off surplus material. If there is no baseboard, secure the cover to the spring case with skewers and then sew the squab to the spring case with twine and a 4 inch circular needle, stitching at each flute line. Finally, remove all skewers.

The rear seat cushion cover is fitted over the spring case and secured with skewers. Check that the ends fit correctly and that the flutes are square so that they will line up with the flutes on the rear squab (see **FIG 6:34**). Turn the cushion face down on the bench and fill the borders with stuffing where necessary. Stitch to the spring case at 2 inch intervals. Where there is a board, tacks take the place of skewers and stitching.

The cover can be sewn to the top frame of the spring case before it is turned. First sew black felt to the frame as a sewing base. Skewer the piping tape to the frame for a temporary hold. Sew with twine using a loop stitch. This method can be used in all types of trimming where there is a piping line. It gives a better finish and fit (see

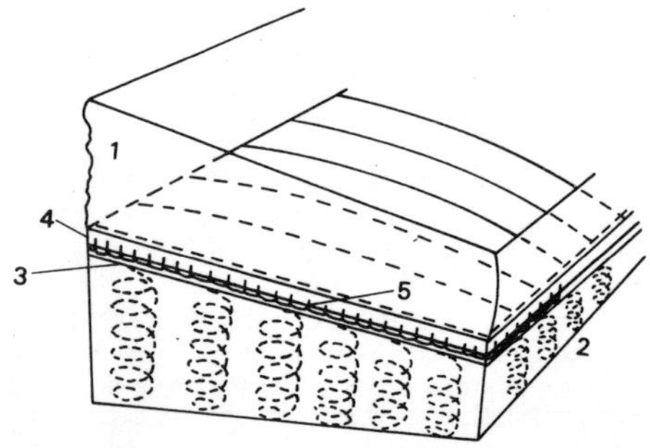

FIG 6:35   Method of sewing top piping to spring case

Key to Fig 6:35   1 Turned-up border   2 Spring case
3 Felt hold   4 Piping tape   5 Loop stitching

FIG 6 : 35). Black canvas is sewn on the bottom of the cushion for a finish. Place felt in position and sew on canvas, with a 1 inch frenching stitch, using twine and a 4 inch circular needle. Air holes must be made in all cushions. These may be made by means of eyelets in the back of the border, or a square hole may be cut in the canvas and turned in. Finally, remove all skewers.

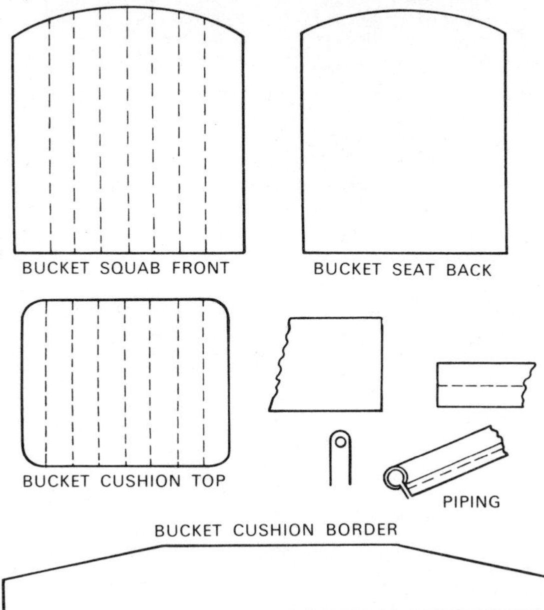

BUCKET SQUAB FRONT   BUCKET SEAT BACK

BUCKET CUSHION TOP   PIPING

BUCKET CUSHION BORDER

FIG 6 : 36   Components of a bucket seat cover

The centre armrest is usually in two pieces, one being the armrest surface when down and the other forming part of the squab when up. The two pieces are joined at the centre of the wooden armrest. The armrest does not usually have a spring case, but a pad of hair or rubber latex. The underside usually has a spring case, shaped to match the squab. It does not matter which of these sides is trimmed first. Fit the armrest so that it folds evenly into the squab. Follow the previous trim. Cover the line where the two sides meet with beading to give a neat finish. The tab for pulling down the armrest can be made as a replica of the old design. Do not leave the tab until last, otherwise some of the work may have to be undone to fix it.

In the pull-on type of bucket seat, the bottom opening is placed over the top of the bucket-back and the cover pulled down tightly. Make sure the cover fits squarely and the piping comes in the right place round the edge of the frame. Tack off at the bottom. In the case of bucket seat squabs which are in two pieces, do the front piece first. Fix it squarely with temporary tacks. Working from the top centre, strain down the flute lines and tack off (see **FIG 6 : 37**). Wadding has to be placed in the outermost flutes before fixing with temporary tacks. Gimp pin round the finishing line and cut off surplus material. Then do the back piece, not forgetting any felt or millboard taken from the old job (see **FIG 6 : 38**). Cover the tack line with double cord piping or beading. Cover the valance the same as the old style.

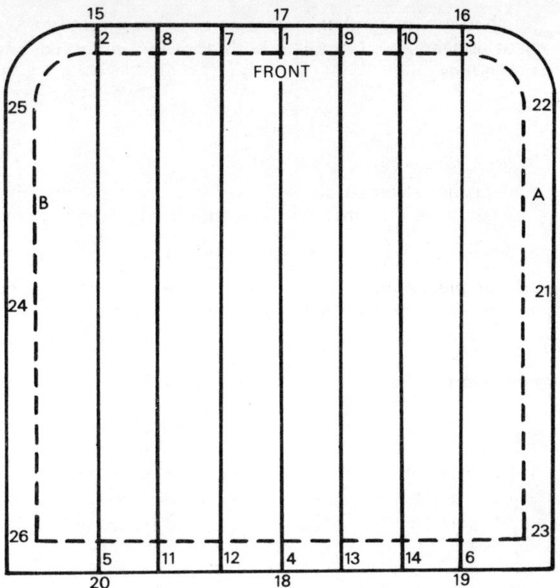

FIG 6 : 37   Bucket seat squab

Key to Fig 6 : 37   (A) Edge of material   (B) Finishing line
1-16 Temporary tacks   15-22 Temporary tacks replacing 16 tacks for further straining

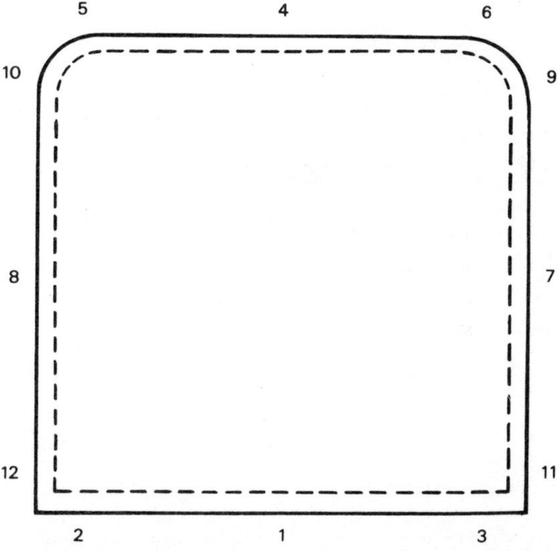

FIG 6 : 38   Order of placing temporary tacks for back of bucket seat squabs

The lift-out type of bucket cushion is trimmed in a similar way to the rear cushion. Fit the cover in position over the spring case and manoeuvre it into shape by straining the piping lines (see **FIG 6 : 39**). When it is properly arranged, skewer it to the spring case (see **FIG 6 : 40**). Turn the cushion face downward, fill out the borders with stuffing where required and proceed as for the rear cushion (see **FIG 6 : 41**). The fixed cushion is trimmed in the same way, except that it is tacked on to the base. Remove all skewers.

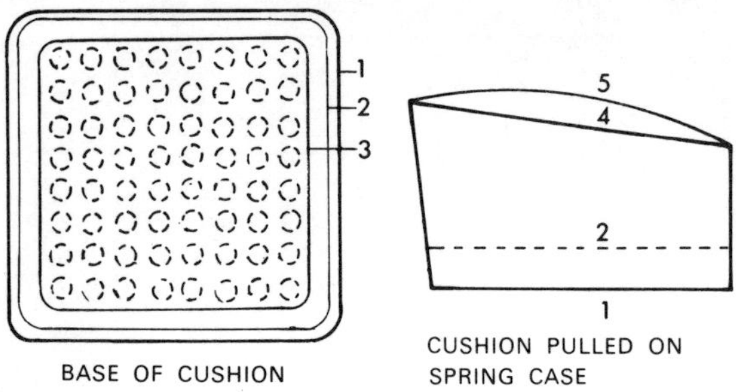

FIG 6:39   Bucket seat cushion

Key to Fig 6:39   1 Edge of leathercloth   2 Edge of board of spring case   3 Join of canvas (frenching stitch)   4 Piping line   5 Fluted pad

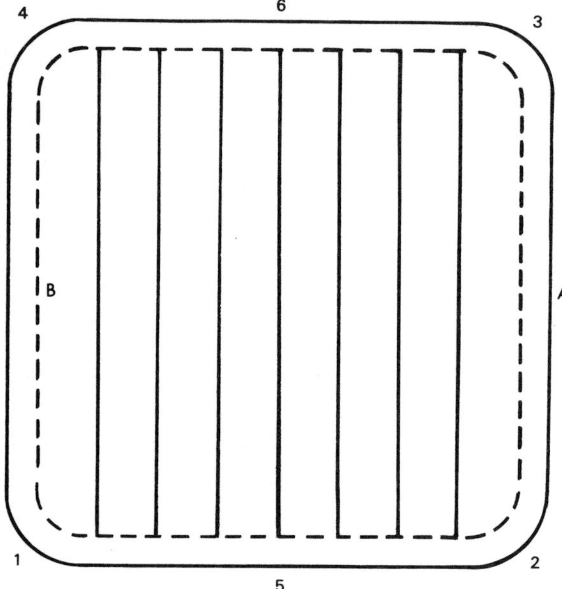

FIG 6:40   Bucket seat cushion showing order of placing skewers. (A) Edge of cushion; (B) Machine line

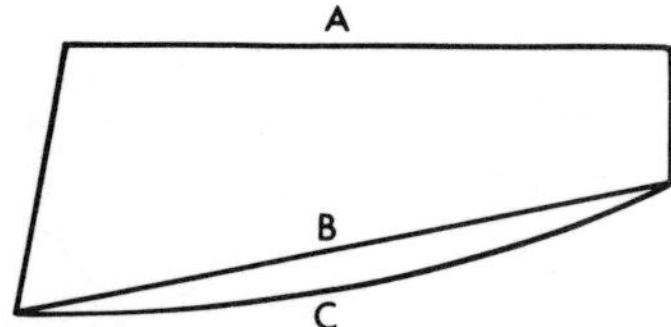

FIG 6:41   Inverted cushion complete. (A) Board of spring case; (B) Piping line; (C) Fluted pad

Door casings:

There are many designs of door casings. Those with pockets are usually machined round the pocket opening. Others have additional lines machined right through the plywood and require a special sewing machine. Pockets may be tacked on from the back of the casing. If no pockets are required, the pocket opening may be covered with wadding and another piece of wadding placed right over to make a plain door pad. To cover the door casings, place the leathercloth face down on the bench. Put the padded side of the casing centrally on top of the leathercloth, wadding side down. Temporarily tack the centre of the sides to the back of the casing, slightly stretching the material. Stretch to corners and fix with 12 temporary tacks. The sides can now be solutioned or tacked with $\frac{3}{4}$ inch tacks. Keep the material tight, fold it in at the corners and cut out the surplus.

If a pocket is to be fitted, do not tack off the sides yet. Cut out the pocket opening, leaving enough material to turn over the pocket edges. These edges and the overlap material are stuck down.

Insert the elastic in the top seam of the machined pocket. Place the machined pocket centrally and temporarily tack it from the back of the casing. Lay the piece of leathercloth which covers the inside of the pocket and forms the lining, so that the face side shows through the opening. Stretch and tack 1 inch apart about $\frac{3}{4}$ inch in from the pocket opening. These tacks should be riveted as follows. Lift one or more of the outer sides of the door casing and push a thin metal strip, such as an old valance plate, between the leathercloth and the plywood (see **FIG 6:42**). Then, placing the metal strip where the point of the tack comes, knock home the temporary tacks. If the tacks were not riveted, their points would stick through the cover. With this method the pocket is held by the riveted tacks alone. Now the sides of the casing are stretched and solutioned down or tacked off with $\frac{3}{4}$ inch tacks. Do not cut the holes for the handle or winder at this stage.

Dash casings and facia panels:

Some cases are not padded, including dash casings on old cars. The leathercloth is stuck directly to the plywood. Nearly all fillets are trimmed in the same way. To cover these, solution the cloth with a scraper and the wooden part with a brush and allow to dry. Lay the cloth on the bench with the solutioned side uppermost. Stretch it slightly. Place the flat of the fillet on top so that the cloth will stick to the wood. Solution the other side of the wood, turn the cloth over and stick. Cut surplus material from the corners and rub the fillet all over with the hand. With large fillets, such as that above the windscreen, stretch the cloth more and temporarily tack the corners to the bench before solutioning. Place the wood on top and remove the temporary tacks. Turn it over and stick down the inside. Do not forget to recover the sun visor if necessary (see **FIG 6:44**).

Reassembling:

The car has now been completely retrimmed and it remains to reassemble all the parts. If the advice in this chapter has been followed throughout the worker should know where everything came from and the operation can be tackled with confidence. It is in fact the reverse of the stripping process. The car should be cleaned out with a vacuum cleaner before starting assembly.

The sliding roof is assembled first and the door casings are fitted next. When the door casing has been fitted in its correct position, the shafts of the door handle and

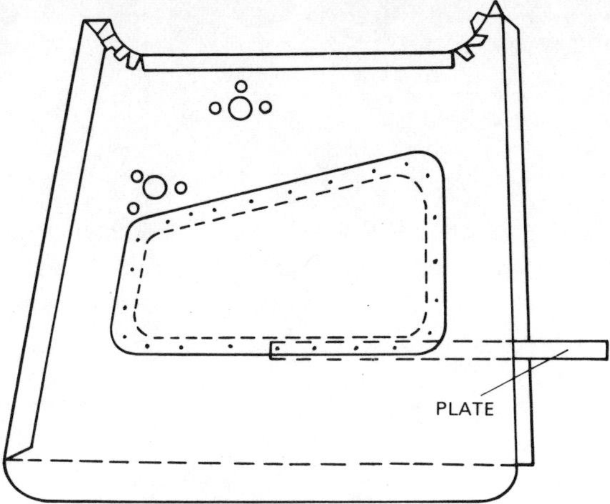

FIG 6:42 Rear view of door casing, showing riveting plate inserted between leathercloth and plywood

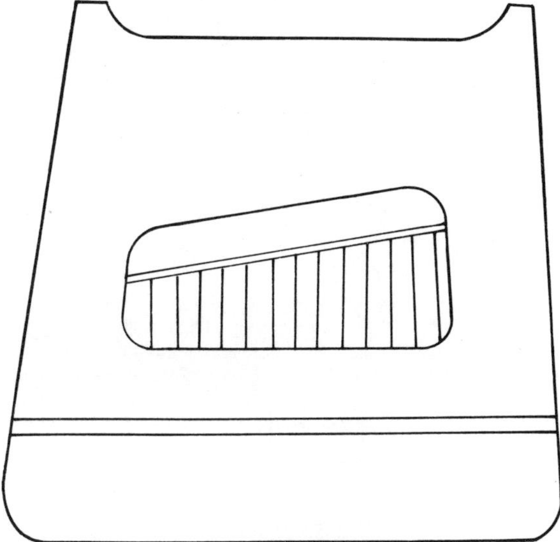

FIG 6:43 Front view of completed door casing

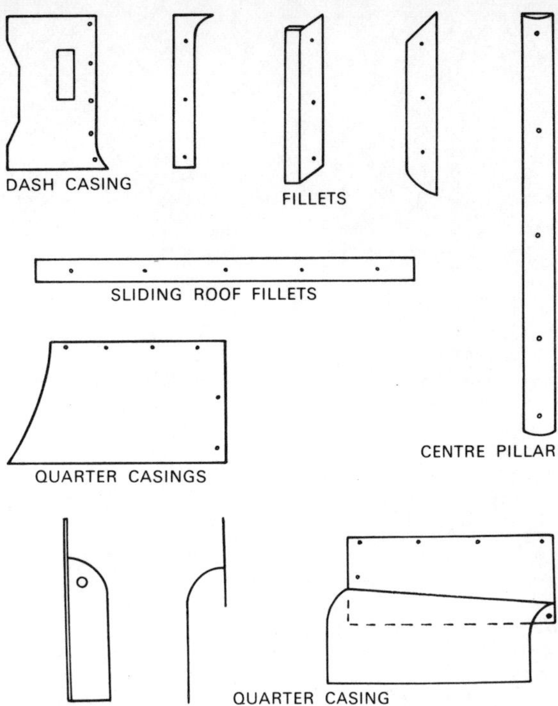

FIG 6:44 Casings and fillets

winder will protrude. Lightly tap both these shafts with a hammer so that they pierce their own holes. Screw, nail or clip the casing in its final position and refit the handle lever and winder. If the casing was previously clipped on and the clips are damaged, use Parker Kalon metal-cutting screws to fix the casing on a metal-lined door, or wood screws for a timber-framed door.

Metal screws can be put in by knocking a hole in the metal with a garnish awl, or by drilling a slightly under-sized hole; the screw will cut its own thread. Equalise the screws around the door, using cup washers to hold the casing firm. Fillets are then fitted and fixed with $\frac{3}{4}$ inch panel pins placed 4 to 6 inches apart.

Any small fitting which has not already been assembled should now be attended to. If there is a rear blind, it may be tacked or stitched to the roller. If it has to be renewed, make sure that it is rolled the correct way; an arrow usually

indicates this. When fixing the blind, see that the spring is wound up sufficiently to give a quick return when the cord is released and that the stick on the bottom of the blind has been inserted and sewn in properly. The cord must run freely in the fittings which run round to the driver's seat. All that remains is to fit the rear squab, cushion and carpets, and to slide the front seats into position.

6:4 Button pleating

Buttons and tufts of hair were used in Victorian carriage work, both for squabbings and seat-backs and this style is coming back into fashion for customised trim. **FIG 6:45** shows four Victorian squabs illustrating the most commonly used patterns. Morocco leather was sometimes used for squabbings on the inside of the doors and hide for the seat-backs.

The geometry for these patterns is best worked out on paper and then transferred to a sheet of canvas or whatever forms the base of the cushion. **FIG 6:46** shows the ratio plan of a full diamond pattern and a cross-section of the finished pad. The 6 inches by 3 inches pattern shows the button anchorage points on the canvas base and the $6\frac{1}{2}$ inches by $4\frac{1}{2}$ inches pattern shows the button positions on the top cover.

FIG 6:47 shows the plan of a half-diamond pattern and a cross-section of the completed pad. The top righthand drawing shows the pattern of the base and the bottom drawing shows the button positions and pleats of the top cover.

On the base the distance between button marks is $4\frac{1}{2}$ inches in both directions. The top cover marks allow

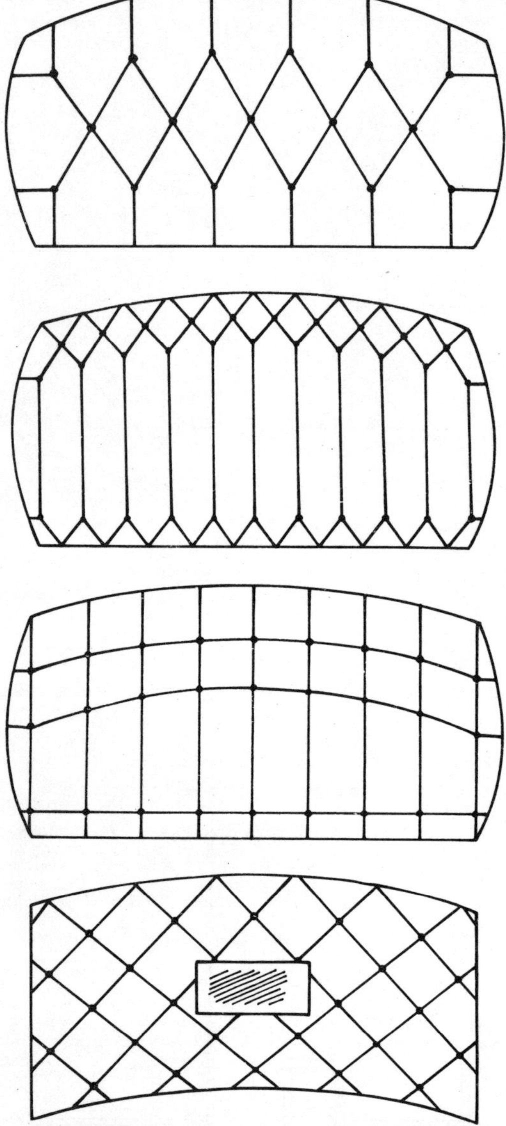

FIG 6:45 Victorian squabs. Top to bottom: Diamond, organ pipe, square, squabbing

$1\frac{1}{2}$ inches extra for fullness across the flutes and only $\frac{1}{4}$ inch down the flutes. Sometimes even this $\frac{1}{4}$ inch is omitted to get a tight pull down each pleat line. The amount of fullness is a matter of taste, but generally less fullness is required for leather than for fabrics. Line A in **FIG 6:47** is the base line for the pattern. The part below this line will be hidden by the seat cushion.

The conventional method of stuffing button-pleated upholstery, which may be encountered in restoring veteran and vintage cars and carriages, was to stretch a canvas backing cloth on a wooden frame laid horizontally on the bench, using temporary tacks. A length of twine was sewn through each button position, pinching up about half an inch of canvas and leaving two ends of

twine each about 10 inches long. Then horsehair was spread evenly over the entire surface, teasing it out a handful at a time, until it was piled up 9 or 10 inches high. If the horsehair was to be covered with cloth, then a layer of wadding was laid over the horsehair to prevent it working through the cloth. Holes were broken in the wadding to enable each pair of twines to be threaded through.

The next step was to punch holes for the button rings

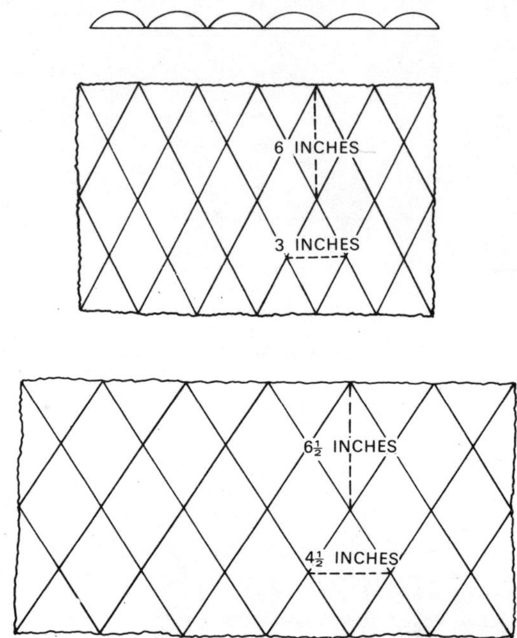

FIG 6:46 Ratio plan of full diamond pattern. Top, cross-section of finished pad. Centre, canvas base; bottom, top cover

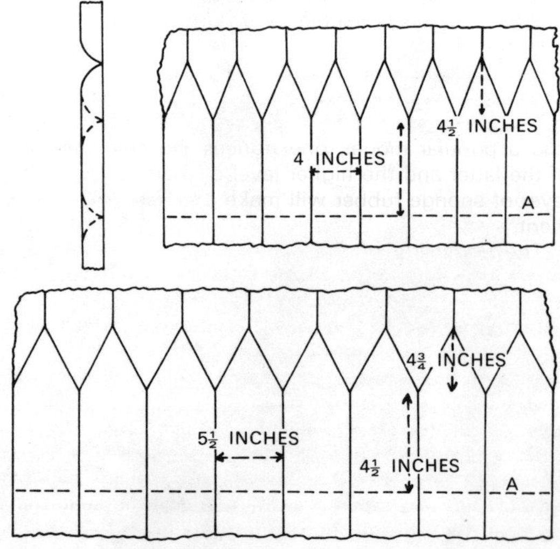

FIG 6:47 Plan of half-diamond pattern. Top left, cross-section of finished pad; top right, canvas base; bottom, top cover. (A) bottom or back button line

in the top cover. If the cover were leather, the pleats were beaten in with a mallet on the bench, wetting the leather first. Fabric pleats were shaped with a needle or regulator.

Now the top cover was threaded on to the bottom canvas, each double twine going through the corresponding button hole. A button was tied to one of each pair of twines. Starting at the middle row, each buttoned twine was tied round the other with a slip knot. Then came the gradual process of lowering the buttons into the pad. Starting at one end, the buttons were lowered about 1 inch all over, then farther and farther until all the buttons were down on the canvas. The pad was then ready for fixing to a spring case or to the squab frame.

Should one of the twines break in service, it is possible to make a repair without dismantling the whole squab. The trick is to tie a nail in the middle of a length of twine and insert it in a small metal tube. The tube is pushed through the button hole and hammered through the backing canvas. The nail is then pushed out of the bottom of the tube with a piece of wire and the tube is withdrawn, leaving the twine anchored behind the canvas by the nail. The twines are then passed through the button ring, pulled tight and tied off. The short ends are finally tucked away under the head of the button.

The use of polyether foam greatly simplifies button pleating (see **Section 6:6**) for the modern trimmer.

6:5 Renewing carpets

The choice of floor covering in a car is partly a matter of price and partly dependent on the use to which the car is put. For heavy work, where the driver is wearing gumboots and jumping in and out all day, heavy rubber flooring is probably the best choice. It can be taken out quickly, hosed and brushed down and replaced directly the underside is dry. It can be obtained moulded into small squares so that it can be cut to an approximate fit very easily.

Less austere, but reasonably cheap and hard-wearing, is haircord carpet. This and other canvas-backed carpets must be protected by an underfelt or sponge to prevent wear against the car floor. If the cost is acceptable, a good quality rubber-sponge-backed carpet is almost ideal. Underlays are not essential in this case, although still a good idea. When stepping out of a luxurious car into a popular model, one notices the cold, hard floor of the latter and the higher level of road noise. An extra layer of sponge rubber will make a remarkable improvement.

The underside of the sponge may be covered with calico, scrim, hessian or similar material to protect it from wear against the ribbing in the floor pan. The covering is simply stuck to the sponge with rubber solution, but make sure you solution the correct side of the fabric. It is very easy to make mistake here. Ordinary carpet can be converted into sponge-back in the same way.

Assuming that the car has been fitted with carpets previously and that these have worn out, the first thing to do is to take out the front seats. Some seats have a stop on the side of one of the runners and this must be removed. Others are bolted to strong points on the floor. If the bolts are rusted, soak them in penetrating oil. If this fails, resort to the methods described under 'Re-

moving bolted wings' in **Chapter 3**. It may be possible to cut the nuts with a 'nut cracker' or a hacksaw.

With the seats out of the way, lift out the old carpets, noting whether any of the fasteners are missing from the back and whether any of the corresponding anchorages on the car floor are missing or damaged. It is not unusual to find that those subjected to the heaviest wear have disappeared, leaving a gaping hole through which one can see the road. Such holes should be welded in or filled with polyester or epoxy putty. A simple substitute for a missing fastener is a self-tapping screw with a washer under the head.

Take out the underfelt, if any, and see whether it is worth keeping. Probably it will be in tatters, damp and rusty, and ready for the dustbin. Remove any other fittings likely to get in the way and sweep out the floor. Have a good look round for patches of dampness and rust and signs of water leaking in from the underside. Clean off rust and flaking paint and repaint as necessary.

In some cars there is a heelboard, or vertical panel, under the back seat, covered with the floor carpeting. Allow for this when buying new material, also for the material on the lower parts of the doors and inner sills if these are to match the new floor covering.

If the old carpets can be extracted in one piece, they can be used as patterns when cutting out new material. A typical arrangement is shown in **FIG 6:48**. Regardless of condition, the old carpet should be kept for reference until the new carpets have been made. If the old carpets fitted badly or are incomplete, new patterns should be made from thick brown paper or wallpaper. Work forward from the back of the car, cutting the paper to

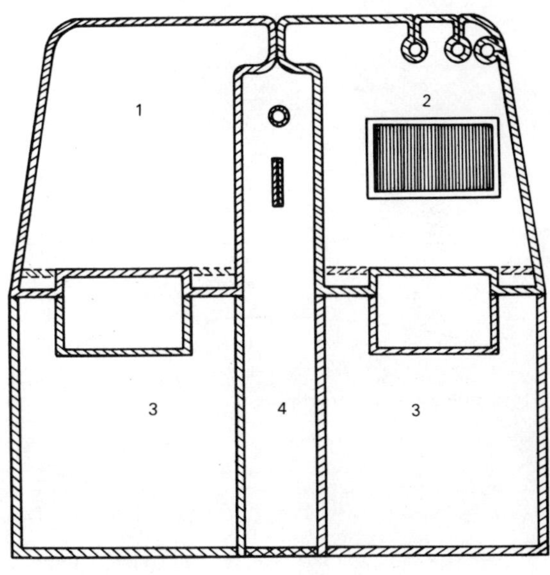

FIG 6:48 Typical carpet layout. (1), (2) and (3) are of the lift-out type, (4) is sometimes fixed, sometimes in two pieces

shape and marking the position of steering column, pedals, gearbox cover, seat runners and any other obstructions.

An electric torch or wander lamp is useful when looking up behind the pedals to see how high the carpet needs to go. This dark corner is a source of draughts, particularly in old cars with no rubber gaiters around the pedals. Make sure that the top of the carpet cannot curl down under the accelerator or brake and clutch pedals and prevent full travel. Such unexpected interference can be extremely dangerous.

The completed pattern is now laid **face down** on the **back** of the carpet. Mark the cutting lines on the carpet with chalk around the edge of the pattern and mark the slots for the controls and other projections. Before starting to cut the carpet with a Stanley knife or shears, check that the pattern is face down. It is the easiest thing in the world to lay a pattern the wrong way up and get a useless mirror image of the shape you need.

The edges of the woven carpets must be bound in some way to prevent fraying, but this is not necessary in the case of rubber-backed carpeting. The traditional binding for first-class work is hide, which is supple, hard-wearing and available in strips for the purpose. There are various ways of binding and three are shown in **FIG 6 : 49**.

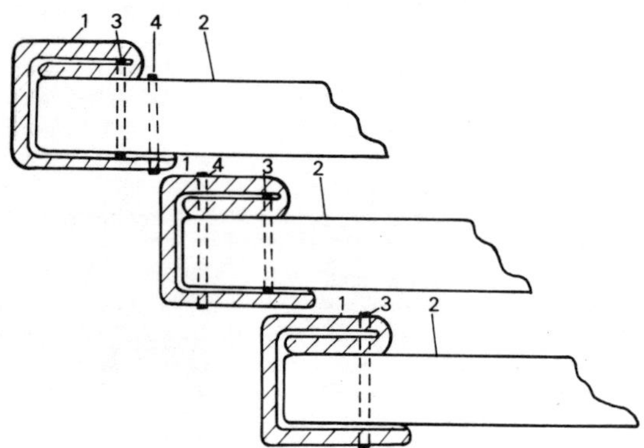

FIG 6 : 49   Three ways of binding the edge of a carpet

Key to Fig 6 : 49   1 Binding   2 Carpet   3 First row of stitching   4 Second row of stitching

1 The method shown on the left of the illustration has no stitches visible in the binding on the upper, or face side, and this is preferred for high-class work.

2 The method shown in the centre sketch has one row of stitches showing, but is useful for rounding difficult corners.

3 The type of binding shown on the right has only one row of stitches and these are visible on the face. This method is used on light carpet.

The width of binding visible on the face should not be less than $\frac{5}{16}$ inch, and it will be noted that in all three methods there is no raw edge showing on the face side of the carpet. It is not easy to sew through hide and carpet and probably it will be impossible on a domestic sewing machine. A Singer 31 or heavier machine is needed, or the binding can be hand done, using a sewing awl to make the holes. Cheaper and more easily worked materials are leathercloth and binding tape, which are available in matching or contrasting colour. A heavy sewing machine is desirable even for leathercloth, but the work might be done on a domestic machine, using a leather needle and oiled thread. The work is easier with two helpers, one to turn the handle very slowly, another to pull the work through, while you guide it under the foot.

In modern popular cars the tendency is to dispense with fasteners and to lay down rubber-backed carpet stuck to a layer of underfelt. The same material is used without underfelt to cover the sills and the lower parts of the doors.

6 : 6 Foam materials

Rubber latex foam :

Latex foam is made up of multitudes of small interconnecting air cells encased in pure rubber latex. It is considerably more expensive than polyurethane foams, so it is mainly used in luxury cars and in public service vehicles where its long life in rugged conditions is appreciated. Car and bus seats are made by pouring the latex into metal moulds, which are very expensive. Consequently 'one off' or short-run mouldings are out of the question for the home constructor. He must either modify stock mouldings, or build the required shape from blocks and sheets. If desired, this work can be done by handbuilders who hold stocks of latex foam and act as agents for the latex manufacturers.

Moulded cushions :

The degree of support given by a factory-moulded cushion depends on three factors; the density of the foam, the overall shape and size of the unit and the shape and size of the internal cavities. Large cavities give a softer feel, so these are positioned in the central area, while smaller cavities and a greater depth of foam gives the necessary support around the edges.

To simplify hand-building, the leading British make, Dunlopillo, is now supplied in a 4 inch thick conversion block in which many small pencil-shaped cavities are located in such a way that it can be cut in any direction without the need for applied side walls. These blocks, known as Dunlopillo SP, are supplied in the standard size 76 inches by 60 inches by 4 inches or slit into sheets of 1 inch, $1\frac{1}{2}$ inches, 2 inches or 3 inches thick. The material is supplied in six hardnesses, as shown in the accompanying table and these, in the six available thicknesses, give almost unlimited scope for individual designs.

Latex foam is pleasant to work and there is no danger from mildew, moths or vermin, nor is it harmed by moisture, but it should be protected from sunlight which ages the rubber. Its use eliminates much tedious filling and shaping and it can be folded, rolled, bent or cemented together to form various shapes. The original contours are not easily distorted, because the material springs back to shape when the load is removed. The material is light in weight and has a very long life, unless grossly overloaded. The material absorbs body heat and exhales it through the cellular structure. In common with other foams its tensile strength is low.

Grade	Super soft (SS)	SQ	Soft (S)	Medium (M)	Firm (F)	Extra firm (EF)
Approximate mean hardness						
Thickness						
4 inch	10	13	24	31	41	50
3 inch	*	**	21	27	37	45
2 inch	*	**	19	25	34	41
$1\frac{1}{2}$ inch	*	**	19	25	34	39
1 inch	*	**	17	23	32	37

* Super Soft. ** Very Soft.

The hardness figures are in accordance with BS 3129 method of test. The SQ grade is primarily designed for the back squabs of domestic furniture. The SS grade is intended for pillows.

Cutting latex foam:

No complicated equipment is needed to cut latex foam. Use a fine-tooth hacksaw, an electric carving knife, a long kitchen knife, or a pair of shears dipped in water. The edge of a bench and a steel straightedge can be used as guides when making angled cuts. To cut a circle or irregular shape, make two templates of hardboard. Sandwich the foam between them, pulling them together with wire and then cut round the templates.

The smooth surface of moulded latex foam, which is formed by contact with the mould or cover plate, provides a good surface for marking-out with ball-point pens or china-marking pencils. To obtain a snug fit for the covering, the latex should be cut slightly oversize. A $\frac{1}{4}$ inch allowance on all sides is recommended for single-seat cushions and other small pieces, rising to $1\frac{1}{2}$ inches for long, four-place cushions. Very soft stock needs a larger upholstering allowance than very firm stock. The combination of thickness and compression determines the cushioning effect of the latex.

Solid slab and cored stock up to 2 inches thickness may be cut clean through with 6 inch shears at one stroke, but with thicker material it is advisable to cut in two stages to assure a truly vertical cut. Dip the shears in water frequently when cutting very firm latex. Make the first cut from the smooth top surface, of sufficient depth to separate the top of each core. This leaves only the core separations joined. Then cut through each core wall to complete the separation and trim off any rough spots. If a bevelled or slant edge is required, it is best to make the first cut vertical and then trim back to get the desired contour. With a little practice it is possible to get a perfect rounded edge by snipping with scissors and buffing smooth with sandpaper.

Attaching latex foam:

An outstanding advantage of latex foam is its ability to form a strong bond to itself, also to wood, metal, tacking tape, plastics and fabrics, when the correct adhesive is used. The maker's recommended cement should be used. Most manufacturers of latex foam supply a fabricating cement in two containers. One is the cement proper and the other is the activator, which speeds up drying. The mixture has a pot life of 24 hours, which may be prolonged by keeping it in a refrigerator. The mixture will provide a good bond until it has gelled, but after that it cannot be reclaimed by the addition of solvent or fresh mixture. The best practice is to mix up only sufficient for the day's use. The activator has some thinning action, but if a more fluid cement is desired it may be thinned with lead-free petrol. Add the thinner to the unmixed cement and then add the activator.

For anchoring latex permanently to a wood, metal or plastics base, another type of adhesive is used. This comes in one can and is used to coat both surfaces, which are allowed to become tacky before they are set together under a little pressure.

Cementing latex to latex. The surface of each piece to be bonded should receive a light coating of cement. Allow the surfaces to become tacky – this normally takes three to five minutes. Bring the pieces together lightly at first, so that adjustments in position can be made if necessary. When the pieces are in exact position, press them together firmly for a few seconds. Within a few minutes, the joint will be strong enough to allow working, but rough handling should not be attempted for several hours.

Cementing tape. Tacking tape is available in varying widths, and some makes have a 1 inch coating of adhesive. When applying tape to latex, spread a thin coat of cement on the latex, allow a minute or two for drying and then register the tape in place. For reinforcing two joined sections of latex foam, a special full-coated tape is recommended, but ordinary tape can be used after applying cement to the uncoated portion.

Tacking tape plays an important part in the fabrication of latex foam and it should always be used when securing an edge. Never tack latex directly to a frame. Use tape for reinforcing edges where necessary and along the seam of cemented sections if unusual strain will be encountered. Tape gives extra protection along the front edge of extra-long seat cushions, where severe flexing occurs, especially if the latex is of soft compression.

Latex foam cushions which must withstand heavy wear should have double tacking strips (sometimes called flies) at the front and rear. These are solutioned to the side and bottom of the boxing (uncored margin of the latex moulding) and the outer halves of the strips are then solutioned together, providing a double thickness for tacking or cementing to the baseboard or other hold. This is the approved method for anchoring Dunlopillo; the use of adhesive for fixing latex foam to a baseboard is not reliable, although it is sometimes used for temporary positioning during assembly. The flies should be tacked with $\frac{3}{8}$ inch square shank tacks. The baseboards should be perforated with a $\frac{3}{8}$ inch hole under each cavity of the moulding. If thin plywood is used, the holding-down bolts should have a 2 inch by 1 inch strip of steel under their heads to spread the load, otherwise the bolts may eventually pull through the ply. These strips may be held in position prior to final assembly by two nails clenched through on the other side of the board.

Chalk or talcum powder serves a useful purpose. Dust it on table tops when handling large pieces. Rub it on latex cushions to reduce friction and to facilitate slip cover adjustment. Chalk absorbs excess cement. Dust it over any areas that have been cemented before the cement is dry – especially when the cement is likely to come into contact with covering materials.

Altering moulded cushions:

Moulded reversible cushions are usually supplied complete with a crown tapering to all edges and need only the application of a final covering. The upholstering allowance of $\frac{3}{4}$ inch has been included to provide a snug, slightly compressed fit. It is possible to alter the size of a moulded cushion, or a hand-built cushion. The method recommended by Goodyear is the end splice, which can be used to reduce or increase one, or even two, dimensions of the cushion.

As the term end splice implies, the cushion is cut near one side, if the side-to-side measurement is to be changed. If the front-to-back measurement is to be changed, the cut should be made near the rear. Avoid making a cut through the front edge or through the middle section, because these areas received most pressure in use.

It is preferable to make the splice about 3 inches from the cushion edge. It will be noticed that most of the taper occurs from that point to the edge and therefore a splice in the area beyond is least disturbing to the contour of the piece.

To reduce the length of a cushion by 3 inches, cut through the entire cushion about 3 inches from one end. Now cut away a 3 inch section from the large piece. Cement the end and the main section together, being careful to align them properly. Use chalk in the open cores to avoid excess cement getting in and binding.

It is practicable to increase a dimension up to 2 inches using slab stock. Various thicknesses of stock can be cemented together to make up the thickness of the insert. For increases beyond 2 inches it is preferable to go a larger size of stock cushion, or to fabricate a complete cushion from stock.

To increase the front-to-back dimension of a cushion by 1 inch, make a longitudinal cut across the back area, about 3 inches from the rear edge. Use a piece of 1 inch slab stock for the insert, matching the compression to that of the cushion. Cut the slab in a rectangle to cover liberally the dimensions that will be needed, as the trimming will be done after cementing. Alternatively, the pattern can be made on the insert by placing the fresh-cut edge of cushion on it and marking round.

Cement the slab and the large section together, making sure that the slab extends flush to all edges. Use chalk in the cores of the cushion to prevent binding. Make contact with the cushion in a natural position – do not compress it. Let it dry for a few minutes. Then trim the excess slab stock to conform with the contour of the cushion. This can be done with scissors very satisfactorily.

The next step is to cement the original end piece to the unit. Dust chalk in the cores. With the cemented sections placed on a smooth surface, bring the two pieces together. Align the end section carefully with the original cut at every point. If they are brought together naturally, with no weight applied at the top, they should coincide perfectly. If the register is satisfactory, apply gentle hand pressure from each end.

Cushions which have no curvature may be increased in length or width by cementing sheets of slab stock to the back or sides.

Tapering a rectangular cushion:

To convert a rectangular stock cushion into a cushion tapering from front to rear, say from 24 inches across the front to 21 inches across the rear, make two wedge-shaped cuts. This method is the same as the end splice, except that the excess material will be cut away in the form of two 'pie cuts' to accommodate the taper. Make the first cut parallel with the edge, starting at the back and ending about 2 inches from the front edge. Then mark $1\frac{1}{2}$ inches inwards from the first cut and make the second cut from this point to the point where the first cut ended. Take out the waste and cement the two sections together, carefully aligning the edges. Repeat at the other side of the cushion. Slight tapers can be pulled in by the cover without the trouble of altering the foam cushion.

Reversible seat cushions of unusual shapes and sizes can be built up from cored and slab stock. Here is a typical example. A 20 inch by 25 inch cushion with a $6\frac{1}{2}$ inch crown at the centre, tapering to $3\frac{1}{2}$ inch thickness at the boxing. Length and width dimensions include $\frac{3}{4}$ inch upholstery allowance. Top and bottom are cored stock, $2\frac{1}{2}$ inches thick, measuring 18 inches by 24 inches. The boxing all round is 1 inch soft slab stock $3\frac{1}{2}$ inches wide. An inner filler forms the central crown, made by using two pieces of $\frac{3}{4}$ inch stock, which can be either soft slab or cored. One piece is cut 2 inches smaller than cushion size all round and the other is cut about 4 inches less all round.

The combined thickness of the cushion edges is 5 inches, so that when the boxing is centred on them, the edges of the cushion form a right angle with the edges of the boxing. Apply cement to these edges and press them gently together to give the effect of a full, rounded contour.

Edging:

There are three main types of edging on latex foam cushions; feather edge, cushion edge and square edge. All can be made very simply.

To make a feather edge, cut the stock to proper cushion size adding the usual $\frac{1}{4}$ inch all round for upholstering allowance. Cement tacking tape to the top of the cushion, 1 inch from the edge, as shown in **FIG 6:50**. Then bevel the lower edge with shears to the necessary angle for the desired contour. If you are not sure what the necessary angle is, try a 5 deg. cut, draw the tape down until the bevelled edge of the cushion is flat against the base and note the resulting curvature. If this is unsatis-

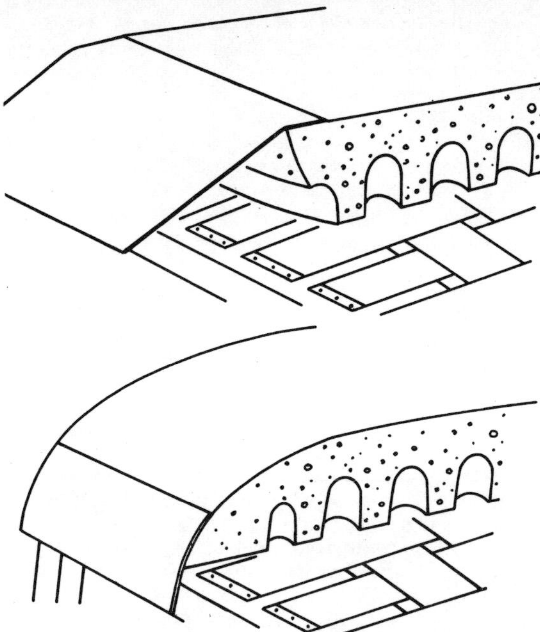

FIG 6:50   Oblique cut to make a feather edge

factory take another few degrees off, and try again, and so on until the desired result is achieved. The tape is then tacked or stuck to the underside of the base.

A cushioned edge is formed by cutting the stock to cushion shape, adding $\frac{1}{4}$ inch all round, plus $\frac{1}{2}$ inch for the edge (a total of $\frac{3}{4}$ inch over base measurement at cushion edge). Cement tape to the top surface of the foam 1 inch from the edge. Tuck the bottom edge of the cushion under so that the edge is flat against the base,

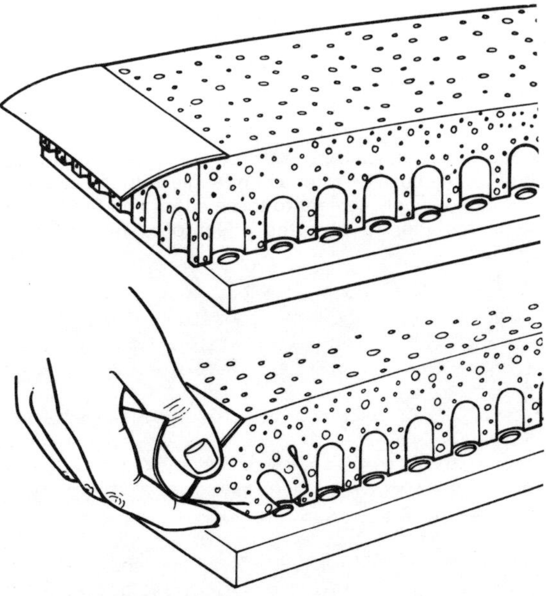

FIG 6:51   Making a cushioned edge

taking care to keep the tape taut, so that the foam does not wrinkle or bunch unevenly (**FIG 6:51**). Finally, tack or stick tape to the base.

For square edges, cut the stock to the desired size, adding the usual $\frac{1}{4}$ inch upholstery allowance all around. Cement tape flat against the vertical edge, covering the entire area and fix the overhang to the base (see **FIG 6:52**).

Heavy-duty latex foam seat mouldings are reinforced by buttresses moulded into the cavities at the front corners and edges. These eliminate the chequer-board marking which can occur on some covers by upward pressure of the walls. Avoid cutting into these reinforced cores if any surgical operations are contemplated. The cruciform reinforcements are clearly visible in the crowns of the cores.

Car manufacturers using buttoned (or 'tufted') cushions in large numbers order latex foam specially moulded for tufting. Tufting can be done from cored stock, but polyether foam is more suitable. When cutting out the cushion, add an extra $\frac{1}{2}$ inch to both length and width for each button.

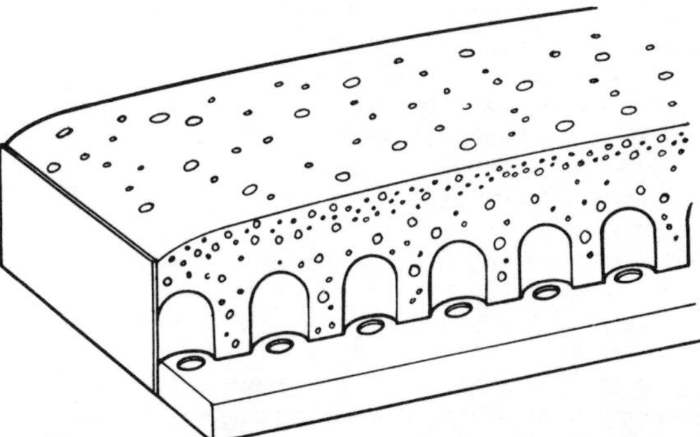

FIG 6:52   A square edge finished with tacking tape

Covering:

Practically any type of fabric is suitable for use over latex foam, but those which stretch excessively should be avoided. When using extremely slippery loose weave or high-pile fabrics, it is generally advisable to cover the foam first with muslin. As opposed to conventional upholstery fillings, latex does not pack down, so no allowance need be made for this. Too much cover tension reduces the depth of the cushion and detracts from its resilient comfort. When covering shaped seats it is some-times advisable to cement the fabric lightly to the latex foam to keep the cover in position. Great care must be taken when solutioning leather and latex, because if the leather is misplaced and the sticking has to be raised, the leather will bring lumps of latex away with it and a neat finish cannot be made at the second attempt.

Interlayers should be used between latex foam and open-weave fabric because the ultra-violet element in sunlight ages rubber. Cloths such as Tygan, woven from polyvinylidene chloride filaments, need an interlayer not only because of the open weave, but also to prevent a chemical reaction between the Tygan and the rubber.

Leather stretches in service and becomes slack over a latex foam cushion. To overcome this fault, a special pre-stretched grade of leather may be obtained, or a fluted design of leather cover should be used, or a thick interlayer of rubberised hair inserted to take up the slack. Leathercloth and moquettes do not need an interlayer or wadding over latex foam.

It is important to drill air holes in the baseboard under each core of a moulded latex cushion. These holes should be at least $\frac{3}{8}$ inch diameter. If they are omitted the cushion will be uncomfortably hard. Whether latex foam needs a spring case under it for the utmost comfort is a matter of controversy and personal taste. Top-quality cars in which headroom is not restricted often employ a spring case. For smaller cars flat springs or Pirelli rubber webbing offer a height-saving compromise.

Polyurethane foams:

Polyester and polyether foams are made from polyurethane, a product of the petrochemical industry. Polyester foam is mainly used in laminated textiles to give warmth with lightness and to impart body to open fabrics. In the motor industry, it is faced with PVC leathercloth and used for crash pads and headlinings.

Polyether is mainly used as stuffing in cheap upholstery and this is the material you see in block form in the DIY shops. A well-known make suitable for load-bearing applications is Dunlop's Dulon. There is also a flame-retardant grade called Dunlop High Resilience, with comfort characteristics approaching those of rubber latex foam. A third type, Dunlopreme D97, is a skeletal foam in which the membranes between the cells have been removed, permitting free flow of air or liquids between cells. It is used in the fuel tanks of racing cars to control surging. The foam filling also damps the ram effect which has been known to rupture fuel tanks in a crash. If the tank is punctured, the foam prevents the rapid spread of flame and so acts as an explosion suppressant.

Choice of foam:

Polyether foams are formulated to give the required characteristics for particular purposes and your chances of picking on the right grade in a DIY shop are slim unless you know what you are looking for. The physical characteristics of polyether foam are quite different from rubber latex foam. The softness of rubber latex depends on its density (weight per cubic foot), which is determined by the air-rubber ratio. The softness of polyether foam can be varied without altering its density and it is not easy to tell the difference between high and low density foams by feel. High density foams perform better in service, but they cost more, so they are not found among the bargain offers. The use of a low-density high-hardness foam in a load-bearing application will lead to loss of hardness and sagging. Choice of density and hardness and the thickness of the foam are the three most important considerations. Remember that rubber latex foam compresses evenly in relation to increasing pressure, while polyether foam shows an initial resistance and then 'gives' almost completely. This disconcerting effect can be modified by crumbling polether foam and mixing the chips with a liquid form of the original foam and compressing the mixture. Several hardnesses are made from chips of different grades of foam and the material is used as a base for polyether or rubber latex foams. Dunlop's trade name for this material is Repol.

Densities of conventional polyether foams range from 1 lb/cu ft to 3 lb/cu ft. Grades from 1 lb to 1.5 lb can be used for squabbing, button-pleated back curtains and other non-loadbearing positions, but should not be used for seating. It is better to use a density of 1.8 lb and above – the higher the better. Once the density has been selected the hardness can be decided to give the type of feel required. Similar densities are usually made in two or three hardnesses. Thickness depends on the type of base on which the foam is to lie. On a plywood or metal base, firm grades need to be at least $3\frac{1}{2}$ inches thick and softer grades need $4\frac{1}{2}$ inches thickness. If a sprung base or rubber webbing is used, these thicknesses may be reduced to 3 inches for firm grades and 4 inches for softer foam. Do not allow the foam to come in direct contact with the seat frame side rails, because it is friable. Where height is a problem, a cushion can be reduced in thickness by laminating different hardnesses of foam together. For instance, 3 inches of soft grade over 1 inch of firm grade, is equivalent to 5 inches of soft grade.

Polyether foams can be moulded almost as well as rubber latex foam, but unless a stock mould is used, the purchaser is expected to pay the tooling cost. The private owner can modify a stock moulding in the same way as latex, or build a special shape from slab and sheet using the latex foam techniques already described.

Button pleating:

Button pleating has been very much simplified by the introduction of polyether foam. All that is needed for door squabbings, back and side curtains and other parts which will not be sat upon, is a $\frac{1}{2}$ inch soft layer stuck to a hardboard casing. The covering is buttoned through to the back of the casing, as shown in **FIG 6:53**. The foam distributes itself evenly under the pressure of the buttoning.

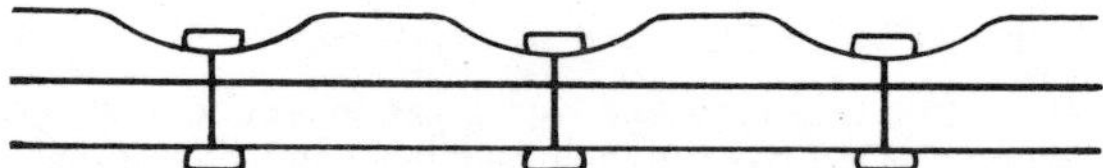

FIG 6:53 Button pleating on soft polyether foam over a firmer layer

Latex foam is not suitable for button pleating. To make button pleated seats and squabs use a layer of soft polyether foam, 1 inch thick, button pleated to a fabric base and lay this over an unpleated cushion of the appropriate firmer grade.

Before embarking on a button pleated upholstery scheme, consider the fact that those deep, tight pleats hold the dust conspicuously, which is why the style fell out of fashion when there were no longer any servants to do the dusting.

CHAPTER 7

Timber bodywork

7:1 Estate car bodywork

7:2 Painting and varnishing

Timber has now been almost entirely superseded by other materials for the construction of car bodywork. The restorer of old cars will meet it, and the attendant rot problems, in the internal framing of steel and alloy panelled bodies on pre-war and some early post-war cars. Careful carpentry, using old parts as patterns for cutting new ones, is called for in renovating such a structure, but the techniques are quite likely to be more familiar to the amateur handyman than welding and panel beating. The visible use of wood is confined to some interior trim and capping pieces, and the bodywork of some estate cars.

7:1 Estate car bodywork

There are two kinds of estate car, shooting brake or 'woodie'. One has a genuine timber frame (traditionally hedge-grown ash) with oak underframe. The other kind is a modified pressed steel body with dummy woodwork attached. In some instances even the dummy 'woodwork' is metal with a grained paint finish, or a wood-grain melamine plastic laminate.

FIG 7:1, which illustrates Briggs Manufacturing Company's Patent No. 656314, shows how a pressed steel door **A** is modified to receive wooden framework **B**, the door pillar **C**, and the horizontal battens **D**, **E** and **F**. The panel portion **A** in section **2** is shaped to support the belt bar **G** and flanged inwardly so that, with a similar flange on the inner panel **H**, a gap is formed for insertion of the sliding glass channel.

The door overlap flange **K** is crimped around the edge of the header strip **L** to support the upper glass run channel. The wood framework **B** is secured by wood screws through the back of the flange **J**. A similar fixing is used for the belt rail **G**. Part of the outer door panel **A** is cut out and set back to provide a recess, and is supported by the upper horizontal strip **M** and vertical angle strip **N** and **P**, as shown in section **3** which is a horizontal section through the forward door pillar, and **4** which is a similar section through the rear door pillar. The cut-out section is also supported by the lower horizontal angle **Q**. The angle **M** has a flange **S** which is spot-welded to the lower edge of the outer door panel. A similar construction is used for the front doors, boot lid, and side and rear quarters of the body.

Many shooting brakes of the 1950's and 1960's were lightly built, and were racked to pieces on flexible chassis frames. Examine the rear floor structure for rot and cracked metalwork, and for cracks in the chassis frame around bolt holes.

Sometimes the front doors of the original body were retained, but if these were too corroded, the original drop lights were mounted in a timber door frame, with an outer panel of 18-gauge aluminium and an inner panel of $\frac{1}{4}$ inch plywood which also formed the inner casing board.

The roof may be metal panelled, or covered with plywood with metal for the sharply curved parts, or it may consist of fabric over closely spaced wooden slats. The upper edge of the cantrail may be swept from front to back, but the curve of the under side has to be restricted to avoid deep grooves for the sliding lights. Generally, a shooting brake body with swept lines and some turn-under to the pillars, all of which means extra work, is made of better materials than the plain box design. When buying timber for bodywork, choose straight grained material without any dark blue or black stains, which indicate incipient rot.

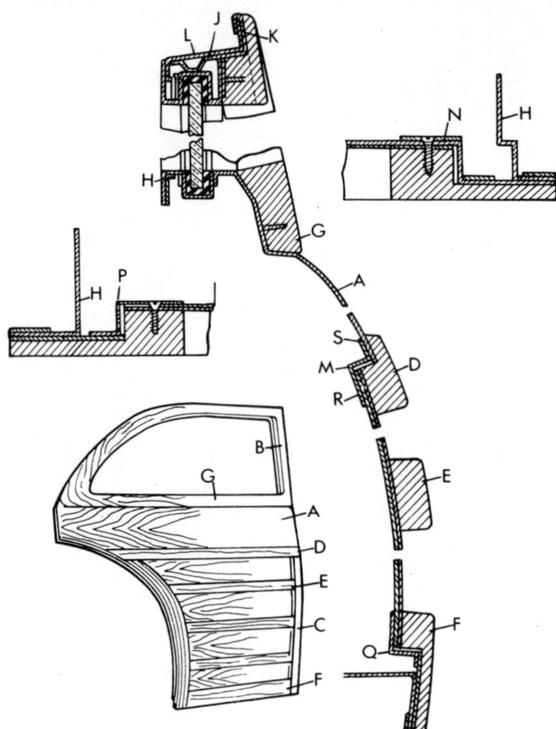

FIG 7:1 Steel door with wooden framing added

A shortage of ash led to the use of various hardwoods after the Second World War, some of which are oily by nature, and will take varnish only to throw if off after a few years. A dressing of linseed oil rubbed into the surface is more effective.

The framework is basic carpentry, most joints being half-laps. If the pillars have broken where the horizontal rails intersect, they may be replaced with pillars notched to take intercostal rails instead of through rails. One of the main troubles with shooting brakes is lack of rigidity in the rear end, which is nearly all door. Angle brackets in the top corners are inadequate, and the racking of the end frame causes rattles, draughts and leaks. The cure for this is to sacrifice six inches of door height and run a 6 inch × 1 inch plank across the top, screwing or bolting it to the pillars at two or more points. Triangular corner plates of $\frac{1}{4}$ inch aluminium alloy bolted to the framing will have a similar effect. It may be possible to place these on the inside of the framework, so that the original doors need not be altered.

Apart from peeling of the varnish on the framing, the commonest fault in old shooting brakes is rotting of the plywood panels. These should be replaced with marine-grade ply or one of the many excellent rigid plastic boards now available. If there are metal panels behind the framing and these are corroded, they must be taken off for rubbing down and repainting. Hardboard was used for the panels of some wartime estate cars. This will probably have bulged due to water absorption and should be replaced with marine plywood, plastic or light alloy. While the panels are off, chamfer the top surfaces of the rails to throw off water.

Some shooting brakes have inadequate door locks, and it is worth looking at these before buying. In some instances it is possible for a thief to remove the back doors complete with nothing more than a small spanner or screwdriver. The hinges should be bolted through and the bolts burred over. Some rear doors have mortice locks with tongues retracted by a square key. These are very easily opened by a thief, and should be replaced with surface locks bolted on the inside of the door. This type of lock is easier to adjust if it rattles, because it can be removed and packed out as required.

When looking round an old shooting brake, see whether the propeller shaft has been fouling the underside of the framing and whether the tyres have been hitting the wings. This is quite a common fault, because many shooting brakes were built on light car chassis, and overloaded.

Cutting wheelarches:

Cutting timber for utility bodywork is very simple, apart from the wheelarches, which may be laminated, steam-bent or cut from the solid. Cutting from the solid is the quickest and cheapest way, but it needs to be done on a bandsaw. Probably the timber merchant will be able to help in this respect.

Some wheelarches are flat on both sides; some are flat on the inside but curved on the outside. We will deal with the flat type first.

The first thing to do is to make a full-scale drawing of the outside of the wheelarch on a sheet of brown paper or hardboard, showing the position of all the joints between the arch and the pillars and rails. The arch cannot be cut out of one piece of timber because it would be too cross-grained to have any strength even if a wide enough plank could be found. An arch is made up of two or three segments spliced together, and now is the time to consider how many sections to use, and where the splices should come. If the wheelarch is a replacement for an existing arch, all this will have already been done, and it is a matter of making a replica. A large number of joints weakens an arch, and a large amount of cross grain weakens it, too, so a compromise has to be found. In practice, an arch of 22 inch radius can be cut from 7 inch wide timber in two segments. The splices should come roughly midway between pillar and rail joints, and if possible all framing joints should be cut out of one side of the arch. In new and replacement work it is far easier to fit a skirt rail and any other intersecting rail right across the bay, and cut out the redundant part after the wheelarch has been fitted, rather than trying to get a good fit with two-part horizontals.

Allow a 6 inch overlap for each splice when marking out the segments on the pattern. Do not cut the curved pattern out of the sheet of brown paper. The flimsy strip resulting from this would be hopelessly inaccurate. Pricking through is the simplest way of marking the wood, but if a template is needed, use hardboard. Mark the pieces of wood N/S 1, 2, 3, O/S 1, 2, 3 on both sides, so that they will not get mixed up. With the bandsaw, cut about $\frac{1}{4}$ inch outside the marked lines to give a margin for error and cleaning up after the joints have been made.

The bevelled splice shown in **FIG 7:3** is stronger than the straight splice, but the latter is easier to make. Whichever is chosen, the cutting lines are gauged from

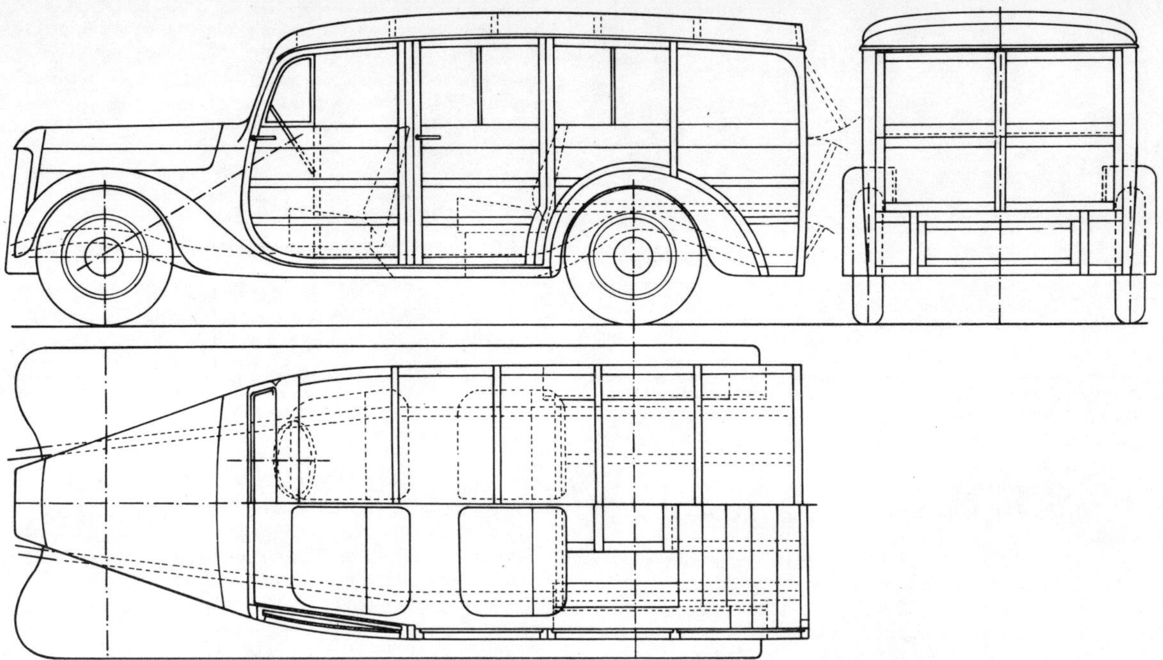

FIG 7:2   Typical shooting brake body of the early fifties with structural wooden framing

the face of the timber. It is very important to cut perfectly square, otherwise the whole arch will be twisted. It is as well to allow a margin for error, by cutting just outside the line. If, on trial assembly, the arch is seen to be twisted when laid down on a flat surface, the offending joint can be pared until correct.

A good fit to the abutments is obtained by clamping them together and sawing down between them with a tenon saw. The spliced joints are usually held together by four No. 10 woodscrews countersunk and $\frac{1}{4}$ inch shorter than the thickness of the wood. Look at the grain of the wood and position the screws so that they go into the straightest part of the grain. This may mean that two screws have to be inserted from one side of the joint and two from the other. Drill pilot holes to avoid splitting cross grain. Do not forget to prime the spliced joints well before final assembly, using old paint or a waterproof sealant, otherwise these joints will certainly rot.

With all the joints screwed up, the arch can be taken back to the bandsaw for trimming (this is a job for two people) or it can be finished by hand. This is not easy, because there is cross grain showing, and the grain at the joints runs different ways. Consequently it is best to use a spokeshave, and not try to sweep right over a joint, which would break off the end grain and spoil the work. A compass plane with an adjustable sole plate can also be used. Do not try to clean up the arch in a spindle moulding machine, as this would tear up the grain, or even break the arch.

Now lay the complete arch on the complete body side frame and mark off the half laps. A large arch may cross three pillars and a side rail as well as the skirt rail, but a half lap is best for all these. Mark the waist rail position at the top of the arch, and drop it into the cuts made for it in the frame members. Mark these on the arch, then take it

out and cut the corresponding laps. Drill and countersink the screw holes for fixing the arch, and it is ready for fitting. It will, or should, need a set of cramps to push it into the joints, not forgetting the primer. Drive the screws from the wheelarch into the straight-grain framing, not the reverse. Finally, clean up the joints and cut away the surplus skirt rail and any other framing which crosses the arch.

Turned-under wheelarches:

Some shooting brake pillars are flat on the inside face and convex on the outer face, and it is not difficult to shape the outside of a flat wheelarch to conform to this line. When the wheelarch as a whole must be curved or 'turned under'

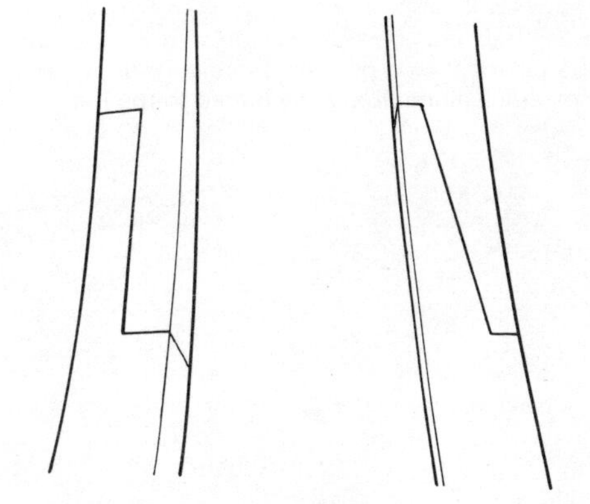

FIG 7:3   A straight splice (left) is easier to cut, but a bevelled splice (right) is stronger

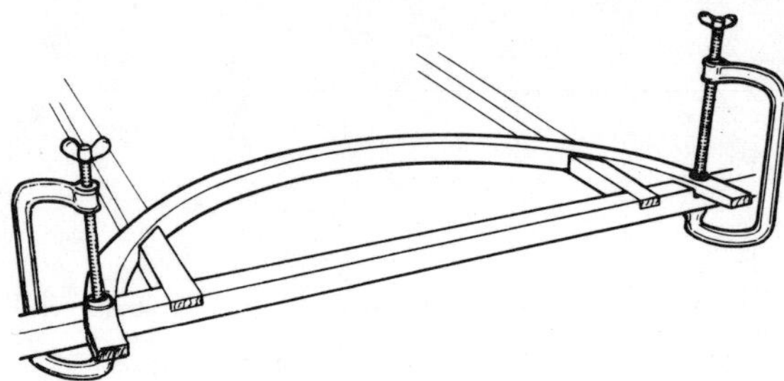

FIG 7:4 Fitting a wheelarch; surplus framing is cut away after attaching the arch

or has a reverse sweep in plan, then it must be cut out of thicker wood to allow for this curvature as well as the finished thickness. For example, a 2 inch thick arch with 1 inch turnunder must be cut from 3 inch thick timber. The method of construction is similar to the flat wheelarch; the difficult part is the marking-out to obtain the correct curvature.

One way is make the arch at full thickness and lay it in position in the side frame without screwing down. Lay a straightedge across two pillars, and use rubber bands to fix a pencil to the end pointing to the wheelarch and just touching the top centre point. Slide the straightedge down the pillars parallel with the skirt rail, and the pencil will mark off the desired shape on the top edge of the arch. Repeat the process on the other side of the arch, then take it out of the frame and trim to shape.

Another method is to mark off 1 inch stations on the pillar and with a straightedge mark corresponding lines across the face of the wheelarch, holding the straightedge parallel to the skirt rail. The lines are continued across the underside of the arch. Each line should be numbered on the pillar and the arch. It is then easy to measure each station on the pillar from the back face, and transfer the measurement to the line on the underside of the wheel-arch. When the marks are joined up, the curve corresponds to the curve of the pillar, and the surplus can be sawn off.

All in all, the timber-framed shooting brake is in-efficient and troublesome. The wooden frame is not readily adaptable to unitary construction, and the type is now superseded by the all-metal utility with a tailgate and folding rear seat, such as the Austin Maxi. It is dangerous to cut the roof off a unit construction car

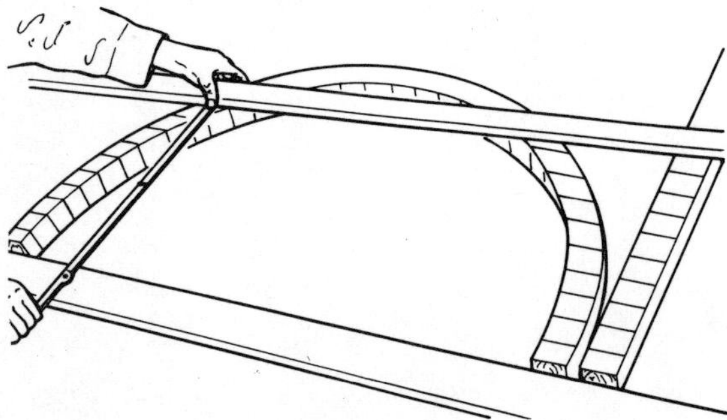

FIG 7:5 Matching a turned-under wheelarch; marking off 1 inch stations

to build a shooting brake, because the shell as a whole is a stressed structure. Cars which appear to be open-top versions of standard saloons have specially reinforced sills and pillars incorporated at the assembly stage, and it is not always practicable to add this reinforcement as part of a conversion.

7:2 Painting and varnishing

It is not possible to paint the panels of a timber-framed shooting brake properly without removing them, because the corners of the panels next to the woodwork are the parts most in need of protection. The panels should be rubbed down or stripped, and treated in the same way as a steel car body.

It is a curious fact that yachtsmen will re-varnish the woodwork of their boat every two years, but expect the varnish on their shooting brake to last for ever! If the varnish on a shooting brake is sound, and not showing any yellow patches or black marks, all it needs is a rubbing down with fine abrasive and a new top coat.

Old, peeling or patchy varnish is best removed altogether, using abrasives or a scraper. One of the best scrapers is a piece of window glass, which costs nothing. Before re-varnishing, fill the grain with a grain filler, preferably of the kind recommended by the varnish manufacturer. Grain fillers may be clear or stained. A stained filler saves time, but it is better to do any staining separately after the grain has been filled and rubbed down. Apply the creamy grain filler across the grain, using a coarse cloth, and wipe off the surplus. A light rub down with medium wet-or-dry paper, used dry, will leave the surface flush. Nothing can be done about black marks where moisture has crept under fittings and penetrated the softer parts of the timber, except to mix some enamels to match the general tone of the wood and paint them over.

At this stage the woodwork can be stained with a diluted naptha wood stain; a dark tone will help to mask imperfections in the wood. Varnish can, of course, be stained, but the disadvantage of coloured varnish is that if it is chipped in service, the lighter colour of the wood shows through.

There is a rather bewildering choice of varnishes today, ranging from the two-can polyurethanes to the phenolics. Two-can polyurethanes are expensive and give a high gloss, but they harden very quickly through the action of a catalyst and do not like anything less than perfect conditions. They are also rather wasteful, because once mixed they start to 'go off' so any surplus must be thrown away. The brushes also need cleaning immediately after use, and once an hour while in use.

It may be found that an alkyd varnish is easier to lay off on the framing of a shooting brake, while a two-can polyurethane can be used indoors for cappings.

Varnishes do not have an undercoat of a different material, but the first coat is often diluted with 25 per cent of the recommended thinner to make it penetrate the timber and so get a better grip on it. The grain filler will in itself have saved a coat of varnish, so three coats will probably be sufficient. Flat the undercoats with fine wet-or-dry paper. When using polyurethane varnish, do not work the brush about more than necessary to spread and lay-off, because with too much working the varnish will cling to the brush and lift off the surface.

CHAPTER 8

Glazing, doors and brightwork

8:1 Glass
8:2 Locks

8:3 Doors
8:4 Brightwork

8:1 Glass

The windows and windscreen of most British cars consist of toughened glass. This is made by chilling the hot sheet in a blast of cold air, setting up surface tension on the principle of Prince Rupert's drops. Toughened glass cannot be cut; any attempt to do so will shatter it. Toughened glass for windscreens is illegal in many countries, and the weight of opinion in Britain too is gradually swinging towards the use of laminated glass. Anyone who has suffered a shattered windscreen while travelling at speed will appreciate the advantage of a laminated screen, although it is more expensive. Plate glass screens may be found in old cars dating from the early 1920's or before.

Cutting glass:

The requisites for cutting glass are a felt-covered table, straightedge, T-square, glass pliers and a six-wheel glass cutter. The jaws of a pair of glass pliers are about $\frac{3}{4}$ inch wide, smooth and parallel when opened about $\frac{3}{16}$ inch. Diamond cutters are unnecessary except for very thin sheet which will not stand the weight of the wheel. Before cutting a sheet of glass, make sure the table is clear of loose nuts, nails or pieces of glass, and that the glass itself is clean and free from grease.

Try the glass cutter on a piece of scrap glass before attempting to cut the sheet. The cutter should be held upright, and run along the straightedge in a single sweep. Never go over a cut twice, and remember that the cut will be $\frac{1}{8}$ inch away from the straightedge. After making the cut, slip the straightedge under the glass with the edge level with the cut. Sharp downward pressure on either side of the cut, using both hands, should now break the glass along the line. Another way to make the break is to put the handle of the glass cutter under the end of the cut and then press down on either side.

When cutting off a narrow strip of glass, up to 2 inches wide, the strip is taken off with the pliers. After making the cut, slide the sheet so that the cut is overhanging the table edge, and parallel with it. Now give a sharp tap with the cutter under one end of the cut. This will start a run along the cut. Grip the strip of glass with the pliers opposite this run and bear down gently. The run should now go right along the cut, leaving the strip of glass in the pliers.

When cutting glass to a paper pattern, a different procedure is used. A one-wheel cutter is used, and the pattern is placed under the glass. The glass is then cut to the pattern, which is followed easily through the glass. A one-wheel cutter is used for this work because it is possible to see the wheel in action, which is not possible with the six-wheel type. The handle of the one-wheel cutter is held between the first and second fingers to keep it at right angles with the glass. The cutter is moved forwards, so that the pattern line is always in view. After completing the pattern, further side cuts are made to assist in breaking out the required shape. The pliers are invaluable for taking off the surplus after starting a run with a tap of the cutter.

The cutting of laminated safety glass is more complicated, because two thin sheets of glass and the acetate interlayer have to be cut. The procedure is much the same, except that both sides have to be cut separately. Cut both sides and break first one side and then the other, with the straightedge underneath. After breaking, the glass must be pressed down over the table edge, and a knife or razor blade used to cut the acetate centre.

Laminated glass is more liable to run off the cut than

ordinary glass, because it is thinner. Care should be taken to get an even continuous score with the wheel. The secret of glass cutting is confidence, so practice on pieces of scrap before attempting to cut a valuable sheet.

The cut edge can be ground with an electric sander, fitted with a fine disc. Fix the sander in a vice, and work the glass across it, using plenty of water. A good ground edge can be formed in a few minutes, and this can be polished with 280 rubbing down paper and Belco rubbing compound, finishing off with a rag. Alternatively the glass may be laid on the table and the sander run over the edges. As the edges of fixed windows will not be seen in position, a polish is not necessary, but all sharp edges should be removed, and the corners rounded.

The successful glass-cutter knows from experience how much pressure to apply to the wheel while making an even sweep right across the sheet. The best way to learn the art is to practice on scrap glass until you have gained confidence.

Glass stiffening rails:

The edges of sliding windows and sidescreens are sometimes stiffened with a metal channel section, which used to be called Gothic channel. It is lined with rubber and is removed by simply knocking it off with a piece of timber slid up the surface of the glass. To replace it, stand the glass on edge, place a strip of sheet rubber about 2 inches wide on the top edge, equalising the rubber on either side. Knock on one end of the channel with a mallet, so that the rubber folds down on either side of the glass and up into the channel. Work along the channel until it is fully down on the glass, then cut off the surplus rubber with a sharp knife.

The thickness of rubber varies from $\frac{1}{32}$ inch to $\frac{1}{8}$ inch according to the size of the channel, and the correct size, if unknown, must be found by experiment. The old rubber in the channel will give a clue, but will probably appear thinner than the new material. Two people should do this job, because it is impossible to hold the glass, the rail, the rubber and the mallet all at the same time. Do not stick the rubber with any adhesive. It is not necessary, and its use will make it impossible to remove the stiffener without damaging the glass or the rail, or both.

Fitting safety glass:

Rubber glazing strips with moulded channels which take the glass and the edge of the body aperture have proved most successful, and of these, the types of strip which hold the glass outside, or opposite, the edge of the windscreen aperture (**FIGS 8:1** and **8:2**) are by far the best.

The disadvantage of glazing schemes in which a rubber section holds the screen behind the lip of the body aperture is that the rubber section is not rigid enough in itself to hold the combined weight of the screen and the wind-load produced when the car is travelling at speed. Assistance from behind in the form of metal stiffening or fillets is necessary, but very undesirable. When this is done, the glass is once more in a channel, but it is an intermittent channel, and the danger of producing high local stresses is very great (**FIG 8:3**).

A soft rubber channel might be thought capable of absorbing irregularities and ironing out local stresses, but

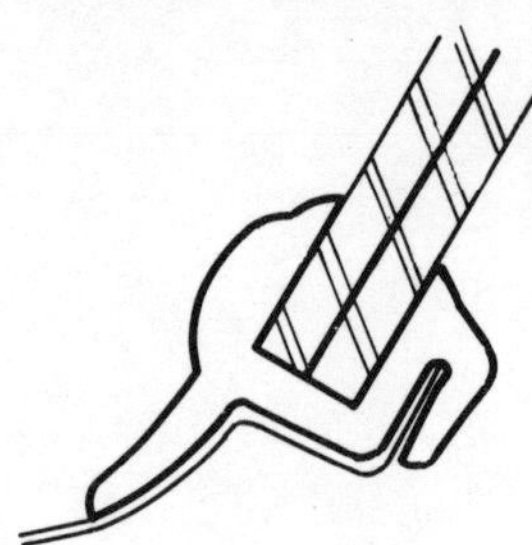

FIG 8:1   Glazing strip: glass outside body flange

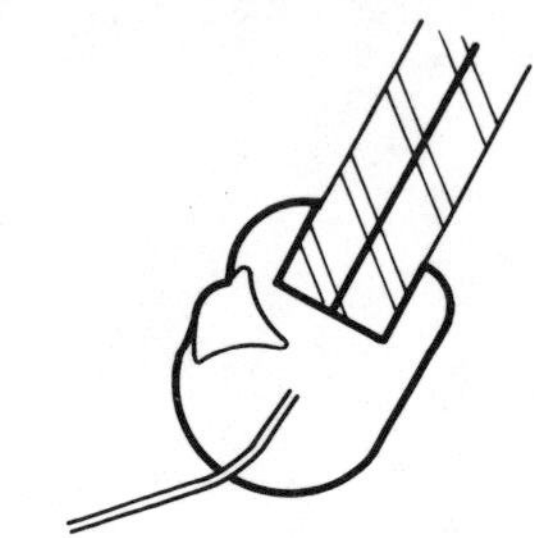

FIG 8:2   Glazing strip: glass opposite body flange

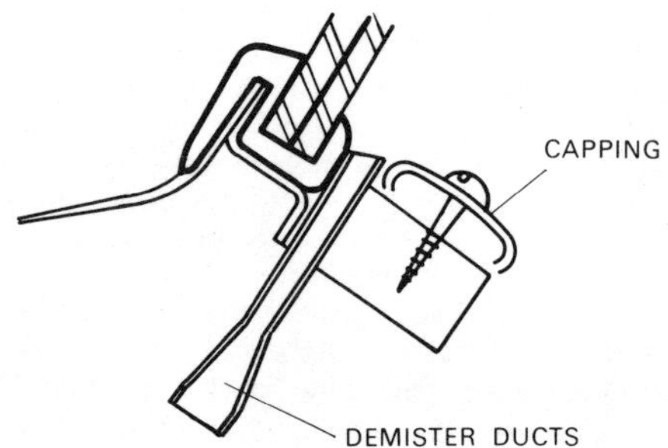

FIG 8:3   Glazing strip: glass inside body flange

the compressibility of rubber is much less than is generally supposed. It requires a load of 30,000 lb to reduce the thickness of one square inch of rubber from $\frac{1}{8}$ inch to $\frac{3}{32}$ inch. No wonder that glass breaks when attempts are made to use the compressibility of rubber to absorb stress or irregularities of shape. It is not the compressibility but the flexibility of the rubber section that matters. Even a fairly stiff rubber will provide sufficient flexibility if mounted as shown in **FIGS 8:1** and **8:2**.

A rubber glazing section should be used in preference to a curved frame, which must be individually checked with the curvature of the screen, and again checked with the curve of the body aperture. The fitting of curved laminated windscreens into separate frames of the type previously used with flat glass leads to very considerable trouble. If only toughened glass has to be considered the problem is simplified because this type of glass may be safely sprung into position, and a metal frame may be used if desired.

For very difficult bends of short radius the design tolerance is increased from plus or minus $\frac{1}{16}$ inch to plus or minus half the thickness of the glass. Curved toughened glass of this type is much more rigid, and it is not possible to spring it into place. If it is desired to use a metal frame, then the channel that takes the glass must be twice as wide as the thickness of the glass, and it will be necessary to use a glazing compound to mount the glass. Suitable compounds are Bostik Glazing Compound and Bostik 1222, Seelastik, and Eldro Dum-Dum.

Because of its low compressibility rubber glazing strip cannot be relied upon to seal the aperture against water. The name sealing strip is a misnomer. Run a bead of sealant around the body aperture before mounting the rubber on the lip. This may be a three-handed job with old designs, needing two people to hold the screen and one to manipulate the rubber. A small screwdriver with the tip softened and bent up at an angle may be useful. Modern designs of strip incorporate a draw-string, and with these it is possible to put a screen in single-handed. The butt joint of a glazing strip should be made at the top of a screen or window.

Before removing a crazed toughened glass screen, cover all apertures in the scuttle and gearbox and seal the covers down with adhesive tape. A few minutes spent doing this thoroughly will save many more minutes picking out tiny fragments. Arrange a dust sheet or old blanket to catch the fragments before knocking the screen in.

Chromium plated beading:

Some glazing strips have a filler strip covered by a chromium beading on the face. To remove this, take off the cover plates to be found at top and bottom centres of the screen and ease the lips of rubber away as the bead is progressively pulled out of the rubber. Remove the rubber filler strip by inserting a small screwdriver behind the strip and easing it out of its channel. The ends of the filler strip will usually be found at the centre of the top of the screen. Remove the glass by pressing at the bottom corners from inside, while another person stands by to take the glass.

Before fitting a new glazing strip, clean off all old sealant. Run a new bead of sealant round the flange of the body and put on the new strip, starting at the bottom corners. Run a bead of sealant round the glass channel of the rubber, before inserting the glass, commencing at the bottom. Ease the rubber lip outwards over the glass with a small screwdriver as the screen is pressed into space.

Clear the channel in which the filler strip fits of all burrs, and lubricate it with soft soap or soapy water. Clayton Wright Ltd., of Wellesbourne, Warwickshire, supplied a special tool for inserting the filler strip. Thread the filler strip into the handle of this tool and about 2 inch through the eye of the tool. Starting about 3 inch from the top centre, press the eye into the filler channel. Hold the short free end of the strip, and pull the tool round the screen, keeping the eye of the tool pressed firmly into the channel. Cut off the surplus and press the short ends into the channel with the spur of the tool. Refit the chromium bead, using the small screwdriver. Make sure there is sealant all the way round under the outer lip, and wipe off the surplus.

Tee-root windscreen rubbers:

FIG 8:5 shows the Tee-root windscreen rubber used on old Humber and Talbot cars with a windscreen frame.

If this rubber has to be replaced, the outer edge **A** should be inserted into the frame first. The tubular section **B** is then deflected to the dotted position shown, and Tee-root edge **C** is then forced into the channel with a blunt screwdriver. Lubrication of both the rubber and the frame channel with Rozalex or soft soap will help. Windscreen frames, originally made for timber bodies, are now obsolete, and a rubber glazing strip is mounted directly on a flange in the window aperture.

Removing windscreens:

In most instances some interior casings have to be removed to give access to the windscreen glazing rubber. In the early Jaguars, for instance, the gloveboxes and instrument panel have to come out as well as all the polished cappings and tacking fillets. A list of the items to be removed is given in the Workshop Manual, but if this is not available, proceed step by step, and do not use force until the glazing rubber is clear and a thin-bladed tool has been run round under the lip of the rubber to break the seal. Prise the chrome finisher from the outside, and if there is a separate rubber locking strip underneath, pull this out, too. Then place a block of wood on the glass and using this as a fulcrum insert a lever between the top of the windscreen aperture flange and the sealing rubber

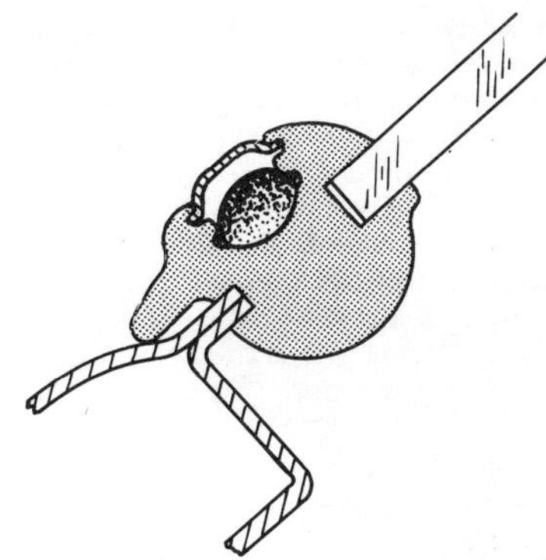

FIG 8:4 Glazing strip with chrome bead

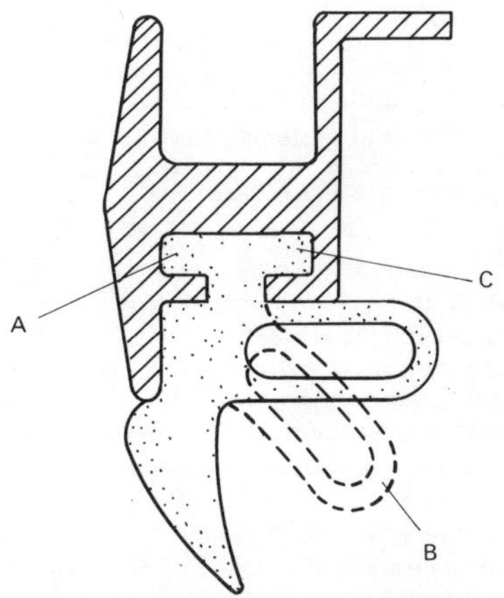

FIG 8:5 Tee-root type windscreen rubber

and push the windscreen inwards. Repeat this along the top edge of the screen until the windscreen can be withdrawn into the car. In some other makes the windscreen lies in front of the aperture flange and must be removed outwards. Locate the flange by poking under the rubber lips with a thin screwdriver.

If the old rubber is to be used again, make sure there are no chips of broken glass embedded inside the channel, and run round the aperture flange with the fingers to find any kinks or rough spot welds. These cause stress concentrations which are enough to break the glass, particularly laminated glass. Such protrusions should be filed flat before refitting the screen. When fitting some types of rubber it is necessary to thread two turns of blind cord around inside the flange channel to keep it open. These are pulled out as the screen goes in. In most cars the screen goes in top edge foremost. Do not try to fit one end first and then the other. Some manufacturer's recommend that the sealant should be injected under the outer lip after the screen has been installed, using a copper nozzle to avoid scratching the glass. If there is a separate chrome finishing strip, the underside should be coated with Bostik 1251 and allowed time to become tacky. Wipe off surplus sealant with white spirit, not cellulose thinners which damages the paintwork.

Removing door glasses:

There are two main types of windows on car doors; one is mounted in a separate frame screwed or bolted to the inner pressing, while in the cheaper type the glasses slides in channels between the inner and outer pressings. To remove the separate frame, take off the door trim casing and look for the screws or bolts holding the window frame to the door. There may also be two more screws holding the lower ends of the glass runs. Collect all packing pieces and washers and make a note of where they came from. Unclip the weatherstrip before withdrawing the window frame.

Vent panes:

Small swivelling ventilating windows, often mis-called quarter lights, usually have a frame of their own, screwed into the window frame. Strip out the rubber to find the retaining screws. The pivot can be tightened by the nut on the shaft, which will be found in an access hole under the trim casing. A broken ventilator usually has to be replaced as a unit.

Removing frameless door glasses:

1 Wind the window down, remove trim casing.
2 Unscrew regulator mounting screws, leaving regulator dangling.
3 Slide regulator arm out of glass holder, and take out the stop limiting downward movement of the glass. In some models it may be necessary to slacken the window runner on the hinge side of the door. The retaining screw will be found near the bottom of the door.
4 Unscrew the bottom of the window runner on the lock side of the door (the screw will probably be found near the bottom of the end of the door) and push the runner aside. The window glass can then be lifted upwards out of the door. Some glasses need turning endways to get

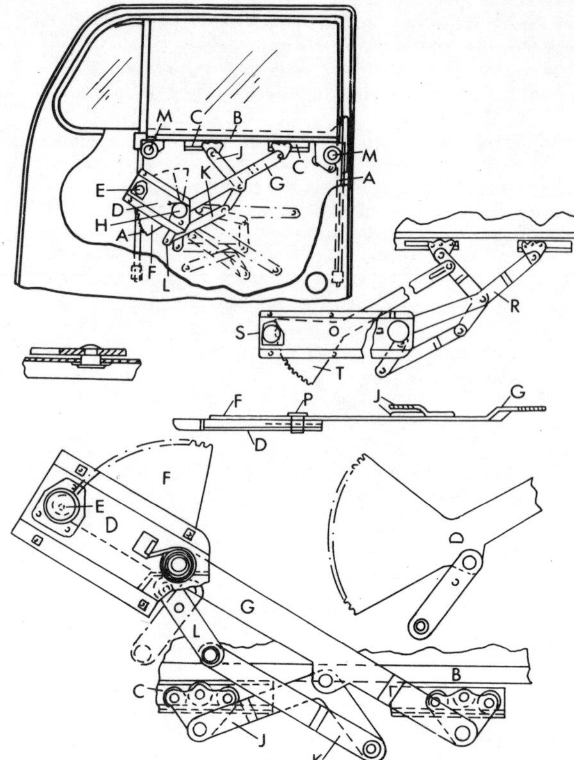

FIG 8:6 Typical window winder mechanism; the components are described in the text

them out. If the runners are very rusty and the felts are worn or swollen, they should be renewed.

Missing window glass:

If a sliding light is missing and a replacement has to be made, it will be necessary to measure the width between the channels in which the glass is to slide. This is done with a trammel, consisting of two laths with pointed ends. One is slotted down the middle, and the other has a clamping bolt passing through the slot, and a wing nut. A piece of tubing and a rod inside it can also be used.

Window winders:

Modern window winders often employ a 'lazy-tongs' system of levers, in which the weight of the window glass is counterbalanced by the force in a coiled spring, as shown in **FIG 8:6**, which is a drawing of British Patent 610142 (Roethel Engineering Corporation and J. H. Roethel). In this system the vertically sliding glass has a metal bottom channel **B** fitted with roller guides **M** in the glass run channels **A**. The main lifting arm **G** is pivoted to a roller guide **C** running on the underside of the bottom glass channel. The balance arm **J** is pivoted to a second roller guide **C** on the same glass channel.

The window mechanism is operated by a handle which turns a driving pinion engaging the toothed sector **T**. The toothed sector, integral with the main lifting arm, is pivoted on a mounting plate **S**. The outer end of the lifting arm is pivoted to a hanger bracket on one of the roller guides. The mounting plate is fitted with a counter-balancing spring **H**. Mounted below the main lifting arm and pivoted to it is an elbow-shaped balance arm **J**. One end of this balance arm is pivoted to the second roller guide, while the other end is pivoted to a control arm **K** which in turn is pivoted to a lever **L** the other end of which is centred on the mounting plate.

There are many other designs, but nearly all consist of a system of levers and one or more balance springs. The systems are lubricated with grease when they are assembled, and the rollers and slides get dry after several years. A little lubrication works wonders.

8:2 Locks

There is a steady flow of new patent specifications for car door locks. It seems that every new model has to have a new kind of lock, or at least a lock that looks different, although most of them are made by the same company. In recent years, safety legislation has taken a part in this process, leading to the development of 'burst-proof' locks. **FIG 8:7** shows a comparatively simple example of a 'child-proof' safety lock (British Patent 641,871 by Wilmot-Breeden Ltd. and H. J. Spicer). The main object of this design is to make the inside handle inoperative when required, so that a child cannot open the door while playing with it.

The mechanism consists of a sliding bolt **A** loaded by the compression spring **B**. (Compression springs are preferable to expanded springs with hooked ends, which may fail through wear or fatigue). The bolt is slid back against the action of the spring by the bolt lever **C** which is mounted on the pivot **D**. The bolt lever is actuated either by the lever **E** attached to the outside handle and pivoted at **F** or by the rear lever **G** pivoted at **H** and operated by the inside handle. The rear lever **G** has a stud **J** which engages a notch **L** in the bottom lever **K** which is pivoted at **M**.

The front edge of this lever projects from the free edge of the door similarly to the lock bolt, and the front end has a slot **R** which may be engaged by a coin or the edge of a car key. The lever **K** has an over-centre spring **N** which will hold the lever in its forward operative position or in its retracted inoperative position. If the bottom lever is moved to its projecting position while the door is open, this locks the lever and after closing, the door can only be opened with the outside handle.

The lock is also designed so that it may be locked by the inside handle and then it cannot be opened by the outside handle. This is done by the gap **P** in the rear lever, which by rotation of the inside handle in the reverse direction, engages the tail **Q** of the bolt lever. Should the base lever be inadvertently moved to its projecting position when the bolt and rear levers are interlocked it will be ineffective, because its notched end will not engage the stud on the rear lever. The base lever will be pushed back automatically to its non-projecting position, when the rear lever is returned to normal, by the action of the stud on the inclined and rounded portion of the upper surface of the base lever.

Another form of safety catch described in the same specification and shown in **FIG 8:8** has a spring-loaded forked member **S** pivoted at **T** and engaging a stud **V** on the standing pillar. When the door is moved to its closing position the fork is rocked by engagement with the stud to hold the door closed. For opening the door, the fork can be rocked by either an inside or outside handle. Associated with the inside handle is a lever **W** operated by a spindle **X** parallel with the inside face of the door. This lever has a shoulder **AA** which engages with the toe of another lever **Y**. This upper lever is exposed by a gap in the edge of the door and can be actuated by a coin inserted in the notch in the outer end. When these two levers are in contact the lock cannot be operated by the inside handle.

Push-button door latches:

Push-button door latches, separated from the barrel lock into which the key is inserted, have largely replaced the turning-handle type. An example is shown in **FIG 8:9** which is based on British Patent 633,252 (Morris Motors Ltd. and R. Welton-Cook). A claw-shaped latch **E** is

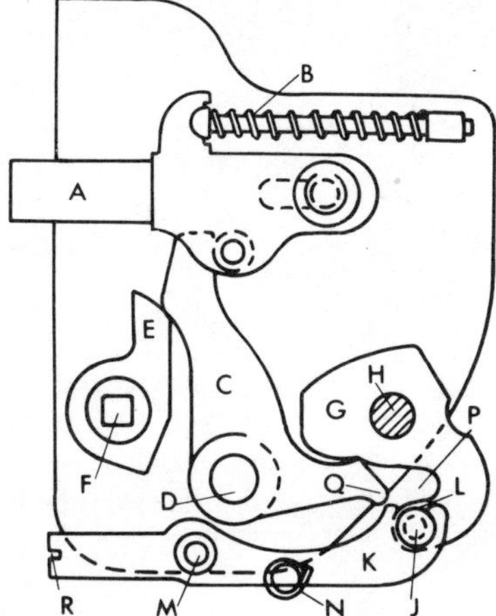

FIG 8:7   Child-proof safety lock; the components are described in the text

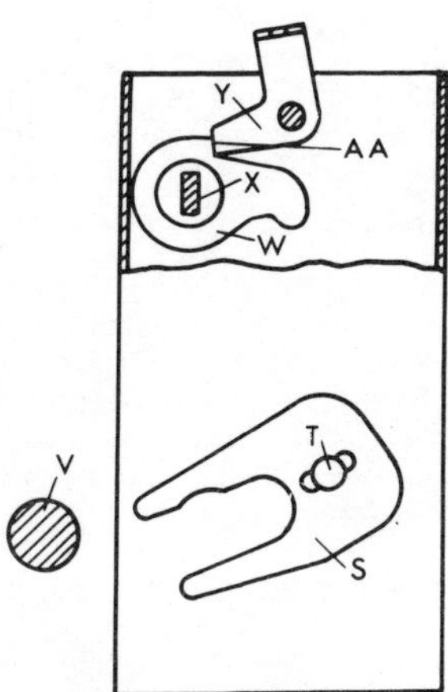

FIG 8:8   Another form of safety lock; the components are described in the text

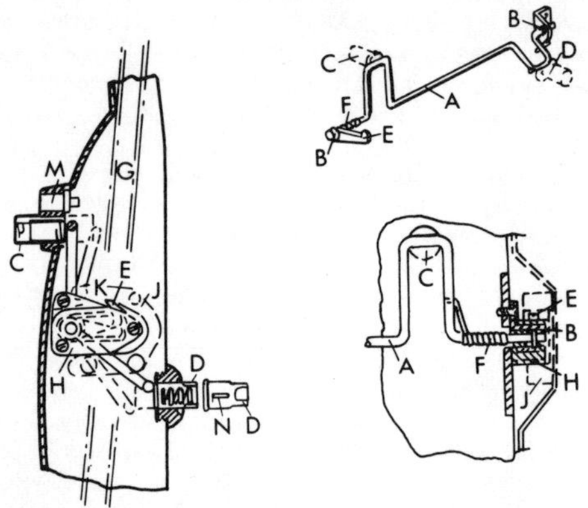

FIG 8:9 Push-button door latch mechanism, as described in the text

mounted on a two-throw crankshaft **A** which is rotated by the outside push-button **C** acting against one throw of the crankshaft, while the inside push-button acts against the second throw. A torsion spring **F** maintains the cranks against the buttons, which are hollow and fitted with anti-rattle springs.

An external barrel lock **M** is fitted with a plate which prevents the push-button being depressed when the barrel is in the locked position. The door is fitted with a fixed external handle, in which the push-button can be mounted.

To prevent unintentional opening of the door through accidental depression of the interior push-button, the button is fluted so that it can be partially rotated in its escutcheon. A pin fixed diametrically across the inner end of the escutcheon passes through the L-shaped slot **N**. When the button is turned clockwise, the pin enters the leg of the slot, and is prevented from being depressed.

Push-button locks are characterised by remote control from the inner side of the door. **FIG 8:10** shows the locking mechanism of the Austin Maxi, in which the lock is at rightangles to the control rods, and sliding latches have replaced internal push-buttons.

8:3 Doors

Dismantling a door:

A modern car door (**FIG 8:11**) consists of two steel pressings, the outer clenched over the edge of the inner; everything else is removable. In the event of trouble with locks or winders, remove the winder handle and the door pull handle or elbow rest. This may be a plastics foam moulding with a hard skin, held by two coarse-thread screws entering nylon captive nuts. Remove the latch surround or bezel, which should leave the door trim panel held only by its top edge, which is tucked under the waist rail capping, and by the spring clips around the sides and bottom edge. These engage in nylon cups in the door inner pressing. If a screwdriver is inserted under the edge of the trim pad a slight angle above the surface of the pad, it will be possible to prise the spring clips out of their cups without scratching the visible paint on the inner pressing.

You may find that the whole of the inner pressing is covered with a sheet of transparent plastics sheet, secured with adhesive tape around the edges and trapped under the nylon cups and captive nuts. This is a sure sign

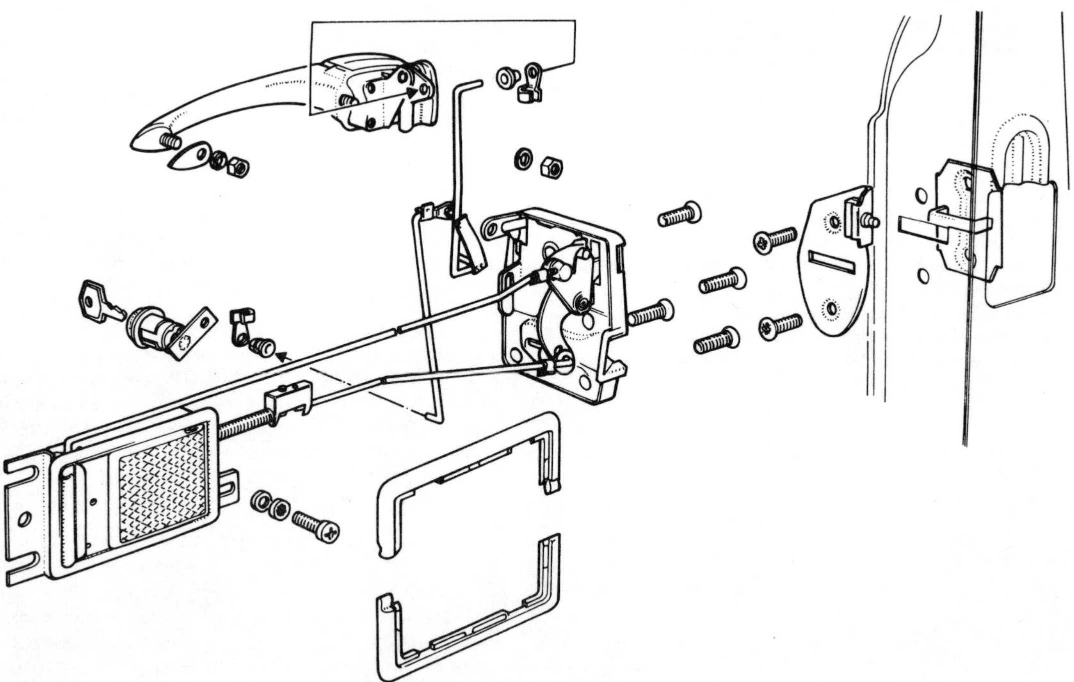

FIG 8:10 Austin Maxi door lock components

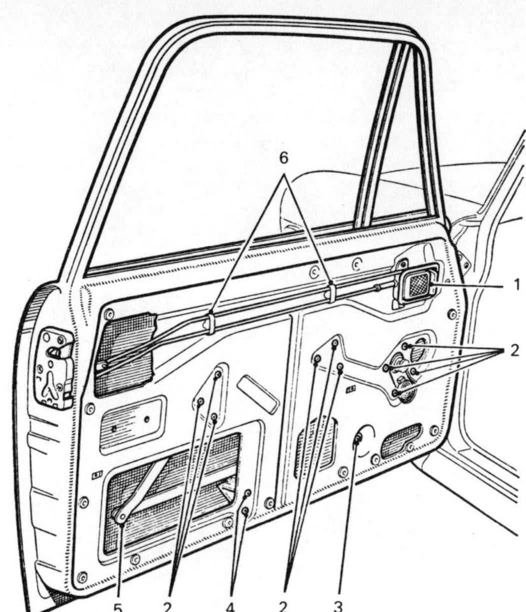

FIG 8:11   Typical pressed steel door (BLMC 1100)

Key to Fig 8:11   1 Door lock remote control   2 Window winder mounting screws   3 Ventilator screw   4 Door stop screws   5 Window winder linkage   6 Anti-rattle clips

that the door mechanism has not been lubricated since it left the factory. The first thing to do is to look carefully for any loose secrews, nuts or washers which have fallen out of place and become wedged between the plastic sheet and the inner panel. Their position will give a clue to their original purpose. Then peel away part of the adhesive tape to make a hand-hole and grope around inside the lower part of the door. Surprising items may be found there—anything from a packet of sandwiches to strips of sound-insulating material which have come adrift from the inner side of the outer pressing. It is quite likely that you will find all the screws holding the winder mounting plate are loose or fallen out. Tighten these by pushing a screwdriver through the polythene sheet if you do not wish to remove it. The polythene can be refixed in place easily with a sealing compound, so do not hesitate to strip it off if necessary.

It will now be possible to see what, if anything, is wrong with the winder or lock mechanisms, by actuating the controls and watching the result. Rear door locks are sometimes put out of action by passengers' attempts to open them from the inside, not knowing that a child-proof safety catch is in operation. Check that the safety catch is in the 'off' position. If the door cannot be opened from the inside with the catch off, it probably means that the remote control rod operating the bolt has been pulled away from its lever at the lock end. The pin is held in the lever by a minute spring clip, which may not be damaged. Check that the other remote control rod operating the locking lever is functioning correctly. There is provision for adjustment at the ends of these rods, but before altering the setting make sure that the trouble is not due to loose mounting screws.

If the barrel locks are stiff and dry, now is a good opportunity to take them out and apply a little graphite grease or oil through the keyhole. The result of overdoing this will be an oily key in your pocket or in your wife's handbag, for which she will not thank you. The barrel lock assembly is held in place by a spring clip on the inside. Door push-buttons simply actuate a plunger rod connected to a lever. They are returned to place by a coil spring around the rod. If the outer door handle is broken, not much can be done about it. They are not worth the trouble and expense of trying to braze and re-plate.

A clean break might be repaired with epoxy resin, but this could be held against you if the joint parted suddenly, causing a passenger to fall. It is safer to buy another handle, either new or from the scrap yard. Ventilator catches are not readily repaired either, but in this case it usually means buying a complete ventilator assembly.

Replacing the trim panel:

To replace the trim panel, tuck the top edge under the capping, then snap the spring clips into their cups with a smack of the hand, having previously ascertained that their points are resting in the cups. If one of these clips is badly bent through being forced against the door pressing instead of the aperture in the cup, it will never fit properly, and must be replaced, which means lifting the leathercloth from the casing board. Remember that hardly anything on a car body is flat, so that there is a right and a wrong position for the collar under the winding handle.

Removing a lock:

1 Disconnect the spring clip holding the remote control rod to the lock. It may also be necessary to slacken or remove the outer, or lock side, window runner. The screw holding this will be found in the end of the door, near the bottom.
2 Push aside or remove the window runner through access hole.
3 Unscrew the lock-mounting screws in the plate on the outside of the end of the door, holding the lock mechanism with the other hand.
4 The retaining screws holding the door handle are now accessible from inside the door, and the door handle complete with push-button plunger is removed. If a new door handle plunger is to be fitted, the length should be adjusted by comparing the setting with the old plunger.

Removing window winder:

Wedge glass in the up position and remove the arm from the glass channel. Undo winder mounting screws and withdraw the mechanism through the lower access hole. Winders are replaced as a unit, but it may be possible to mend a broken spring by softening and reshaping the end, then tempering dark blue.

Adjusting doors:

Timber-framed doors, which may be found in vintage cars and some post-war sports cars, consist of an ash frame with steel gussets and a strut screwed to them, as shown in **FIG 8:12**. The timber frame of the door may have warped, or the whole body may have settled on the chassis, with the result that the bottom (or rocker bar) of the door fouls the tread plate. The proper way to rectify

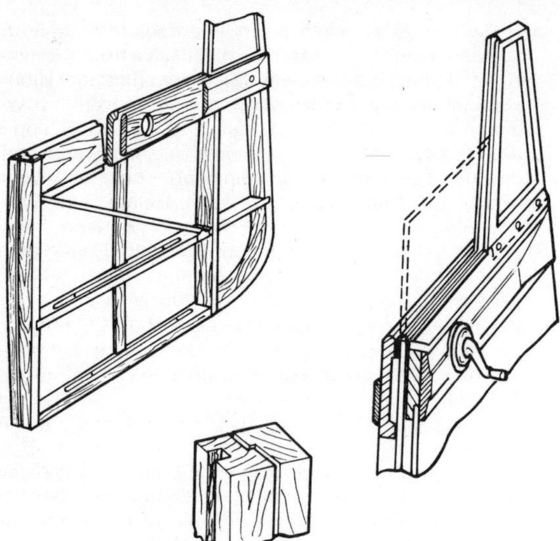

FIG 8:12   Construction of a timber frame door

this fault is to take off the tread plate, ease the rocker panel with a plane or chisel, and refit the tread plate.

Alternatively, it may be possible to lift the door by re-seating the hinges, packing out the lower hinge and cutting the upper hinge rebate a little deeper. If brass hinges have been used, a quick way of achieving the same effect is to put a small spanner between the plates of the bottom hinge and slowly close the door on it. This bows the hinge plates and increases the clearance between the bottom of the door and the hinge pillar, so raising the outer end of the door. This trick should not be tried on modern welded bodies with steel hinges, because the steel hinge plates are too thick to bend easily, and the pressure may fracture a weld.

Pressed steel doors, which consist of inner and outer pressings and a trim panel, do not drop out of shape. If a steel door is binding, either the body shell has been distorted, the hinges are loose or the notched striker plate engaged by the lock bolt needs adjusting. Even a comparatively light rear impact, such as a 'bump up the back' at traffic lights, can distort the door openings. This is put right with a body jack. Wear of the hinge pins is often a problem, too, the process being speeded up by lack of lubrication. While the pins can be replaced, wear of a hinge leaf may be more difficult to rectify.

Door hinge adjustments:

Car door hinges, even on popular cars, used to be more elaborate than they are today, and many of the older types are still in service. **FIG 8:13** shows an elegant design patented by the Pressed Steel Company and L. R. Morphew (British Patent 638,798). Each hinge leaf **A** is pivoted on a bush **B** drilled eccentrically and held in engagement with a ball bearing **D** by a pin **E** passing through the bushes and the ball. The bushes are rotable in the hinge leaves and can be locked in position by the set screws **H**. A coiled spring **F** surrounds the base of the pin to give a resilient thrust on the ball. Each eccentrically-drilled bush has a collar **C** with a number of holes which can be engaged with a C spanner or similar tool, so that the bush can be turned to give lateral as well as fore-and-aft door adjustment.

There are several variations of this idea, using cones or half balls. If one of these hinges has to be dismantled, be very careful not to lose the cone or ball, as spares may no longer be obtainable.

Modern door hinges are very much simpler (see **FIG 8:11**), consisting of a steel hinge pin with two phosphor-bronze washers to take the wear. One arm of the hinge is welded to the door or to the hinge pillar, while the other is attached to the hinge pillar or door inner pressing with three screws. There is no provision for adjustment except at the striker plate.

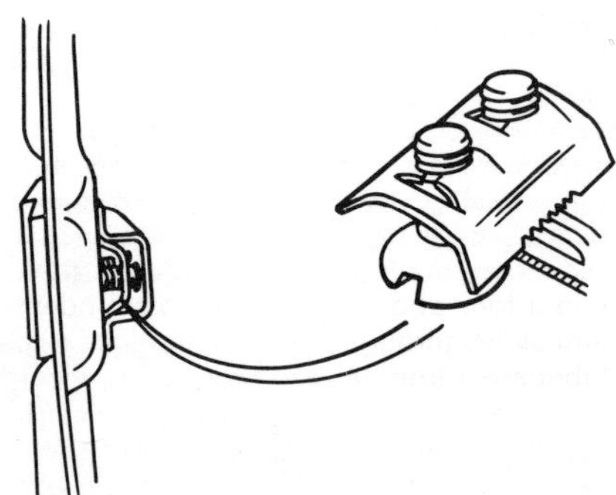

FIG 8:14   Striker plate held by a serrated twin spire nut (right) inside the pillar

Striker plates:

FIG 8:14 shows one design of striker plate, using a twin Spire nut to engage sheared ribs on the inside of the pillar. Note that more than a friction grip is provided to withstand continual slamming of the door. There are various designs of striker plate, but they all provide vertical and horizontal adjustment. These plates are often grossly over-lubricated with graphite grease, which soils clothing.

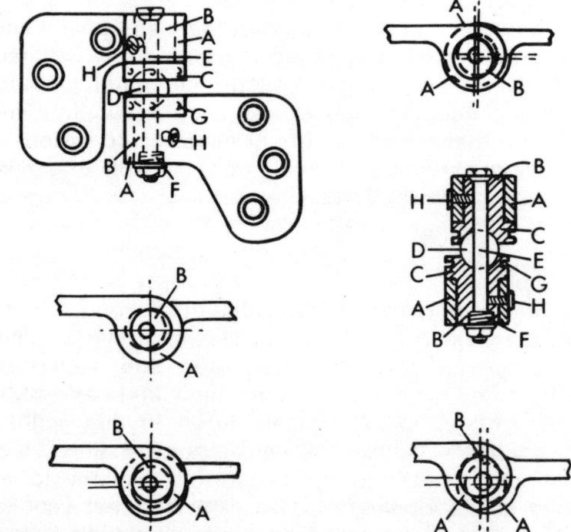

FIG 8:13   Adjustable door hinge; the components are described in the text

Adjusting door locks:

First make sure that the catchpawl mounting screws on the end of the door are tight. Then adjust the striker plate, by loosening the screws and moving the plate inwards or outwards, up or down.

Bonnet lock:

The bonnet lock striker plate is adjustable by slackening the screws in their slotted holes. The bonnet lock bolt has a screwdriver slot or flats on the end, and a locknut at the base so that its length can be adjusted.

Boot lock:

The boot lock striker plate or U-shaped rod has slotted holes for adjustment. The boot lid hinges should be lubricated periodically.

Tailgate:

The tailgate lock striker plate is usually adjustable, and the tailgate hinge retaining bolts are also adjustable. Rattles and leaks can be stopped by step-by-step adjustments at both ends of the tailgate.

Door checks:

Older cars have door checks made of thick rubberised fabric or belting, secured to the door and hinge pillar by screwed or bolted plates. These fabrics used to rot, and if the door were caught by a strong wind, they would break unexpectedly, and the door would fly beyond its normal travel, doing considerable damage to the pillars and surrounding panels. If you acquire an old car with this kind of door check, it will pay to renew them if they are frayed.

Modern door checks usually consists of either a straight or a jointed folding strut, with a rubber buffer which is compressed against the inside of the inner door pressing. The outer end of the strut is attached to a lug welded to the hinge pillar by a clevis pin, which is secured by a splitpin in a hole in the small end. Garage mechanics often fail to replace this splitpin after taking a door off. Clevis pins have been known to rattle out, with disastrous results, so make sure that yours are secure (there are four of them in a four-door saloon). In most modern cars the check arm slides through a slot in the door pressing and needs lubrication from time to time.

Leaky doors and windows:

The sealing of door and window openings has been vastly improved, and they should now be watertight, not merely draughtproof. Leakage under the bottoms of the doors leads to corrosion of the floor pan, and the cure is to renew the sealing strip. Do not use latex foam or polyether foam strips for this; they have interconnecting cells which pump water into the car as the door closes. Non-intercellular sponge rubber such as Sorbo can be obtained in $\frac{7}{16}$ inch $\times$ $\frac{3}{8}$ inch strips for the purpose.

An annoying fault on modern cars is the solid rubber sealing strip which falls away from its mounting flange in the door opening. Attempts to stick it back in place by local additions of adhesive are sometimes unsuccessful, and the best thing to do in such cases is to remove the strip completely. Clean off the old adhesive from the metal and the channel in the rubber. Make sure that both rubber and metal are dry and free from grease all round. It will probably be noticed that the original cement was slapped on carelessly, with too much on some parts and none on others. Take time in spreading rubber cement evenly on the mating surfaces, allow the recommended drying time, and then replace the rubber strip, working it well into the corners, and close the door on it until the cement has set. The butt joint between the two ends of the strip should be a force fit so that the strip is in effect pre-loaded to spring it out against the body shell. If it is on the short side, or worn along the sill edge, scrap it and buy a new piece. The overlap at the butt joint of the rubber strip should be $\frac{3}{8}$ inch at least.

Leaking windscreen and window rubbers do not always respond to local injections of sealant. Here again, the best thing to do is to take them off and reseat them. It may be found that the outer flanges have perished due to the action of sunlight on the rubber, and in this case replacement by new material is called for.

Draught excluder:

Draught excluding strips such as Furflex form a second line of defence. On some cars this strip is trapped under a pop riveted tread plate on the sills. To renew this strip the pop rivets must be drilled out. They should be replaced with self-tapping screws, preferably of stainless steel. If ordinary steel screws are used, they should be well bedded in primer to prevent rust.

8:4 Brightwork

Chromium plate:

It is possible to do electro-plating at home, and text-books on the subject will be found in most large public libraries, but chromium is the most difficult of all the plating metals, and it is not economical to set up a plating bath and gain the necessary experience merely to restore the brightwork on a single car – assuming that it is restorable.

Chromium protects against tarnish only, and a substantial underlayer of nickel or copper is required on steel. Nickel is preferable, because chromium plate tends to peel off copper. Copper also accelerates pinholing of pressed steel – a type of bi-metallic corrosion. The deposit of chromium is very hard, so all polishing must be done on the underlayer before plating.

Alternatives to chrome:

Periodical shortages of nickel after the Second World War led to experimental use of stainless steel, stainless chrome iron, bright tin, bright zinc, and 'super-bright' finishes on ultimate-purity aluminium, and some of these may be found on modern cars. Bright tin and bright zinc failed because they are not hard enough. Stainless steel is good but costly, and not the easiest material to work. Super-bright aluminium is an alloy of 1 per cent magnesium and 99 per cent high-purity aluminium, which is brightened electrolytically, followed by anodising, which imparts a hard oxide film, almost equal to chromium.

There followed the metallisation of plastics by the high-vacuum metal evaporation process, which proved better than electro-plating of plastics. The end product is a sandwich of metal between two layers of lacquer. The underlayer seals pores in the plastic and provides a suitable base on which to deposit vapourised metal, and the top coat protects the thin metal film. A well-known example of metallised plastic is the trim strip which runs around the wheelarches of the BLMC Mini. It outlasts the pressed steel body, but it is soft and liable to mechanical damage, and it is not as lustrous as chromium.

Restoring brightwork:

Examine a rusted-out chromium-plated part such as an overrider and you will see that the mild steel pressing has degenerated into swollen laminations of rust, from which the plating can be peeled off as a springy sheet, showing the chromium flash on one side and the typical greenish-grey surface of tarnished nickel on the other.

It is a waste of money to re-plate pin-holed steel pressings, because new rust will soon lift the plating. If the underlying metal is sound, as in the case of accidental damage which has been repaired, then the best course is to take the part to a plating firm, whose address can be found in the yellow pages of the telephone book, and get an estimate for re-plating. In some instances it will be cheaper to buy a replacement part.

Various faults occur in the plating process itself, not least being inadequate degreasing and deoxidation of the article to be plated. Imperfectly-plated bumper blades are sometimes passed off on an unsuspecting customer as part of an insurance repair job, and a substantial allowance should be claimed before accepting the car or signing a satisfaction note.

A practical way of extending the life of blemished window frames which are not worth re-plating, is to rub off the chromium with abrasive paper, de-rust and prime both sides of the metal, and then paint it, either black to match the rubber, or in the body colour.

Corroded trim strips:

The simple cure for corroded trim strips which serve no function is to throw the silly things away, fill in the attachment holes with Cataloy or epoxy resin, sand flush and paint over. Their purpose was principally to help sell the car. The owner cannot even see the bright exterior trim while using the car, but if he discards it the car becomes non-standard, giving the dealer a plausible reason for knocking down the trade-in price. This will not worry an owner who intends to keep the car until the end of its life. Trim strips may well be replaced by a painted line in gold, silver or some contrasting colour. An alternative is the stick-on stripe, but this has a short life compared with painted lining (see **Chapter 9**).

Bi-metallic corrosion:

It is noticeable that bright metal trim strips mounted in glazing rubber outlast those clipped directly to the steel body shell. The lesson from this is that a metal trim strip should be separated from the body of the car by zinc chromate primer, or by sticking it on with epoxy resin. The only merit of the trim clips used by motor manufacturers is that they save time on the assembly line. Any horizontal trim strip, however well mounted, forms a pocket along its top edge, in which water can lie, creating a corrosion trap. Fortunately, there is a trend to eliminate trim strips from popular models.

Bumpers:

Originally bumpers were intended to take bumps and were made of spring steel, even on cheap cars. Apart from new models complying with American safety codes, bumpers on British cars are little more than trim strips, made of mild steel and plated. Repairs undertaken on behalf of an insurance company seem to include a new bumper blade as a matter of course, but a private owner can save money by repairing a bumper if it is not too badly mangled. The main requirement is a dolly block fitting into the back of the blade. This block can be made of body solder cast into an undamaged part of the blade. If you go carefully and use a polished hammer it may not be necessary to re-chrome the bumper. If the shape of the bumper is suitable, and you have access to a wheeling machine, but plenty of grease on the chromed face and run the blade through to reduce the hammer marks. This treatment will take the sheen off the chrome, but polishing the whole blade afterwards will make the repaired area less conspicuous.

Bumper guard strips:

Rubber bumper guard strips are not glued on, but held by $\frac{1}{4}$ inch bolts, the heads of which are concealed under the rubber. They pass through a metal strip which is dovetailed into a channel in the back of the rubber moulding. These strips are not difficult to fit, but you will need a sharp centre punch to form a starting pop for the drill on the slippery metal. A strip of masking tape stuck on the chromium temporarily makes marking-out easy, especially if you have to make cut-outs in the rubber to accommodate overriders. Vauxhall supply the type of strip fitted on the Magnum in the form of a kit. The bolts should be fitted with lockwashers, and not over-tightened because this will form bulges in the rubber. Unwanted bulges can be removed by bending the rubber in the opposite direction.

CHAPTER 9

Customising

'Custom-built' is the American equivalent of bespoke bodywork and the term has been extended to any after-sale additions, or alterations, to a stock car, whether the object is to improve performance, increase comfort, impress other people, or merely to make the car easily recognised in a large car park. Some of the extraordinary touches such as dummy exhaust systems slung between the wheels on either side are expressions of the American sense of humour, which is sometimes misunderstood abroad. A point to bear in mind is that wild colour schemes reduce the trade-in value of a car.

Increasing comfort is largely a matter of putting in what the maker left out in order to keep his selling price down. A comparison between the De Luxe model in a range with the popular model at the basic price will illustrate this. The seats will be thinner and harder, the floor will be hard, the amount of sound-proofing will be reduced and all non-essential instruments and lights will have been omitted. The interior fittings and trim will probably be made of black plastics, because this pigment masks the discolouration caused by ultra-violet rays in sunlight.

Acceptable trim is a matter of taste. Some people loathe being surrounded with plastics and yearn for polished wooden fillets and facia and leather seating. Others think this is fuddy-duddy and that the place for polished timber is the drawing room. Certainly many motorists would consider ornamental timber out of place in a high-performance car because it means carrying unnecessary weight. For those who do not regard their car as a racing machine, a remarkable feeling of luxury can be achieved on the principle of substituting natural materials for synthetics and painstaking hand craftsmanship for cheap, rapid mass-production methods.

9:1 Legal requirements

Conversions and alterations to cars must conform to Government regulations; otherwise the car will fail its next DoE test, or it may be ordered off the road at a police spot check. Alterations also invalidate the insurance policy unless the insurer is informed and agrees to the work.

The principal Government regulations are the Motor Vehicles (Construction and Use) Regulations 1969, the Motor Vehicle Lighting Regulations 1971 and the Road Traffic Act 1972. These are continually being amended to meet EEC standards and export requirements and most large public libraries have an updated copy among the law books in the reference department. This should be consulted before making any alterations to the following; overall dimensions, weight, position and power of lights, minimum diameter of wheels, front view from driver's seat, windscreen wipers, windscreen washers, speedometer, mirror, audible warning instrument, direction indicators, seat belts, speedometer, wings, tyres and fuel tank. The latter must be made of metal and cars first used after January 1st, 1959 must have safety glass at the sides and back as well as at the front.

9:2 Structural modifications

Cutting down saloons:

It is not safe to cut the roof off a chassisless car to convert it into an open sports car or tourer. Although the manufacturer's open version may appear to consist of the same pressings below the waist line, the sills and hinge pillars will have been specially reinforced to compensate for the absence of the roof pressing and such reinforcement is not always easy to introduce into a completed shell. If such a conversion appears practicable, ask the manufacturers for their advice before cutting any metal.

The 'roof chop' or lowering of a saloon roof to make a customised car faster is another matter. In theory, at least, the lower roof should improve the strength of the structure. The older the car, the more scope there is for lowering the roof.

Upgrading a popular model:

Press tools are costly and take a long time to make, so motor manufacturers use the same basic pressings for a range of models sold under different names; for instance, the Austin 1100, 1275, 1300 and GT and the MG, Riley, Wolseley and Vanden Plas variants. As the bodyshell is the same, a private owner can convert a simple 1300 into one of the other variants, according to his liking for comfort or speed.

As the range has been in service since 1963, many of the early models have rusted out and it is possible to buy Vanden Plas reclining seats, armrests, wooden facias, leather-bound steering wheels and many other extras from the breaker's yard. Flaring the wheelarches will permit the use of 13 inch wheels and 185 section radial tyres to team up with a tuned engine such as the 1300 GT. It should be remembered that some small mass-produced engines will not stand a great increase in power output. A broken crankshaft and a wrecked engine has often been the outcome. It is better to fit a larger engine at a lower stage of tune than to try to get the ultimate output from a small one.

Improving performance:

Many of the measures that can be taken to improve a car's performance are beyond the scope of this book. Details can be found in the companion Autocare manual **Tuning for Economy and Performance.**

Apart from engine tuning, weight-saving and reduction of frontal area are the principal means of improving car performance. Less weight means better acceleration and deceleration. Reduced frontal area improves maximum speed because air resistance increases as the square of the speed. For instance, if a car with a frontal area of 13 sq ft has a top speed of 115 mile/hr, a reduction of the frontal area to 12 sq ft will increase the maximum speed to 118 mile/hr. It would need an additional 10 brake horsepower to reach 118 mile/hr with the 13 sq ft body and this extra output might not be obtainable from an engine already highly tuned.

The first step towards reduction of frontal area is to lower the driver's eye point, by fitting a thinner seat cushion and, if possible, dropping the bottom of the seat below the main underframe members or chassis. This will make it necessary to lower the scuttle and bonnet, and the limiting factor in older cars is the height of the radiator, not the height of the rocker box. One soon finds oneself with a major rebuilding job, which should not be undertaken without the help of an experienced welder. If the roof is to be lowered, it is better to choose a body with flat glass at front and rear, otherwise it may be necessary to make a pattern for specially curved glass, or to try to make the bodyshell fit an existing glass curve, which is not easy.

Streamlining:

Not only are aerodynamics largely unimportant at normal road speeds, but there is little the amateur can do to improve an existing car. Costly prototype development work using wind tunnel facilities is the only accurate way of finding the right compromise between low drag, stability and everyday practicality. Avoid adding projections like mirrors and roofracks if they are not essential as they will generate wind noise as well as drag.

Converting a saloon into an open two-seater does not necessarily improve maximum speed because of the drag of turbulent air in the open cockpit. Turbulence in the wheelarches is impossible to eliminate and it is doubtful whether an undershield gives any measurable improvement. The high-pressure areas around the nose of the car will best repay modification. A smooth front end or 'entry' can be achieved by mounting the radiator transversely and drawing air through it from the wheelarch by means of an electric fan.

It is just as important to lead the air out of the engine bay without turbulence after it has taken away heat from the radiator. This was discovered many years ago by the French car designer Gregoire, who cut down radiator drag by half by using ducts from the output side of the radiator to vents in the body sides.

Fairing-off the front end must not starve the front brakes of cooling air and the front wheels must clear the bodywork at full bump on full lock in both directions. The body must be wide enough to prevent mud being thrown up by the tyres and not so shaped that it tends to drive air under the car, causing the front wheels to lift at high speed.

Spoilers:

A spoiler is an aerofoil mounted above the rear end of a car to create a downward thrust on the rear wheels, which improves tyre adhesion but creates some drag. A wind-tunnel test on a model will show whether a spoiler is necessary. Spoilers are usually painted in a contrasting colour, to make sure everyone notices them.

Saving weight:

There is not much scope for saving weight in stock cars, because so much depends on choice of materials at the design stage. If speed is the goal, choose a light car to work on – some are considerably heavier than others in the same horsepower category. Substitution of GRP doors for metal, Perspex for window glass, removal of nave plates, polished cappings and interior trim and fitting rudimentary seating are among the racing tricks which together may yield a measurable improvement in acceleration.

Lightening body panels by cutting holes is not recommended, although it may make the car look more track-worthy. Manufacturers' cut-outs are nearly always flanged while the panel is being pressed and this is not practicable with hand tools. The most likely result of such efforts will be to start a crack. The webs of chassis frames are well peppered with holes already and any new ones should be made well away from the spring shackle mountings and placed near the centre of the web. Do not cut away the upper or lower arms of a channel section; this acts as a severe notch in stressman's parlance and will cause the collapse of the frame under shock loads.

Wheel and tyre sizes are so closely bound up with engine tuning that there is no point in discussing them separately. Suffice it to say that rubber is heavy and that unnecessarily big tyres will not improve performance. Light alloy wheels should be weighed against steel wheels to see whether there is any advantage apart from good looks.

Lowering:

The car as a whole can be lowered by altering the suspension, not forgetting that the new sunken seat pans may now be the lowest part of the body. Cutting the front suspension coils, fitting lowering blocks and longer U-bolts under the back axle and fitting smaller wheels are ways of achieving this, but problems of clearance, damper travel, suspension geometry and gearing make the process less simple than it may seem. It is safest to consult someone with experience of the model.

Wheel modifications:

Wider wheels are necessary to take wider tyres, which, in principle, give better roadholding, cornering and braking performance, but these ambitions are not necessarily fulfilled on a popular model. Fitting larger diameter wheels and tyres has the effect of raising the overall gearing, so making possible some increase in maximum speed if the engine can pull the higher gear. Conversely, smaller diameter wheels and tyres reduce the maximum speed but improve acceleration at lower speeds. Changing wheel sizes may lead to unexpected difficulties, such as rims fouling the brake gear, so take specialist advice before spending your money. The better-looking your new wheels the more you need anti-theft locks.

Flared wheelarches:

In many cases wider road wheels need wider wheelarches to comply with the law against mud and water being flung up. The simplest way is to fit a GRP wheelarch flare, which can be obtained ready-made, together with pop rivets and a riveting gun. The joint is faired off with a GRP stopper such as Cataloy. One does not need to go very far to find an example of how **not** to do this! The stopper should be sanded down neatly and then painted in a colour, matching or contrasting, with the remainder of the body side.

GRP flares are not very satisfactory in service, because they are brittle compared with sheet steel, and tend to develop cracks in the paintwork at the ends and over the rivet heads. Welded steel flares are better in the long run and, although they are beyond the capacity of the non-welder, they need not cost much more than GRP flares. Either an entirely new flare can be made on a wheeling machine, or the original wheelarch lip can be cut off with a padsaw and welded back in place after adding an extension strip of the required width. Wet rags or asbestos should be used to prevent warpage while the tack-welding is being done and the new work treated with rust preventer, particularly at the back after the asbestos has been removed.

A third way, not requiring any heat, is to cut away the original lip of the wheelarch, then slot the edge. Drill bolt holes between the slots and then turn the tongues into the arch to form mountings for a bolted flare, filling the joint with wing piping.

Competition regulations:

Cars intended for sporting events must conform to FIA rules, which are closely followed by the RAC competition rules and some additional requirements are specified for British events. The rules cover body width and height of sides, seats and dimensions, wings and positioning, windscreen and hood, size of windows, the height of the roof, provision of a fireproof bulkhead. Copies of these rules are obtainable from the RAC and should be studied if you intend to go in for any form of competitive motor sport.

GRP panels and wings:

GRP wings, panels and complete front ends are available for many popular cars. Although the wings are made to the same shape (a steel wing is used as a master pattern for the moulds) they are not the same thickness. GRP has to be much thicker than steel to acquire the necessary rigidity and without going to vast expense it is not possible to reproduce some of the small radii found on a pressed steel wing. The polyester resin is coloured and, although the colours are sometimes described as 'factory matched', they will not match the faded colour on a car which has seen some years' service. The increased thickness and different colour make a single new GRP wing appear very odd on an old car. Consequently, it is better to fit a pair, or four GRP wings and make a virtue out of necessity by painting the rest of the car in a contrasting or toning colour.

A complete front end consists of front wings, bonnet and apron. On transverse-engined cars like the Mini range the front is hinged on the front channel of the subframe. No welding is involved and the old metal is cut away by drilling spot-welds and cutting with a padsaw as described in **Chapter 3**. Most of the moulders offer a fitting service for about £12, or they will send a kit with instructions. Those who wish to do the fitting themselves should collect the parts from the factory if possible, because large GRP mouldings sent by public carrier are often scratched in transit.

A hinged front end vastly improves engine accessibility, and the moulding can be sold when the remainder of the car has to be scrapped. The snag is that the bumper will be fouled unless it is mounted on the moulding and the heavy strap-iron two-point bumper brackets are unsuitable for GRP. They will be punched straight through the moulding at the first impact. The bumper blade should be mounted directly to the edge of the valance if it fits, or backed with a piece of shaped timber, to distribute impacts over the moulding as a whole. If this is not practicable, a rubber bumper guard should be bolted to the edge of the valance as described in **Chapter 8**.

Apart from replacing corroded wings, GRP front ends can be used to upgrade older models, for example Mini to Clubman, Herald to 13/60, Spitfire to GT6 and so on.

Ford Anglias, Cortinas and Escorts need a tie bar between the top suspension plates after the bonnet has been cut away. This is supplied by the moulder, or it can be made at home by flattening the ends of a length of water pipe and drilling bolt holes in them.

A new front end moulding will be thicker than the original metal and will not lie level with the top of the scuttle. A thick rubber moulding, such as a door seal, which stands proud of the bonnet, will divert attention from this joint.

Sound-proofing:

The noise in a car comes from several sources; engine and gearbox; back axle; exhaust system; tyre treads on the road; wind eddying round the outside of the body; and drumming of body panels and roof.

Scientifically, there is no substitute for mass to stop some of the sound frequencies. Submarine engines, for instance, have sound-deadening cowls consisting of sheet lead, plastic foam and GRP. The weight of sheet lead is unacceptable for use in a car, but the self-adhesive sound-proofing materials sold in motor shops are easy to apply. There are various asbestos-based compositions which are normally applied by spray which are not convenient for the private owner. Undersealing and the proprietary rust-proofing processes mentioned in **Chapter 1** will reduce the level of noise to some extent.

A plastic-faced sound-proofing felt is obtainable from coach trimming suppliers in 54 inch rolls. It can be spotted on at 6 inch intervals with Dunlop S480 solution. This makes it easier to remove if necessary and allows some ventilation over the surface of the metal. Sometimes this is sufficient to eliminate panel resonance, but persistent drumming is best cured by stiffening ribs of similar metal or wood stuck to the inner surface with epoxy resin. Sometimes a piece of leathercloth glued down all over with upholstery cement will do the trick.

A plastic-faced felt, or a carpet with a felt underlayer is the conventional way of soundproofing car floors. A layer of up to an inch of non-intercellular sponge rubber (not latex or polyurethane foam) under the carpet is better than felt, because it does not transmit moisture and if dried out occasionally it will prevent the footwells from getting wet.

9:3 Converting a van

Converting a commercial van into a utility by the addition of side windows behind the driver's seat changes the van into a private car from the taxman's point of view. Car Tax, which is the successor to Purchase Tax (not to be confused with the vehicle excise licence) must be paid on conversion. Details will be found in Customs Notices 77J and 672, obtainable from the local officer of Customs and Excise, whose address can be found in the telephone directory. The Car Tax payable is based on the capital value of the van at the time of conversion, so the Customs Officer will have to see the van to determine its value. You should, therefore, take it along **before** you make any proposed improvements. There are heavy penalties for failure to pay tax on van conversions.

Thanks to rubber glazing strip, the insertion of fixed side windows is a straightforward job, but it needs planning if the result is to look neat. Ideally, the windows should be the same depth as the door windows and the space between the door window and the first side window should be the same as the space between the first and second side windows. If possible the space between the rear edge of the second side window and the rear end of the van body should be the same also. The original back windows may be enlarged, but they should have the same base line as the side windows and be evenly spaced across the back doors.

The length of the side windows will probably be governed by the pillar positions, but if there is any latitude one cannot go wrong in making them the same length as the door windows. If such perfection is unattainable, the insertion of chromed plastics filler strip in the rubber glazing will attract the eye and divert attention from the difference in size between the old and new side windows.

Several firms offer complete kits for putting side windows and seats in the current range of commercial vans and will also lend metal cutters for making the apertures in the van side panels. If there is a kit ready for the van you intend to convert, then all the planning and glass cutting will have been done for you and much time, trouble and expensive running about will be saved. The kits are supplied with fitting instructions.

For those who are not so lucky, here are the main points to consider. First, one must distinguish between pillars which are part of the structure and stiffening ribs or struts which are put in to prevent drumming of the side panels. It is permissible to cut out alternate pillars and anti-drumming ribs are not necessary where there are side windows because the combination of glass and rubber glazing strip serves the same purpose.

With care it is possible to cut the window apertures without spoiling the paintwork, which means that the vehicle need not be off the road for a repaint. Special metal cutters greatly simplify the operation but a padsaw can be used with care. Remember that it is easier to cut more metal away than to replace it if it is cut too far.

On many vans there is a waist moulding which can be used as a base line for marking-out. If not, a line can be snapped on with chalked cord. The radii of the corners depends upon the type of glazing rubber to be used, because a minimum curvature is recommended for each type. If you compare your proposed curve with that of a windscreen glazed with the same type of rubber there should be no difficulty. If you wish to keep equal distances between windows, make sure you measure from the rear edge of the cab window, not from the front edge of the shut pillar; this is a common mistake.

Choice of glass:

It is impossible to cut toughened glass and having glass cut and toughened to order may mean an unacceptable delay, although the glass manufacturers will do toughening for you. Laminated glass can be cut, as explained elsewhere in this book. If you are doubtful of your ability to cut laminated glass, this can be done for you by the glass merchant, who will need an accurate pattern to work from. This is made of paper and stuck down on the glass before cutting. The glass merchant will also grind the edges.

Perspex:

Acrylic sheet, such as ICI Perspex or American Plexiglas and Lucite, is permissible in lieu of safety glass and it can be curved to follow sweeps which would be impossible with toughened or laminated glass. Perspex is easy to cut, but its disadvantages are that it is soft and liable to scratches and needs occasional polishing with fine metal polish to restore its surface.

Rubber glazing strip:

The types of rubber glazing strip readily available for van conversions are:

1 $\frac{5}{32}$ or $\frac{3}{16}$ inch glass on $\frac{1}{16}$ inch body panel.
2 $\frac{5}{32}$ or $\frac{3}{16}$ inch glass on $\frac{1}{8}$ inch body panel.
3 $\frac{1}{2}$ inch glass on $\frac{1}{4}$ inch body panel.
4 $\frac{3}{16}$ inch glass on $\frac{3}{8}$ inch body panel or vice versa.

All these rubber strips need a clearance of $\frac{9}{32}$ inch to accommodate them, so the aperture in the body panel must be $\frac{9}{16}$ inch deeper and $\frac{9}{16}$ inch longer than the glass.

Marking-out:

Marking-out from glass windows already in hand can be done simply by holding the glass against the panel in the desired position and drawing a line $\frac{9}{32}$ inch outside its perimeter. This can be done with a pair of calipers, or with a piece of wood carrying a nail protruding at a point $\frac{9}{32}$ inch from its edge. Alternatively you can make a template of cardboard the same size as the glass and run round it with a scriber, or pencil. If you are working single-handed, hold the template in place by two self-tapping screws driven into the part of the panel which is to be cut away.

To mark-out for glasses which have yet to be cut, cover the window area with brown paper, the reverse side of wallpaper, or old posters, held in place by sticky tape and draw your window with snapped chalk line or pencil.

Cutting the apertures:

Window apertures in sheet steel or aluminium van sides can be cut with power-driven tools such as the nibbler or jig-saw, or by means of a metal cutter or shears or a fine flexible hacksaw blade in a padsaw handle. GRP panels should always be sawn. Shears or a power-driven nibbler will crack the gel-coated outer surface. Arm yourself with a sharp centre punch before drilling any padsaw or nibbler starting holes. Blunt centre punches will cause the drill to run off beyond the marked margin of the aperture.

The edges of the aperture should be cleaned up with a half-round file, but it is a good idea to leave the top edge somewhat rough so that the rubber glazing strip will hang up while you are working it round the corner radii.

Fitting the glazing strip:

Cut one end of the rubber glazing strip at right angles and push the narrow channel over the edge of the panel, starting at the top centre. The filler strip channel is usually on the outside of the van, but if the van is likely to be left outdoors where thieves have an opportunity to break into it by removing the filler strip and glass it may be better to have the filler channel on the inside.

Press the glazing strip well into the corners of the aperture as you work around it. Unless you are sure of getting a very good fit, it is as well to run a bead of sealing compound around the bottom of the channel. When you come back to the starting point at the top centre of the window, cut the rubber strip off square, allowing $\frac{3}{8}$ inch overlap. Then push the two ends together to make an interference fit which will be watertight.

Installing the glass:

Starting at a bottom corner, slide the glass into the larger channel and ease the rubber lips around it with a screwdriver, finishing off along the top edge. This job is easier if two people can work, one on either side of the window. A bead of sealant inside the glass channel should not be necessary for side windows, but it will prevent leaks if the aperture is irregular.

Fitting the filler strip:

The filler strip, which locks the rubber and glass assembly in place, may be of rubber or chromed plastics. Both are inserted by means of a special tool, which resembles a curved screwdriver blade with a hole in the middle. The strip is threaded through the hole and placed in position as the tool is run round in the locking channel. These tools can be bought for about 30p from the rubber suppliers.

Soapy water or washing-up liquid will help to lubricate the filler channel. Pull about an inch of rubber through the eye of the inserting tool and start near the top joint of the glazing strip. Holding the tool at right angles to the glass, press the end of the tool into the channel. Then hold the short end of the filler strip and incline the tool in the direction of travel, working it from side to side so that the filler strip sinks into its channel. Take it slowly, otherwise the lips of the glazing strip may be torn. When the circuit has been completed, allow $\frac{3}{8}$ inch overlap and butt the ends together in the channel with a screwdriver.

Chromed plastics filler strip is rather brittle when cold, so it is advisable to make it flexible by warming it in hot soapy water and to carry out the fitting in a warm atmosphere so that the strip does not cool down before the circuit has been completed. Some fitters have a hair-dryer ready to hand to keep the plastics strip warm and soft in the event of any hold-up.

Flanged windows:

Flange-fit windows, widely used in American for customising vans, are more expensive than the rubber-mounted type. They consist of a split flange sandwiching the glass and the body panel between them, with screws entered through the inside flange into blind holes in the outer flange. They look well in burnished aluminium and their superior rigidity makes them more suitable than rubber for mounting large sliding lights.

Utility seating:

As a rough guide, allow 3 ft headroom between the top of the front edge of a seat cushion and the roof. To allow passengers to sit in the normal knees-up position, the top edge of the cushion should be 1 ft above the floor. This may be reduced for younger passengers who are willing and able to adopt the racing driver's pose.

If the utility is to carry passengers only, ready-made

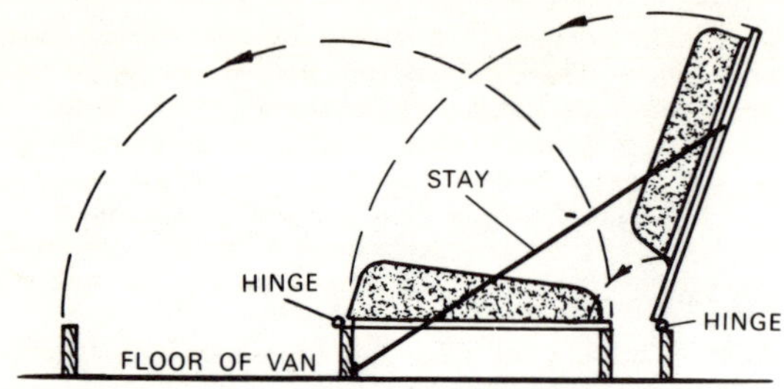

FIG 9:1 Folding van seat, side elevation

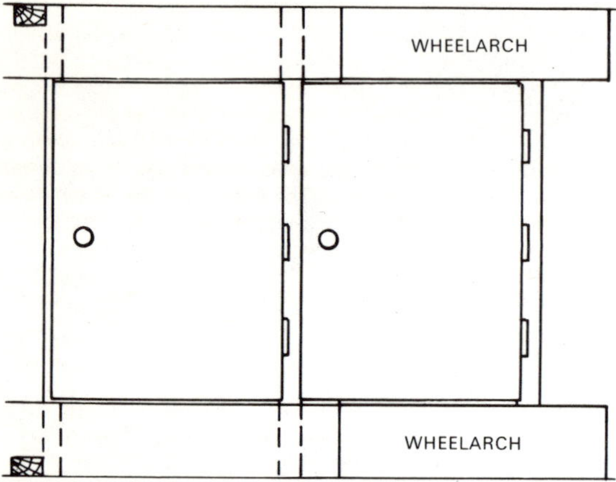

FIG 9:2 Folding van seat, plan view

seats can be bolted to the floor after strong points have been located or provided by welding on load-spreading plates. Workmen's bench seats and seat-backs can be obtained ready to fit into the larger commercial vans.

If the vehicle is required for carrying goods and passengers, the seats can be arranged to fold flat, so that their backs form part of the goods-carrying floor. There are two ways of doing this: **1** cutting away part of the original floor of the van and fitting floor pans which form footwells when the seat is raised; **2** building up a false floor, either fixed or removable as shown in **FIG 9:2**. The disadvantage of the fixed false floor is the permanent step in the floor over the rear axle, which will prevent heavy loads being slid right up to the back of the front seats. The false floor can be made removable by anchoring it to the underframe by bolts welded to the underframe which pass through angle-iron brackets screwed to the frame of the false floor. The bolts are fitted with wingnuts, so that the false floor and its seating can be lifted out bodily, leaving the van in its original condition. Two longitudinals, not shown in the sketch, will be needed to hold a removable frame together.

The false floor system is easier for the home constructor because no welding is required, but in very small vans such as the Mini there is insufficient headroom and floor pans must be fitted. Conversion kits are available for these, and it is more economical to buy and fit them than to make them specially.

The wooden false floor shown in the drawing (**FIG 9:2**) is made of $\frac{1}{2}$ inch plywood or 1 inch chipboard.

The two folding traps cover all the space from the back of the front seats to the centre of the wheelarches. If the van is to carry heavy goods, the edges of the trap boards should be armoured with $\frac{1}{8}$ inch angle iron. Aluminium angle is not hard enough and breaks away from the attachments screws after a few years' rough treatment.

The cushion should be $\frac{1}{2}$ inch thinner than the depth of the false floor, so that it does not pick up dust when folded down. The cushions can be made up on a plywood baseboard (see **Chapter 6**) and screwed to the trap. If headroom is precious, a conventional spring case can be omitted and the seat cover filled with a pad of rubberised hair, Dunlopillo or polyether foam. Such seat pads are strictly 'utility' and for long journeys something better is needed. Pirelli rubber webbing, which is interlaced to form a hammock, takes up little vertical space, although some clearance is needed, otherwise the passenger will find him or herself 'bottoming' on the surface of the trap. Pirelli webbing is obtainable from coach trimming suppliers complete with anchoring metalwork and fitting instructions.

There is no need to make the cushions the full width of the trap. A 2 inch gap at each end will make it easier to attach the cushions and to mount seat-back stays.

It pays to use a good welded link chain for the seat-back stays, and to attach them to tailboard hooks. Hide leather sewn round the chain gives a good, durable finish. An alternative is wire rope. If this is bought from a yacht chandler he may be able to make the end splices, or supply a type of compression collar which eliminates the need for splicing. This is preferable to a splice covered with cord whipping, which soon wears out, leaving sharp ends of steel wire which will scratch hands and tear clothing.

Converting a pick-up:

An open-back pick-up truck can be converted into a van by cutting out the back panel of the cab, moving it to the rear and welding in new roof and side panels. The installation of side windows behind the driver's seat converts the vehicle into a private car from the taxation point of view. The Customs Inspector will need to examine the vehicle, as in the case of a van conversion already mentioned in this chapter.

There will be a considerable amount of oxy-acetylene cutting and tack-welding to do, so this is not a job for the private owner unless he is an experienced welder. Sheet metalworking plant will be needed to shape the roof panels, which should be formed with $\frac{1}{2}$ inch inward flanges. These are tack-welded at 2 inch intervals and the outside Vee filled with body solder. The side panels are flanged and tacked in the same way, to prevent distortion. The pick-up floor may need lowering to give sufficient headroom.

If drip rails are required, the new side panels should be outwardly flanged to provide sufficient metal to form these channels, while the roof sheets are flanged inwardly to provide anchorages for additional list bars. The roof sheets are joined with interlocking flanges, with the opening on the trailing edge. Joints between dissimilar metals should be primed with zinc chromate primer. Steel-to-steel joints should be phosphated and filled as necessary before painting. All additional panels can be made from 18 swg sheet and the same material can be used to form channel sections to make seat frames, reinforced at the corners with gusset plates cut from $\frac{1}{16}$ inch metal. The additional list bars can be made from $\frac{5}{16}$ inch round, which should be primed before the headlining is sewn around it.

Window openings in the side panels should be cut out after the panels have been welded in position. The marking-out procedure is similar to that already described for van conversions.

9:4 Custom painting:

Under this heading is included artistic embellishments on a base coat, and some of the many kinds of 'trick painting' used to brighten cars and vans. Most of this work is done with pigmented and clear acrylic lacquers, which are readily obtainable in small quantities from art shops. Acrylics are easy to both brush and spray. Each coat must be given time to 'flash off' or surface harden before the next coat is applied. A very high, durable gloss is obtained by burnishing the final coat of clear acrylic lacquer.

An alternative is synthetic enamel, also readily available in very small quantities. This dries with a high gloss which needs no rubbing-out, but the disadvantage is the long drying time, which makes it impossible to do any masking for a second colour without a long wait while the enamel hardens.

Preparation for acrylics:

If the vehicle is fairly new and the factory paint is in good condition, it may be sanded down to remove the surface gloss, treated with a corrosion inhibitor and used as a base for two coats of primer-sealer. If there is any doubt at all, it is better to strip the panel, or the whole vehicle, down to bare metal as described in **Chapter 5**. It would be a pity to spend many hours on artistic endeavour only to find the whole scheme peeling. GRP bodies should not be sandblasted or stripped with chemical paint strippers, but rubbed down with abrasive paper. Do not use a blowlamp on metal or GRP bodywork.

Masking:

Masking tape 1 inch wide is used in ordinary car refinishing to fix masking paper covering the glass or second colour. In custom painting a tape only $\frac{1}{8}$ inch wide, which can be curved in two planes, is used for bold lines. This is the narrowest stock width, but it can be cut narrower on a meat slicing machine and used to mask-up the base colour to make 'spaghetti swirls'. This very narrow tape is used to give a sharp edge to the outline and the narrower the tape the smaller the radius that can be negotiated before the tape buckles up. The area outside the narrow tape is protected with wider tape or paper. It pays to use good quality masking tape which will come away cleanly after use.

Stencils:

A stencil is a form of mask, but in a more elaborate form. They can be cut from any paper, but a particularly useful form is Frisket paper, obtainable from art shops. This is very thin paper, adhesive on one side, with a backing sheet, which is peeled off after the design has been drawn and cut out. The great advantage of Frisket paper is its transparency, which makes positioning much easier.

The air brush:

For fine work, the artist's air brush is used to obtain the vignette or half-tone effect. An air brush is a miniature spray gun and the double-action type suitable for car painting costs about £22. This has an adjustable spray, a $\frac{3}{4}$ oz paint jar and a 6 ft air hose. It is powered by an air compressor or a 13 oz can of aerosol propellant. The minute passages in these guns become blocked with acrylic lacquers unless they are frequently cleaned with thinners, which should be kept handy in a spare jar. Air brushes must always be cleaned out directly after use.

The procedure for cleaning, stopping and priming is the same as described in **Chapter 5**, but the primer should preferably be obtained from the maker of the acrylic base coat. Wet sand the primed surface with 600 paper to make it as smooth as possible for the base coat. Three coats of primer are recommended as a base for most metallics.

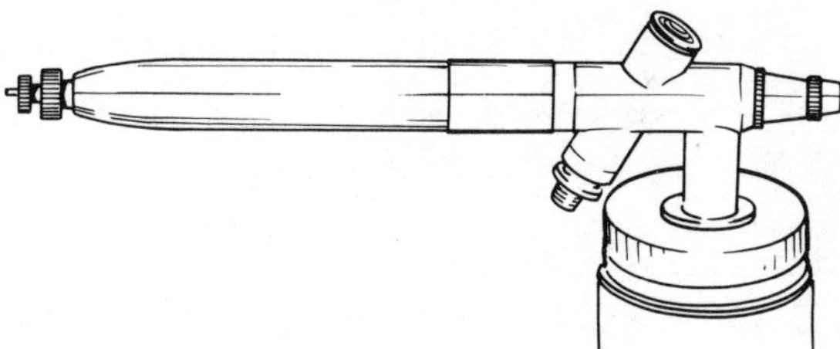

FIG 9:3   Air brush for special paint effects

Metallics:

Metallic paints contain minute particles of metal in various colours and mixtures of colours. They are mixed into clear acrylic lacquer in the proportion of 3 to 4 oz of flake per litre. As the flakes tend to settle, the mixture needs constant stirring. One way to do this is to put two ballbearings in the paint cup of the spray gun and shake the gun after every pass. Metallics do not cover very well and need a coloured base coat to fill the voids. The makers supply appropriate coloured primer-surfacers which also serve as a base coat.

The makers of Metalflake, one of the leading brands, recommend a Devilbiss 043, 30 or 306 nozzle or Binks equivalent on a production spray gun for spraying metallics. If you do not have this equipment, use the spray-can. The clear acrylic will need considerable thinning, perhaps as much as 4 or 5 parts of thinner to one part of colour. The air pressure should be reduced to 24 lb/sq inch so that the flakes lie flat and do not bounce off the work. Apply three or more coats depending on the degree of coverage and allow 10 minutes drying time between coats. After the final coat has dried for half an hour, rub off the loose flakes with the flat of the hand. Remember that metallics can be stained by metal treatment solutions such as Jenolite, so be careful not to splash them when doing any subsequent work on adjoining metal.

Top coats:

Metallics such as Metalflake need a thick layer of clear acrylic lacquer to protect them, particularly where they have to be petrol-proof. Spray 7 to 9 medium-wet coats, allowing 10 minutes, drying time between each. Then leave the surface for 12 hours and apply 7 to 9 more top coats. After two days of air drying, sand with 400 paper until the 'orange peel' disappears, but do not expose any flake. Apply three more coats of clear lacquer, then wait a month before wet sanding with 600 paper. Then spray a light coat of thinner with 15 per cent of acrylic clear lacquer added. Finally apply a cutting compound and burnish as described in **Chapter 5**.

Candy Apple:

Candy Apple is a translucent acrylic which is sprayed over a metallic base coat. It is available in 15 tints and the depth of colour depends on the number of coats applied. It is a difficult paint to use, so some practice with a spray can is indicated. Unlike an opaque colour, Candy Apple cannot be sanded if a run should occur, and it is very sensitive to dust particles, which cause lumps and specks. If anything goes wrong, the whole film has to come off.

The preparation of the metal and priming is the same as for Metalflake, followed by two coats of acrylic base colour. Candy should be applied in three thin coats at 45 to 55 lb/sq inch allowing 10 minutes' drying time between each and spraying alternate coats at right angles to each other, to prevent streaking. If a deeper colour is wanted, spray another three coats at 10 minute intervals and leave for a week before compounding and polishing.

Pearlescents:

Acrylics loaded with pearlescents also give an iridescent effect. They are sprayed in the same way as Candy Apple and need stirring constantly. Pearl paints are supplied in various tints and they are sprayed over a coloured base, usually white. A particular kind of pearl paint known as Flip-Flop radiates changing iridescent colours as the point of view is shifted. Pearls can also be covered with Candy Apple to enhance the tint.

Scrolls, ribbons and murals:

Scrolls, ribbons and skylines for murals are first sketched on the primer or a base coat of acrylic, using an eyebrow pencil, which is easily washed off after spraying. Simple outlines can be masked in the usual way, but for elaborate designs a separate stencil is cut for each colour, using transparent stencil paper. It is very easy to spray the wrong area when working close up to a large design, so it is a good idea to mark each area **L** for light, **D** for dark and so on. Air brushwork should be covered with several coats of clear acrylic, which is left for a fortnight before rubbing down with 600 paper used wet, followed by burnishing compound and a wax polish.

Fish scales:

Fish scales are sprayed by means of a mask of cardboard, with a series of circular adhesive patches stuck along the

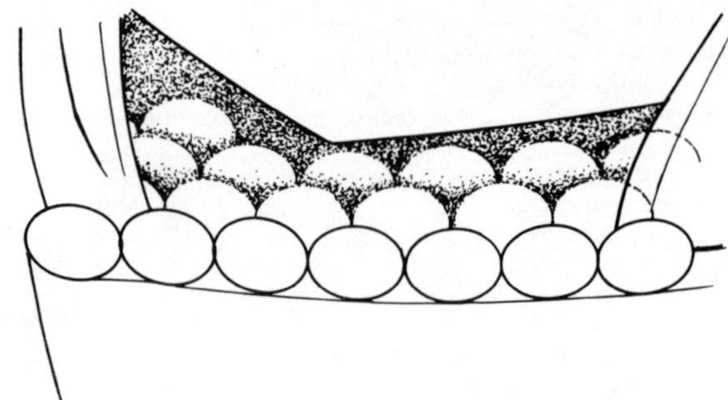

FIG 9:4   Special paint effects: fish scales

FIG 9:5   Special paint effects: card masking

edge, as shown in **FIG 9:4**. These patches may be obtained ready-made or cut from a sheet of pressure-sensitive material sold by art shops. The mask is placed on the base coat and the area around the edge of the line of patches is 'fogged' with the air brush. Then the mask is moved half a patch diameter back and half a diameter to one side and the fogging repeated to give the overlapping effect.

Card masking:

A similar fogging effect is obtained by holding a pack of old playing cards or business cards arranged in fan shape and fogging around the edges. For convenience the cards forming the fan are riveted so that the angle between them can be altered, or they can be stuck together and the fan as a whole is rotated or moved along after each pass of the air brush.

Lace:

Another form of masking is lace painting, in which any kind of lace fabric is used as a stencil. Stretch the lace as tightly as possible over the base coat and stick it down with masking tape. Either an air brush or a spray can may be used. A succession of thin fog coats is preferable to one wet coat, because if the lace becomes saturated with paint it may not pull away cleanly.

Flames:

Designs of waving flames, in red or orange, have long been popular. They are simply done by drawing the flame pattern on Frisket paper, cutting it out, sticking it down on a red or orange ground and spraying round with a contrasting colour. A black outline can be made by laying down $\frac{1}{8}$ inch masking tape on a black ground, then spraying the orange or red inside the line with an air brush. Then the area outside the $\frac{1}{8}$ inch tape is sprayed with a contrasting colour. The tape is peeled off, leaving orange flames with a black border. Alternatively, the contrasting colour may cover the whole ground and after the orange has been sprayed, the $\frac{1}{8}$ inch tape is peeled off and the exposed strip is touched in by hand with black.

Freak drops:

Making freak drops is a trick performed with a double-action air brush. The paint is made watery by adding thinners, then the gun is held 2 inches away from the surface and a short burst deposits a spider-shaped pattern on the surface. A short burst gives a large nucleus with short tentacles and a longer burst will make the tentacles spread. This is followed by straight air (not carrying any paint) to make the drop spread out. If too much paint is deposited, the pattern will collapse and the paint will run off the work.

Cobwebbing:

A cobweb effect is obtained by blowing undiluted paint through a spray gun. The paint is too viscous to atomise and comes out of the gun in long strings. The gun should be held about three feet away from the work and as the strings fly wild, extensive masking is necessary. When dry the cobwebbing is protected by clear acrylic.

Crackle mosaic:

Crackle finishes such as Metalflake's Vreeble are manufactured without the usual ingredient which inhibits shrinkage. This paint is sprayed in the same way as other acrylics, but the size of the crackle pattern can be controlled. A thin coat gives a small crackle pattern and a heavier coat gives a larger pattern. The largest squares are formed by spraying a second heavy coat before the first has started to dry. The cracks in the Vreeble coat are then filled with 8 to 10 coats of clear acrylic.

Catalysed acrylic top coat:

Metalflake offer a flexible, clear acrylic named Crystacryl, for top coating other acrylics. It is less prone to chipping and cracking and one coat of this material is said to be equal to five coats of ordinary clear acrylic. It needs a special undercoat, called a tie-coat, to unite it with the ordinary acrylic and it is activated by a catalyst, which is stirred into the paint just before use. It is recommended for covering metallics. Two clear coats should be applied with 30 minutes setting-up time between them. These should be left overnight before sanding and the application of a final coat, which will not need waxing. One of the limitations of Crystacryl is that no further painting of any kind can be done on its surface.

All the materials and equipment mentioned above are obtainable from Calbrook Cars Ltd, whose address will be found in the list of suppliers.

Lining:

Fine lining, or pinstriping, needs to be done well or not at all. The craftsman uses a small long-haired brush called a lining pencil, the size of which corresponds to the width of line desired, or a versatile long-haired brush called a sword liner or dagger brush, which is more difficult to use. The lining pencil is held between the first two fingers. The remaining fingers take the weight off the

FIG 9:6   Lining pencil (brush)

FIG 9:7   Sword liner or dagger brush

brush, because variations in pressure will produce variations in the width of the line. If possible the supporting fingers are run along a body moulding as a guide. The brush is long-haired because it has to carry a heavy load of paint for a long line. The brush should be dipped in thinners first, then filled with paint, pinched out between finger and thumb to remove the surplus.

When running a line freehand, the eye is fixed some distance ahead of the pencil, which is swept across the panel in one steady stroke. The best lining is always done quickly. When following a chalk line, the brush may be held between the fingers and thumbs of both hands, using the little fingers as supports. Lining is not quite as difficult as it sounds. It needs practice which builds up confidence.

Straight lines which do not run near a body moulding should be snapped on with a chalked cord, or marked by the brown paper and compass method. Cover the rough side of a piece of brown paper with chalk and hold it against the panel, chalked side down. Then one leg of a pair of compasses is run against a guide and the other is pressed against the paper, which leaves a fine chalk line on the work.

Lining machines:

Small, wheeled lining machines are used in factories for new work, but these do not give very good results on refinishes and are hardly worth purchasing by private owners who will have no regular use for them.

Lining with tape:

Lining can be done by sticking down two pieces of cellulose tape, such as Sellotape, about $\frac{1}{8}$ inch apart, and running paint between them. Patience is required to lay the tape in the right position and this tedious task is made easier if an assistant holds the reel and maintains the strip tension, while the painter presses it down firmly, so that paint cannot run under it anywhere. The tape should be laid down against a single or double chalk line. Painting between the tape is done carefully and when the paint is tacky, not hard dry, the tapes are peeled away and the line is left to harden off before any traces of chalk are removed.

As an alternative to using two strips of cellulose tape, it is now possible to buy a special lining tape which has a removable centre strip. The tape is first applied as a

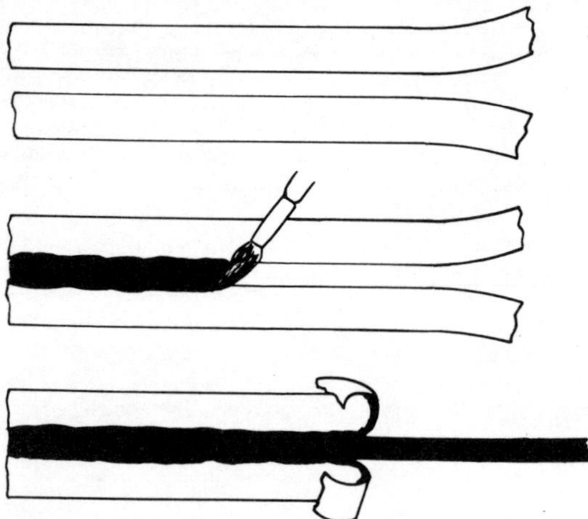

single piece and then the centre strip is peeled out leaving an accurate gap for painting. The rest of the procedure is as already described.

Paints for lining:

Lining may be done with cellulose slowed down in drying by a retarder or castor oil, but as this mixture cannot be wiped off if a mistake is made, it will be better for an inexperienced person to use a synthetic enamel.

There are two ways of lining in gold. One is to mix gold or bronze powder in a medium which is sold with these materials and to line with this mixture, keeping it well stirred. The other way is to run the line with gold size to which a little chrome yellow has been added and when it is tacky dust over it with gold powder on a piece of cotton wool, then wash off the surplus gold and varnish over.

In high-class bodywork the lining is done after flatting the first coat of varnish or the second coat of colour, so that the final coat of varnish will seal the line. Varnish is not used on mass-produced cars, so the simplest thing is to leave the line exposed to the weather (and the cleaner) and renew it when it wears off.

Transfers:

Colourful representations of fish, flowers, fruit and cattle in the form of water-slide or varnish transfers were once commonplace on tradesmen's delivery vans and some of these transfers may still be obtained. The water-slide type is used only where accurate positioning is not important, because the water slide prevents proper setting-out lines being used.

It must be emphasised that the panel to which a transfer is to be applied must be completely clean and free from grease or polish if the decoration is to be permanent and not peel.

Varnish transfers are printed on a Duplex paper, the corners of which must be separated before applying any gold size. Pin the transfer to a board so that the design can be coated with gold size or varnish. Be careful not to let the varnish overlap the design. The position of the

transfer on the body will have been marked beforehand and when the coating is tacky offer it up to the panel and press home with a clean rag. When the transfer is in correct position, the outer and thicker paper is peeled away. The transfer which will now show under the tissue paper, should be well rubbed to remove air and wrinkles.

After half an hour the tissue paper should be soaked with clean water from a sponge until it slides away easily. Wash the area around the transfer before drying with a chamois leather, otherwise some of the mucillage from the transfer may dry on the panel and show up as a nasty defect under varnish.

Water-slide transfers are easy to apply, but not so easy to position accurately. Clean the panel by wiping over with a damp chamois leather. Soak the entire transfer in clean, cold water for half a minute and then lay it aside for another half minute. Hold the transfer up to the approximate position with the right hand and with the left hand commence pulling the backing paper away. At this stage the transfer can be moved slighly to correct its position. The backing paper should now be replaced on the transfer with the sticky side outside and the transfer squeegeed to expel surplus water and air. When the transfer has dried it will be irremovable and safe to varnish.

Both water-slide and varnish transfers should be protected against the weather by a coat of clear varnish. This may not be necessary for the small plastics stickers and stripes sold in motor shops. In these cases the makers' instructions should be followed.

Only the best exterior quality varnish should be used, and scrupulous cleanliness should be maintained, because varnish tends to magnify defects.

Sand-blasting windows:

Car windows can be decorated like Victorian gin palaces by sand-blasting through a paper stencil. It is possible to do this on toughened glass if care and the right grade of sand is used. Engraving, which is done with a rotating copper wheel, is not applicable to toughened glass, but it can be done on ordinary 5 mm glass which is then taken to a safety glass manufacturer for toughening. An alternative to wheel engraving is the use of an electrically-operated engraving needle, which gives an effect similar to sand-blasting, but inferior to engraving. A third method is acid embossing, which is done by firms who also undertake silvering and gilding on glass.

For a cheap etched-glass effect, transfers similar to the 'Bond bullet holes' which were popular at one time, can be applied to the inside of the glass. These transfer kits include flower designs and stripes.

Tinted glass:

Tinted glass is available as flat laminate sheet in a range of tint shades. The very dark shades make night driving difficult, if not dangerous. This material is not generally available for curved windows, except BLMC Mini rear windows. There are also tinted toughened screens for some popular models. A new rubber moulding will be needed with each replacement window and a special tool is required to fit the metallised plastics trim strip into the rubber.

Tinted Perspex:

Tinted Perspex acrylic sheet, which has been curved after gentle heating, is available commercially for the Vauxhall Viva and Magnum side windows and can be supplied to order for other cars. The old windows will be needed as patterns.

Spray-on window tints:

Window-tinting paint can be obtained in an aerosol and sprayed on to the inside of the glass after thorough cleaning and dusting. The surrounding trim will need masking to catch the overspray. This material has a limited life, but is comparatively cheap.

Custom windows and portholes:

The American type of split-frame side window is available in the UK from importers and some are now being made by British manufacturers. The American types consist of inner and outer light alloy frames which clamp the body panel, window and interior trim together. A spacer can replace the trim thickness if necessary. The screws are entered from the inside, so that the outside fits flush with no screw heads showing. The lights are either flat or bubbled Plexiglass (an American equivalent of Perspex) and the frames are available in a large number of plain and fancy shapes such as tear-drop, heart, cat-eye and football.

Generally, glass is preferable to any make of acrylic. Acrylic is easily scratched and it is by nature thermoplastic. This means it will soften in extreme heat and bulge in the frame. It tends to yellow with age, but the surface can be restored with metal polish or jeweller's rouge, which is used to polish out scratches.

Forming Perspex sheet:

Acrylic plastics sheets, commonly called Perspex in the UK, can be formed by at least a dozen methods, from the one-off to mass production. If the compound curve is not excessive and the number of parts does not warrant expensive equipment, it is practical to stretch the heated material by hand over a rigid form, with the help of a disciplined crew. The sheet must be heated to about 250 deg. F, so the size of the oven will be the limiting factor. Wooden carpenters' clamps are fixed to the edges of the sheet at 6 inch centres. Holding the sheet by these clamps, the crew slowly stretches the material over the form and holds it until it has cooled. As the first attempt will probably be unsuccessful, it may be cheaper to buy a ready-formed shape and save the cost of the male mould as well.

9:5 Seat design

Car seat design is a complex matter, particularly if overseas safety regulations have to be considered. The resilience of the seat should be related to the suspension of the car, damping out road shocks but not causing excessive movement of the driver's eye in relation to the screen. The object is not to make a seat conforming to the driver's body in the curved or slumped position, but to support his back in the upright position where he feels alert and can best absorb road shocks.

The task is obviously simpler if the seat can be constructed to suit an owner-driver instead of the average man. If the body position is correct, comfort can be provided without great depth of padding in the squab, but fully reclining squabs need as much upholstery as the seat if they are to be used as beds.

In default of a general formula for calculating cushion thickness, we suggest trying a 2 inch medium core of Dunlopillo with a 1 inch soft overlayer. This should be sufficient on a resilient diaphragm or rubber webbing. Additions can be made before the cover is machined. On a spring case, a 2 inch soft core with 1 inch Super Soft or SQ overlayer is suggested. Further details on the use of foam materials can be found in **Chapter 6, Section 6:6**.

Seating and headroom:

Special bodies for sports cars used to be designed around the owner, who was invited to the factory to sit in a specially designed fixture while his 'measures' were taken. In arranging new seating in a car, take the underside of the steering wheel as a starting point and allow 5 to 7 inches between the bottom of the wheel and the uncompressed surface of the cushion and 13 to 15 inches from the bottom of the steering wheel to the driving seat squab. The distance from the top surface of the seat cushions to the underside of the roof should be at least 34 inches.

9:6 Accessories

Exhaust trim:

The American show pipe or sidewinder, slung between the front and rear wheelarches, is named after a nasty, mean American snake, found in Arizona, which propels itself with a peculiar sideways winding motion. Show pipes are dummies, but the genuine sidewinder becomes an open exhaust when a muffler cut-out is operated (beyond city limits). The outlets can be arranged to deafen the passengers, reducing them to a state of near-paralysis. Exhaust cut-outs are illegal in the UK, but there would be no objection to show pipes provided they did not protrude beyond the maximum permitted width.

Replacement silencers with stainless steel or chromium-plated tail pipes are available for most popular models and these smarten-up the only part of the system normally visible. A tuned engine will require a freeflow exhaust system and the use of stainless steel or aluminised steel is recommended for long life.

Roof racks:

Apart from a few Continental cars which have mounting points welded into the car roof, all roof racks are clipped to the drip rails. A complete rack can be bought for less than £10, so it is not worthwhile making one, unless all the materials and equipment are ready to hand. A point to remember is that roof racks should not be overloaded, not for fear of damage to the rack, but because the shock loads caused by the vehicle hitting a severe bump can distort the roof of the car and even jam the doors. The manufacturers will advise the maximum safe load to be carried on a roof rack.

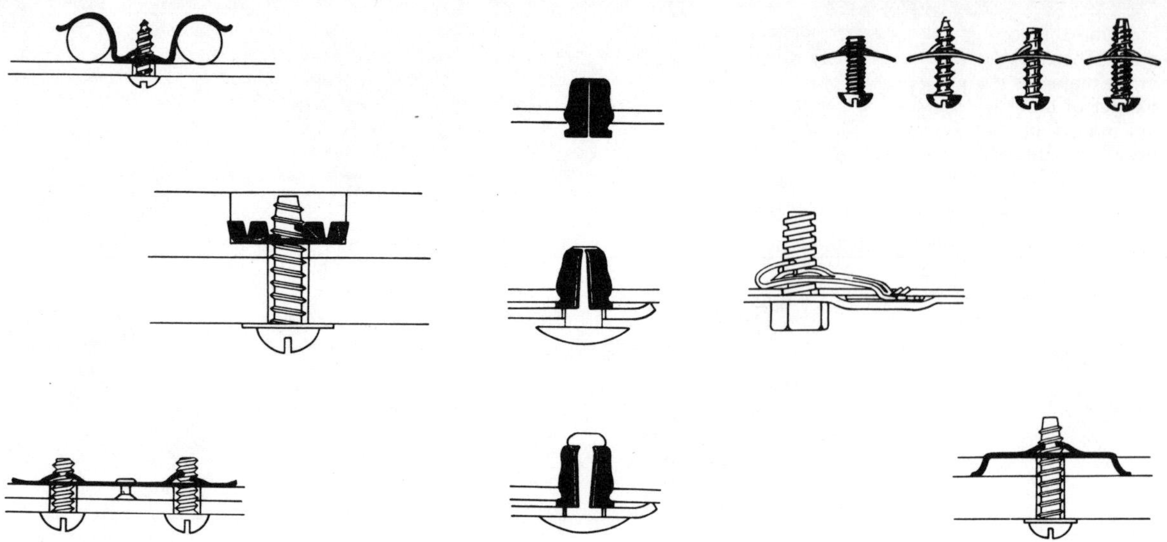

FIG 9:9   A selection of Spire Speed Nut fastenings

Dog guards:

A quick way to reduce the value of a car is to leave a dog in it, scratching to get out. Dog guards, usually fitted behind the rear squab of the estate-car type of body, can be bought for less than £10. They are designed to be quickly removable, with extensible vertical or horizontal members capped with rubber pads which bear against floor and roof, or against the waist rail or side windows. The advantage of the adjustable type is that it can be taken out if you decide to sell the car.

A semi-permanent dog guard, to fit one car and needing a screwdriver for its removal, can be made very simply with wood or metal slats, or PVC-dipped wire mesh, fixed to the bodywork with self-tapping screws. If guard dogs are likely to be left in a car for long periods an aluminium or zinc tray should be provided to cover the entire floorspace.

Consoles:

Consoles, mounted above the gearbox and housing radio or stereo equipment in the forward end, are very simple plywood structures, glued together and covered on the outside with leathercloth and underlayer of wadding or polyurethane foam. They can be bought ready-made to fit popular cars, but making one's own console offers an opportunity for individual design – for instance to make a stowage for carrying bottles upright, a convenience lacking in many modern cars.

The simplest way of mounting a console is to drive self-tapping screws through angle brackets into the floor of the car, but as the points of the screws will pierce the underseal they will make starting points for corrosion. If a dry mounting point cannot be found, it is better to make the mounting bracket a permanent fixture, bedding it in epoxide resin. The mounting brackets are then attached to the sides or end of the console with wood screws, or bolts with cage nuts on the inside of the console.

Speed nuts:

Speed nuts are used in very large quantities by the American and British motor industries. They are very useful for additions to consoles and for fixing 'bolt-on goodies' of all kinds, because they give a vibration-proof lock, require no heat, and some of them do not require access to the back of the surface on which they are used. There are several competing makes and new types are continually being introduced. The accompanying drawings show some of the commoner types of Spire Speed Nuts, which are made in the UK by Simmonds Aerocessories Ltd., of Treforest, Glamorgan.

The basic type consists of a spring steel pressing, designed to suit a particular application and a screw with a special thread. Two separate forces are exerted on the screw as it is tightened. First, the two arched prongs move inward to engage and lock against the flanks of the screw thread. These free-acting prongs compensate for tolerance variations. Second, a self-energising spring lock, created by compression of the arch in both prongs and base, as the screw is tightened. These combined forces eliminate loosening by vibration.

Unlike threaded nuts, Spire nuts do not have to be tightened with a great amount of torque. Their holding power and vibration resistance are dependent solely upon spring tension. Excessive tightening will distort the arch of the prongs and affect resiliency. The standard material is spring steel, tempered and dipped in a rust preventative, but cadmium plate, zinc plate and walterised finishes are also available. There is also a stainless steel version. One of these more resistant types should be used on the underside of a car and of course the principle of bi-metallic corrosion applies to these nuts.

The use of a screw of the correct length is important, because the locking prongs must grip the full root diameter of the screw if they are to be effective. These nuts eliminate lockwashers and spread the load over a greater area than an ordinary nut and they may be re-used indefinitely unless they are overtightened. Unlike small, machine-thread nuts, they do not become clogged with paint. Their resiliencey makes it possible to screw down brittle materials like glass or unreinforced plastics without danger of breakage due to vibration. The push-in types eliminate the need for threaded inserts and these are useful if a threaded insert has been stripped. The insert can be drilled out and a speed nut inserted to take a screw of the same, or slightly larger, diameter than the original. A word of warning; some of the tubular clips, such as the SLC for use with rivets are intended for final operations. This means that they are not intended to be taken out again. They are used for fixing escutcheons and such emblems cannot be removed without breakage. If necessary, the heads should be drilled away.

KNOW MORE ABOUT YOUR CAR

with an Autobook Workshop Manual

Includes detailed information about:

The Engine
The Fuel System
The Ignition System
The Cooling and Heating System

The Clutch
The Transmission
The Rear and Front Suspension
The Steering System
The Electrical System
The Bodywork

AUTOBOOKS are car workshop manuals specially written for the do-it-yourself motorist. They feature easy-to-follow, step-by-step instructions, clear illustrations, fault diagnosis tables and practical working hints. There is an Autobook for most British, Continental or popular Japanese cars.

IF YOU ARE enthused with the idea of tackling the repairs and maintenance of your motorcar, you will find financial savings and the satisfaction of knowing that the work has been thoroughly and properly done have led a third of today's motorists to become do-it-yourselfers. Many rely on an Autobook for detailed, accurate instructions.

AUTOBOOKS may be obtained from all good motor accessory shops or bookshops, or from Autobooks Ltd., Golden Lane, Brighton BN1 2QJ, telephone Brighton (0273) 721721.

Other titles in the Autocare series:

Electrical Systems – including Tapes and Radios

Tuning for Economy and Performance

Glossary of terms

A-post	Forwardmost upright of a steel saloon
Accelerator	A substance that enables polyester resin to polymerise at room temperature and contact pressure
Aerosol	A can of paint under the internal pressure of a propellant gas
Anti-bleed sealer	A special coat made by paint manufacturers to prevent underlying reds and maroons showing through new colour coats
B-post	Pillar standing between the doors of a steel saloon
Back curtain	Interior trimming material around the rear window
Back tacking	Tacking fabric face downward and folding it back again over a straight-edge
Base	Bottom line
Batten	Wooden crossmember in a car roof
Beading	Any strip used for covering a row of tacks
Bench trim	All trimming work done on a table or bench (see Body trim)
Bezel	A metal ring which holds a headlamp or instrument glass in place
Bleeding	Underlying colour showing through new colour
Blushing	A white cloudy surface on cellulose caused by excessive humidity in the surrounding air. Sometimes called blooming or fogging
Body trim	All work tacked or solutioned to the body (see Bench trim)
Bonnet	Hinged lid over engine
Bonnet surround	Cut out to receive bonnet
Boot	Luggage compartment
Boot lid	Lid of luggage compartment, sometimes called deck lid
Bridging	Paint which does not follow a sharp curve faithfully, forming a hollow blister
Bulldog head	Thickset jaw of strainers used for straining piping lines and other trim
Bump out	To knock dented sheet metal back to approximate shape before planishing
Burnish	To smooth a surface by rubbing it with a very fine abrasive compound, as distinct from wax polishing
C-post	The rearward of two centre pillars (now rare)
Cant rail	Timber rail running across tops of pillars and carrying hoopsticks (roof bows). In pressed steel bodywork the cant rail is a U-section running across the pillar tops
Capping	A polished strip of timber to embellish the interior of a car. Also called a finisher
Casing	Side trimming of car interior
Cataloy	A proprietary brand (Holts) of filled polyester resin used as a stopper
Catalyst	A substance that helps a chemical reaction to take place
Channel	In the USA, to fair-off excrescences by sinking them into channels in the bodywork
Chaser	A panelbeater's tool resembling a blunt cold chisel with a rounded end
Chop	To reduce the height of a stock car body by cutting and welding
Circlip	A circular spring used as a retainer
Clevis pin	A steel pin with a broad head and a transverse hole for a splitpin at the other end. Used in linkwork
Coach cloth	Woollen cloth used for headlining
Cover	Machined piece ready for trimming
Cup washer	Countersunk metal washer

Cutting line	Marked line on fabric for scissors to follow
D-post	The rearmost upright of a steel saloon
Dash casing	Casing on the inside of the car forward of the front door
Dolly or dolly block	A hand anvil used in panel beating
Dum Dum	Proprietary name of black mastic used for waterproofing
Face mitre	In trimming, corner join intended to show on the finished work
Face side	Side of fabric which shows when finished
Fillet	Strip of plywood, generally covered with cloth, used on interior of car; a strip of polished wood
Finishing line	Line of tacks near edge of fabric, often covered with beading
Flange	Overhanging lip of metal
Flatting	Wet rubbing down of new finishing coats
Flitch plate	Steel strip reinforcement running up the centre of a timber pillar; side member of steel front end assembly behind wheelarch
Flutes	Parallel padded strips on seats and squabs
Flute lines	Parallel lines marked out for machining fluted covers
Footwell	An open box welded into the floor to make more leg room
Frenching	Invisible stitching
Fullness	Surplus material, which may be eliminated by straining
Garnish awl	An awl, about $2\frac{1}{2}$ inch long, with a peg-top handle
Gel	Of resin or resin-based stopper, to become jelly-like; first stage of cure
Gel coat	Unreinforced surface coat of resin on a GRP moulding
Gimp pin	A fine cut finishing tack with a small head
Glass run	Fabric-lined channel for sliding window
Go off	To harden
Green	Not fully cured; soft material which will harden in service
GRP	Glass reinforced plastics (often called Fibreglass)
Headlining	Suspended ceiling in a saloon car, forming an insulating air space under the roof
Heelboard	Seat support in timber bodywork
Heel panel	Rear seat support in pressed steel bodywork
Hinge pillar	A pillar on which a door is hinged
Hold	General term for an anchorage for tacks, etc.
Intercostal	A rail running between two ribs or pillars, but not passing through them
Joggle	To indent one member of a lap joint so that the joint appears flush
Light	Any window
Lining	General term for coachcloths and other materials for inside roofs
Lists	Machined folds in headlining attached to roof rails or list bars
List rail	Wooden rail to which list is tacked
Mag hammer	A coachtrimmer's hammer with one end magnetised for picking up tacks
Masking tape	Adhesive tape used to attach masking paper to car bodies
Mist coat	A very light coat of sprayed paint, as distinct from a full wet coat
Mop, polishing	A circular piece of lambskin tied to a rotating rubber disc
Offcut	Material left over after main pieces have been cut out
Overspray	A final coat of thinners tinted with colour sprayed on after flatting cellulose colour coats; surplus paint which settles on adjacent surfaces as dust
Pan, floor	The pressing which forms the floor of a steel saloon
Panel pin	Long thin nail with head only slightly larger than the shank
Piping	A strip of leather, fabric or plastic sheet wrapped round a cord and sewn or stuck underneath. Used to cover stitches in trimming and to fill gaps between pressings
Planish	In panel beating, to work the dents out of sheet metal and bring it up to its intended shape
Polish	To add a thin coating of wax to make a smooth surface shiny
Pop rivet	Proprietary name of a hollow rivet driven with a special hand tool
Primer	The first coat of paint which is designed to give good adhesion to wood or metal rather than covering power. Primers also often have anti-corrosion properties
Quarter casing	Casing at side of rear cushions, sometimes carrying an armrest
Quarter light	A D-shaped window behind rear pillar or D-post
Regulator	A long awl, tapering to a point
Rocker panel	Sill
Roving	Untwisted bundles of glass fibres
Rubbing down	Abrasion of existing paintwork or filler to remove all loose particles

Scraper	A tool used for applying cement to fabric
Scuttle	Panel between engine bay and windscreen, housing heater, instrument panel and so on
Set up	To dry (of paint or varnish)
Sewing base	Hold for hand stitching
Sewing line	Line which the needle enters
Shear	Forces acting in opposite direction in the same plane
Shut pillar	Pillar against which a door shuts
Sill	Horizontal pressing below the doorways; also called a rocker panel from its original shape
Sleeker	A hardwood blade used for smoothing fabric or leather
Spoon	A spoon-shaped panelbeater's hammer with a serrated or smooth working face
Squab	Back rest of seat
Squab shelf	Shelf between squab and rear window
Stone guard	Steel lining in a light alloy or GRP wing
Stopper	Putty-like paste, based on oil, cellulose or polyester resin, used to fill indentations
Strainer	Gripping tool with ribbed jaws used to strain fabric
Straining	Stretching
Striker	Plate against which the bolt of a door lock engages
Stuffing iron	A steel bar, 8 to 24 inch long, with one end pointed and the other flattened and serrated
Surfacer	A filler combined with a primer
Sweep	A curve
SWG	Standard wire gauge, used to measure thickness of sheet metal
Tack off	To knock in tacks at intervals along a line
Tack rag	A sticky cloth used for picking up dust and lint on newly painted surfaces
Tease	Pull apart to loosen lumps
Temp. tack	Tack knocked only halfway in as a temporary measure
Tissue, surfacing	A very fine form of glass mat, used for small repairs and for hiding the fibre pattern of heavier reinforcements
Tonneau panel	Boot enclosure, cut out to receive boot lid
Torsion bar	A bar, fixed at one end, and twisted at the other end by a lever on which the road wheel is mounted
Traffic film	A greasy deposit from the exhausts of other vehicles
Trammel	An extensible measuring rod
Trim strip	A bright metal strip embellishing exterior or interior
Trimmer's hammer	Hammer, with a head about 8 inch long, with one square pein and a flat-edged pein
Trimmer's knife	Straight 4 inch blade with 4 inch handle, often made from old hacksaw blade
Tufting	Deep button pleating
Turnunder	A curved pillar or panel sweeping inwards below the waist
Turps sub	A substitute for American turpentine
Valance	Covered metal strip around base of bucket seat retaining cushion in place; front end panel below bumper
Ventilator	Small triangular swivelling window forward of main front door window. Sometimes misnamed a quarter light
Waist rail	Horizontal rail just below side windows, usually the widest part of a body
Wet-or-dry paper	Abrasive paper coated with silicone carbide, used for rubbing down paint with or without water. Grades run from very coarse 80D to very fine 600A
Wheelarch	A semicircular timber frame around the rear wheel; a semicircular panel above the rear wheel
Wing	A mudguard around front or rear wheels

Suppliers

Air brushes:
Calbrook Cars Limited, Commerce Estate, Kingston Road, Leatherhead, Surrey

Coach trimming materials:
Creech Coach Trimming Centre, 67 High Street, South Norwood, London SE25
Leathercloth and Trimming Supplies, The Old Tannery, Station Road, Otley, Yorks.

Corrosion protection:
Ziebart (GB) Limited, Ziebart House, Dominion Way, Worthing, Sussex
(Local stations in many towns—see telephone directory)
Finnigans Limited, Eltringham Works, Prudhoe, Northumberland
(Waxoyl compound for do-it-yourself use)

Custom paints:
Calbrook Cars Limited, Commerce Estate, Kingston Road, Leatherhead, Surrey

Glass:

Abrasive blasting:
Impact Finishers Limited, Woodson House, Ajax Avenue, Slough, Bucks.

Glass toughening:
Splintex Limited, Nightingale Road, London W7

Tinted glass:
H. G. Shepherd & Sons Limited, 206 Shepherds Bush Road, London W6
Splintex Limited (address above)
Wood & Picket Limited, Abbey Road, London NW10

Perspex (heat-formed and tinted):
Gordon Engraving Commercial Limited, Roper Close, Roper Road, Canterbury, Kent

Reinforced plastics and glass fibre:
Strand Glass Company Limited, Brentway Trading Estate, Brentford, Middlesex
(Branches in Birmingham, Brentford, Bristol, Cardiff, Derby, Glasgow, Ilford, Leeds, Liverpool, Plymouth, Reading, Portsmouth, Southampton, Stockport and Stockton—see telephone directory)

Pop rivets and riveting guns:
Tucker Fasteners Limited, Walsall Road, Birmingham B42 1BP

Replacement body parts (metal):
R. G. Barratt (Auto Sills), 19 Church Street, Blantyre, Glasgow
Peter Rhodes, Monkhill Station, Pontefract, Yorks.
Southern Panel Company, 37-39 Penge High Street, London SE20

Replacement body parts (GRP):
Guy Performance (Alcester), Eclipse Works, Birmingham Road, Alcester, Warks.
Windmill Plastics, Freepost, Coventry

Transfers:

Trade van type:
J. H. Butcher & Company Limited, 498-506 Moseley Road, Birmingham B12 9AL

American style:
Action Automotive, 77 Manor Road, Wallington, Surrey

Van window frames and kits:
Americar Limited, 352-4 Southchurch Road, Southend-on-Sea, Essex
Calbrook Cars Limited, Commerce Estate, Kingston Road, Leatherhead, Surrey
Cooper & Company (Coach Builders), The Old Tannery, Station Road, Otley, Yorks.
D. W. Price (Enfield) Limited, 12 Savoy Parade, Southbury Road, Enfield, Middlesex

Index

Figures in bold type refer to illustrations